Modern Language As... W9-AHQ-102

Approaches to Teaching
World Literature

Joseph Gibaldi, Series Editor

Approaches to Teaching Dickinson's Poetry

Edited by

Robin Riley Fast

and

Christine Mack Gordon

The Modern Language Association of America
New York   1989

Copyright © 1989 by The Modern Language Association of America

Library of Congress Cataloging-in-Publication Data

Approaches to teaching Dickinson's poetry / edited by Robin Riley Fast
    and Christine Mack Gordon.
        p.   cm.—(Approaches to teaching world literature ; 26)
    Includes bibliographical references.
    ISBN 0–87352–525–6   ISBN 0–87352–526–4 (pbk.)
    1. Dickinson, Emily, 1830–1886—Study and teaching.   I. Fast,
Robin Riley, 1948–   .   II. Gordon, Christine Mack, 1947–
III. Modern Language Association of America.   IV. Series.
PS1541.Z5A65   1989
811′.3—dc20   89–12705

Suzanne Juhasz's "Reading Doubly: Dickinson, Gender, and Multiple Meaning" is
a revised and combined version of portions of her essays "Poem 315" and
"Reading Dickinson Doubly," which appeared in the Emily Dickinson conference
issue of *Women's Studies*. Used by permission of Gordon and Breach Science
Publishers, Inc.

Cover illustration of the paperback edition: Mabel Loomis Todd, *Indian Pipes*,
Amherst College Library, Amherst, Massachusetts. By permission of the Trustees
of Amherst College.

Published by The Modern Language Association of America
10 Astor Place, New York, NY 10003-6981

CONTENTS

PREFACE TO THE SERIES

In *The Art of Teaching* Gilbert Highet wrote, "Bad teaching wastes a great deal of effort, and spoils many lives which might have been full of energy and happiness." All too many teachers have failed in their work, Highet argued, simply "because they have not thought about it." We hope that the Approaches to Teaching World Literature series, sponsored by the Modern Language Association's Committee on Teaching and Related Professional Activities, will not only improve the craft—as well as the art—of teaching but also encourage serious and continuing discussion of the aims and methods of teaching literature.

The principal objective of the series is to collect within each volume different points of view on teaching a specific literary work, a literary tradition, or a writer widely taught at the undergraduate level. The preparation of each volume begins with a wide-ranging survey of instructors, thus enabling us to include in the volume the philosophies and approaches, thoughts and methods of scores of experienced teachers. The result is a sourcebook of material, information, and ideas on teaching the subject of the volume to undergraduates.

The series is intended to serve nonspecialists as well as specialists, inexperienced as well as experienced teachers, graduate students who wish to learn effective ways of teaching as well as senior professors who wish to compare their own approaches with the approaches of colleagues in other schools. Of course, no volume in the series can ever substitute for erudition, intelligence, creativity, and sensitivity in teaching. We hope merely that each book will point readers in useful directions; at most each will offer only a first step in the long journey to successful teaching.

Joseph Gibaldi
Series Editor

PREFACE TO THE VOLUME

I dwell in Possibility—
A fairer House than Prose—
More numerous of Windows—
Superior—for Doors—

Of Chambers as the Cedars—
Impregnable of Eye—
And for an Everlasting Roof
The Gambrels of the Sky—

Of Visitors—the fairest
For Occupation—This—
The spreading wide my narrow Hands
To gather Paradise—   (657)

For those who teach Emily Dickinson, "possibility" is clearly an operative word. The variety of courses in which her poetry is taught and the breadth and complexity of her work allow us as teachers to guide our students along many pathways, all leading to that "fairer House" with which she has magnificently endowed us. Dickinson's life and her range of topics and tones suit her for contexts as varied as American literature, Romanticism, realism, nineteenth-century culture, and women's literary traditions. The essays in the second part of this volume describe how she can be located and taught in these and other contexts. Each perspective shows us Dickinson in a different light, inviting us to enter through one of the many doors and windows of possibility.

This book emphasizes instruction at the undergraduate level. Many of the essays, though not all, elucidate methods of introducing Dickinson and her work to students who may have preconceptions about poetry, poets, or both but whose knowledge of Dickinson and experience reading poetry are limited. The approaches and techniques described, however, can be valuable to teachers at any level.

Teaching Dickinson—whether to freshmen in different fields or to senior English majors—poses numerous problems because of the poetry itself, with its compressed style and constant surprises, and because of the biographical questions that fascinate students and critics alike. Answers to some of the questions can be derived from the impressive volume of Dickinson scholarship, but each teacher must finally discover the answers and approaches most suited to the particular teaching situation and students. Teachers of Dickinson almost universally acknowledge, more often with delight than despair, that the answers can never be final, for our poet insists on the mysteries with which she confronts us: "It is true that the unknown is the largest need of the intellect, though for it, no one thinks to thank God" (*Letters* 2: 559).

Our purpose in this volume is to provide insights into and suggestions about both criticism and teaching techniques that have proved effective in presenting Dickinson to undergraduates. While many of our readers may be beginning instructors or nonspecialists, we hope that the materials included here will likewise be helpful to seasoned teachers. We assume that teachers have had graduate training either on Dickinson or in some related fields and that such training, along with wider critical reading in Dickinson scholarship, will supplement our text.

We gratefully acknowledge the interest and generosity of all respondents to our questionnaire on teaching Dickinson's poetry and thank the members of the MLA Committee on Teaching and Related Professional Activities for their sponsorship of the series. Joseph Gibaldi, general editor of the series, has encouraged and advised us astutely throughout the process of putting this volume together.

We thank our colleagues for their support and encouragement. We are grateful to Sarah Lorenz and her Interlibrary Loan staff at the University of Akron and to the staff at the University of Minnesota Libraries for their assistance; to the Department of English and Dean Claibourne E. Griffin of the University of Akron for their generous support of travel; to Deborah Borland, David Allen, Xiaoyang Jiao, and Satinder Randhawa for research assistance; and to Sandy Wehmann and Bonnie Bromley for their able assistance with correspondence. Sonia Smith deserves special thanks for her fine typing of much of the manuscript. Finally, we thank Paul Fast and Bob, Jane, and Jonah Gordon, who allowed us the time and space to enter Dickinson's world while never completely leaving our own.

RRF and CMG

Part One

MATERIALS

Robin Riley Fast and
Christine Mack Gordon

Introduction

To begin work on this volume in the MLA series Approaches to Teaching World Literature, we prepared and mailed a questionnaire to over two hundred scholars in the field of American literature; some names were gleaned from journals in the field, some from the annual MLA bibliographies, while others were randomly selected from the American Literature Division of the MLA. An announcement about the book in the *MLA Newsletter* also requested that anyone interested in responding to the questionnaire write one of the editors.

The sixty-one respondents, twenty-seven men and thirty-four women, represent fairly well a cross section of those teaching Dickinson at the college level: they come from large and small public and private colleges and universities (though public institutions outnumber private ones) and pursue their scholarship both inside and outside the United States (Canada, the Netherlands, Brazil, Turkey, and Israel are all represented).

These teachers reflect the contemporary range of scholarly approaches to literature, although few would narrowly define themselves as critics of one particular "school." The most common method of teaching Dickinson is close textual analysis, which varies according to emphases and assumptions. Whatever its New Critical or formalist origins, this perspective is often combined with others—most frequently historical-cultural and feminist criticism. In addition, our respondents mentioned theological, biographical, and psychological approaches, as well as interest in contemporary critical theories such as deconstructionism. Most of these scholars nevertheless agree that the texts themselves are the most suitable focus for teaching, and many note the risks inherent in spending too much time and energy in class on biographical or historical information at the expense of the poems. Many would agree, we think, that a little background and a little theory go a long way.

In describing what they consider the central concerns of Dickinson's poetry and how these influence their teaching, our respondents mirror the historical development of Dickinson criticism and the preeminent issues of our time. Thus, many cite the widely recognized themes of religious doubt and belief, love and human relationships, the mysteries of pain and death, the significance of the everyday and of the natural world ("the miraculous within the familiar," as one writer phrases it), and the power and responsibility of the poet in relation to her own voice and to the poetic tradition. Dickinson's identity as a nineteenth-century woman and all that suggests about her relationship with her family, her community, and literary traditions are also frequently mentioned as significant, as is the poet's exploration of her inner life.

Such topics are addressed in varying degrees in classes on Dickinson, depending on the course, the teacher's interests, and the time available. Practical considerations may determine the appropriate approach in a survey course that explores the poetry for two or three class periods, while the generous (although never sufficient) time available in a full quarter or semester course on Dickinson allows greater opportunity for diverse forms of analysis as well as the inclusion of more biographical, historical, or critical information.

Courses and Texts

Several events probably explain Emily Dickinson's more visible presence in the undergraduate curriculum in recent decades. Thomas Johnson's preparation and publication of the variorum edition of the poems in 1955, followed in 1960 by the one-volume *Complete Poems* and in 1961 by *Final Harvest*, made Dickinson's entire corpus available to a wide public. The 1950s and 1960s also saw a growth of interest in poetry as both a written and a performing art, as the Beat poets and others took to the road (which often led from campus to campus) to bring poetry to the people. In the late 1960s and early 1970s, the resurgence of feminism in the country at large had a significant impact on the intellectual community: many women scholars began to focus their attention on the sung as well as the unsung women of the past and to reexamine their work from a perspective that viewed gender as a significant variable in the lives women led and the work they produced.

Dickinson's work is now placed in the hands of everyone from freshmen in beginning literature courses to seniors in undergraduate seminars. It is most frequently taught in surveys of American literature or major writers and in introductory courses that focus on literature, literary study, or poetry; courses in women writers and women's literature generally include some of Dickinson's work, and her poetry wends its way into composition courses as well. Most of these courses are taught at the lower-division level. In upper-division classes, primarily though not exclusively filled by English majors, Dickinson is again taught in surveys and courses on major American writers and poets, courses like Forms and Forces in American Literature and Creative Americans. At this level, more narrowly focused courses begin to include Dickinson's work as a major part of the curriculum, in contexts such as American transcendentalism, American Romanticism, the American renaissance, New England literature, classical American literature, and the rise of realism. Our respondents also mention more thematically focused courses such as Poetry as Prayer, American Humor, Experiments in American Poetry, and Poetry and the Creative Mind. Some upper-division classes (often described as seminars) concentrate exclusively on Dickinson, while others examine her in conjunction with other poets. Her most frequently mentioned comrade, not surprisingly, is Walt Whitman, although our respondents also listed courses such as Dickinson and Frost; Emily Dickinson and Her Time; Dickinson and Hopkins; Whitman, Dickinson, Frost, and the Emersonian Tradition; and Dickinson, Frost, and Stevens. At both upper and lower levels she is taught in cross-listed or multidisciplinary courses (most common are American studies and women's studies listings) and in a few courses on world literature.

The text of choice for our respondents is clearly the *Complete Poems*, followed by *Final Harvest*. As one respondent states, "I always use the Little, Brown paperback edited by Thomas Johnson. Although at first I feared requiring the students to spend so much on one book, I am convinced that this is the best (in fact, I'm convinced it's the *only*) way to teach Dickinson." Proponents of *Final Harvest* cite "its general authoritativeness, its generous and judicious selection of poems, and its relatively modest price"; its accuracy and "extensive and representative selections," and its "wide representation," which "makes possible an appreciation of both the unity and variety in Dickinson." But *Final Harvest* evokes some negative comments as well: it is "irritating on two counts: the numbering (J-number, sequence number, page number) and indexing of the book" and the exclusion of "at least *one* poem of a desirable teaching set." Another respondent says, "There is no good text. I use *Final Harvest* for my sophomores, but the numbering is so screwed up that it confuses." (For strong reservations regarding the Johnson edition, see our discussion of Susan Howe's book *My Emily Dickinson* in "The Instructor's Library" section of this part and Alice Hall Petry's essay in part 2.)

Survey courses usually preclude the use of either of these texts. Survey teachers must rely on anthologies; a significant number of respondents report that they often distribute additional poems to complement those in the anthologies. One writer uses *The Norton Anthology of American Literature* (Murphy and Parker) "because it has in one volume Emerson's important essays, all of *Walden*, and OK selections of Poe, Whitman, and [Dickinson]. (Her texts, though, have printing errors! I distribute a list of corrections.)" Commenting on the Macmillan *Anthology of American Literature* (McMichael), two respondents write that it "offers a good selection, a variety of poems comic and tragic, late and early, etc.," and that "it has good texts and a generous sampling with minimal editorial interference." Both the Norton and the Macmillan anthologies include approximately sixty poems (there is considerable overlap between the volumes) and useful but limited introductions—neither mentions Dickinson's important relationships with women or the range of women writers she read, for example. The Norton divides its two volumes at 1865 and puts Dickinson in volume 1, while the Macmillan makes the break between Romantics and realists and puts Dickinson with the latter, in volume 2—choices that clearly may influence the perspectives from which her poetry is taught. One writer, who uses the *Norton Anthology of Literature by Women* in both composition and women's literature classes, states that "Gilbert and Gubar's anthology . . . offers a sensitive, large selection of Dickinson's poetry, some of the most important letters, and a first-rate biographical introduction." The Gilbert and Gubar anthology includes fifty poems (with little overlap with the Norton or Macmillan; it is interesting to compare lists of the poems included in the three anthologies) and six letters.

Two other anthologies mentioned are the *Oxford Book of American Verse* (Matthiessen) and the *Mentor Book of Major American Poets* (Williams and Honig); one writer notes, "The Oxford and Mentor books are comprehensive, but I dislike the editing practices and the lack of notes." One respondent mentions using *Selected Poems and Letters* (ed. Linscott), then demurs, "I chose it for its selection of poems and letters. I would not use it again because it contains 'edited' poems." Correspondents from abroad mention Faber and Faber's edition of the *Complete Poems* and the United States Information Service's *Highlights of American Literature* (the latter available only from the U.S. Information Service offices overseas).

Those who mention using additional poems cite various reasons, including the flexibility that copying allows in the choice of poems (selected according to theme, imagery, "simplicity"). One writer mentions the use of variants from the three-volume Johnson edition to stimulate class discussion. Since reasonably authoritative versions of Dickinson's poems are available, our respondents have little patience with anyone who has tampered with the text—whether it be those early editors who wished to present their versions of Dickinson to the larger world or more recent editors who exhibit simple carelessness or lack of scholarship.

Dickinson in the Classroom

Instructors almost universally observe that Dickinson's unconventional syntax and grammar, unfamiliar language, and apparently fractured style can be extremely difficult for students. Richard Benvenuto describes some of the problems: Students "can't paraphrase her very easily; they can't follow her syntax; and they don't know when she is being simple and literal or when she is being suggestive and symbolic. Some have trouble telling if she is using a word as a noun or a verb." The indeterminacy and opacity that intrigue us as critics perplex our students. Some students initially perceive the poems as simple, often because of their brevity. Respondents who note this tendency suggest that such students be invited to look below the surface, with a "yes, but . . . " or an invitation to try an alternative perspective. Bess Stark Spangler emphasizes the importance of "awakening students to the complexity of her poems, and overcoming their reluctance to value complexity, paradox, wit, uncertainty." Nancy Walker, in a similar vein, remarks that refusing to provide students with the "right answers" about Dickinson's meanings "ultimately empowers them to deal with ambiguity."

A problem for many teachers is students' lack of historical knowledge, including a lack of familiarity with Dickinson's cultural background and her situation as an individual, a writer, and a woman. Impressions of Dickinson gleaned from the poems can also impede students' understanding. The stereotype of the timid, "half-cracked" girl (or "old maid") in white still has wide currency, and even students who have not been exposed to it often see her as odd, foreign, childish, erratic, lacking in "real" worldly experience—hardly the kind of person with whom they can readily sympathize. They may be further alienated by what many perceive as her pessimism and morbidity, as well as by the unconventional religious attitudes she expresses. Several teachers remark on students' inclination to see her as simply Christian or anti-Christian, devout or heretical, and on the disturbing effects, for students, of her contradictoriness about religion. When students have begun to work their way through the difficulties and to see her in her various contexts, they find her meanings challenging, or, as Nicholas Ruddick puts it, "The nakedness of the truths she conveys very often disturbs the beginning reader (so it should!)." Thus for many students, reading Dickinson may seem to begin and end in discomfort and difficulty. Teachers respond to these challenges in different ways, but many share some basic assumptions about teaching Dickinson. Even those who devote only a few days to her agree on the importance of reading the poems aloud and of analyzing some in detail. Several teachers mention preliminary advice they give to students about reading Dickinson: some assign dictionary research; Toni McNaron advises students to "read lots of poems before they try to 'figure out' any single one, to read some poems from bottom to top, to think in terms of riddles whenever they can, to read her under soothing conditions."

To help students deal with the structural and stylistic difficulties of Dickinson's poetry, most teachers spend some time teaching how to explicate a poem, often including work on paraphrasing, making grammatical "translations," and filling in ellipses. In some classes this becomes a kind of game. (But at least one teacher offers a contrasting approach: David Stewart attempts "to get students to react to the poetry's dominant moods, not its logic—phrases and words, not sentences. . . . Trying to 'interpret' a Dickinson poem only reinforces stereotypes about 'hidden meanings.' ") As they gain confidence in reading the poems, students can often see that at her best Dickinson uses her perplexing techniques with care, and they should enjoy discussing why she selects certain words or structures and how her technical choices might be related to her aesthetics and beliefs. Another way to provide a context for Dickinson's now (the teacher hopes) less daunting techniques may be to stress her poetic development. Teachers who do not see significant development in the poetry will define other contexts; most instructors do believe that empowering students to respond more fully to Dickinson requires not only teaching them analytical skills but also suggesting some contexts in which the difficulties can be justified or comprehended. While a few instructors prefer to teach the poems entirely from a New Critical or formalist perspective, without reference to biographical or historical contexts, many find that they can alleviate some student problems in understanding Dickinson by including such material in lectures or assigned readings (see "Aids to Teaching" and "The Instructor's Library"). Finally, learning to explicate a poem will not and should not enable a student to reduce Dickinson's meanings to simple formulas. Dealing with the challenges she offers, in fact, allows us again to stress the value of complexity and variety in poetry and interpretation. Lynn Keller remarks, "I try to acknowledge these difficulties and turn them into opportunities for students to discover and defend their own variant readings." To deal with Dickinson's tendency to "qualify and question rather than to assert," Lynne Shackelford discusses her "intellectual honesty, the variation of her moods, and her conception of 'Truth' as expressed in such poems as 1129." Teachers can further help students by demonstrating the great range of emotions Dickinson describes (in contrast to students' perceptions of obsessive morbidity) and by inviting students to think about feelings and experiences of their own that the poetry recalls or expresses.

In selecting the number and kinds of poems to assign, most instructors assume that students will read more poetry than is actually discussed in class. Although in some freshman courses only 2 to 6 poems may be assigned, the average lower-division assignment for a complete unit on Dickinson is 30 poems (as described in the questionnaires, Dickinson units typically consist of four to six class periods, with 4 to 12 poems—at greater or lesser length—discussed in each class). While in several upper-division courses students are expected to read all of the *Complete Poems*, the average upper-division requirement is 325 poems (when the classes that require all 1,775 poems are excluded, the average is 125; these figures are all approximate, as we have numbers for only about one-third of the classes, and ways of reporting varied.) The tendency to assign more poems than will be discussed reflects the frequently voiced goal of exposing students to Dickinson's stylistic, tonal, and thematic range.

One of our greatest practical dilemmas is how to group the poems, considering the need to acknowledge the poetry's refusal of neat labels and to provide students with a coherent, somewhat controlled experience. The shorter the time, the more important, probably, is the structure: survey classes rarely allow in-class time for students to work out their own ways of coming to terms with the poetry. Thus the double need to give them a kind of scaffolding, but also to help them see the limits of the "props" that "assist the House." Most commonly, teachers assign poems in thematic clusters, selecting poems on a variety of topics. Some label the thematic clusters, while others prefer to have students define the clusters for themselves—such decisions may be related to time constraints. Wendy Bean Barker describes a variation on thematic grouping. She assigns poems in clusters that emphasize different states of mind: the poet's sense of being at odds with her culture; pain and breakdown; and confidence, transcendence, or ecstasy. This grouping allows students to see possible relations between contrasting themes and states of mind and between poems that may build on or subvert one another. Another principle of selection is based on rhetorical, structural, or stylistic devices and traits. Frequently instructors combine rhetorical and thematic groupings of poems. Dickinson's fascicles, as reconstructed by Ralph Franklin, provide some teachers with an alternative way of grouping the poems. The fascicles, too, allow students to speculate on the relations the poet might have seen among her poems. Finally, some select the poems they consider Dickinson's best, or her most famous, and a few—who assign all the poems in the text they use—allow students to select the ones for intensive discussion.

While the essays that follow detail specific classroom approaches, some general remarks can be made here. The traditional lecture is not a common method of teaching Dickinson except in the largest survey courses, where it is supplemented with discussion sections or question periods. The general tendency away from lecturing seems consistent with the widely shared recognition that students initially lack analytical skills and with the emphasis many teachers place on discussion, where students can practice those skills. Of course, most teachers lecture occasionally, especially to present biographical and historical information. Opinion is divided on whether such material should be presented first, to lead into discussion of the poems themselves, or whether one should begin with the poems and later present background materials, which may then help answer questions raised by the poems.

Jean Ferguson Carr describes an introductory assignment that combines attention to poetic detail and cultural context:

> I usually start my Dickinson classes by having students compare Johnson's version of 199 ("I'm 'wife'—I've finished that—") with the version Higginson printed (titled "Apocalypse" and altered in significant ways). This allows us to raise questions about how critics . . . understand Dickinson's poems. This particular pairing suggests her use of "improper" language . . . her "eccentric" sense that what is "spiritual" or "transcendent" to her contemporaries is "palpable" or observable in her discourse. . . . Students also can move from . . . relatively large changes to an interest in Dickinson's punctuation, practice of capitalization, italicizing, quoting—all of which are revised by Higginson in this poem. This encourages them to attend to the small changes in "normal" discourse Dickinson makes in her poems. . . . I find this a useful way of teaching students to read closely as well as to read culturally, to combine these two attitudes and to see that they are inseparable.

Most instructors seem to agree that writing assignments on Dickinson should be as concrete as possible. Nicholas Ruddick comments that "once students learn to read Dickinson, the poems sell themselves, and the problem is usually one of focusing enthusiasm." One way to promote concreteness and clarity is to ask students to write about one poem or a small group of poems. Over half of our respondents, in fact, assign written explications. This practice is consistent with our awareness that students find poetry, especially Dickinson's, difficult and that practical experience analyzing it can increase their understanding and pleasure. It is also consistent with our tendency to emphasize close reading in our teaching of Dickinson, regardless of how we may otherwise define our critical stances.

Another common assignment is a thematic study of several poems, for example, a study of female roles assumed by Dickinson or of her uses of landscape to symbolize inner space. Or students may be asked to study a particular image or stylistic device (e.g., the use of light or dark imagery, compressed language) as it appears in several poems. A variation on this kind of assignment is to have students make up fascicles of their own and analyze the poems and their relations. (See Paula Uruburu's description of such an assignment in the appendix.)

Assignments that ask students to compare Dickinson to another writer or to assess her influence on a later writer appear often in surveys and other multiauthor courses. The other writers mentioned by our respondents are Whitman, Frost, Plath, Sexton, Emily Brontë, Roethke, Emerson, Hawthorne, H. D., Rich, and E. A. Robinson. Alice Hall Petry has asked her students, "What do Dickinson and James Whitcomb Riley have in common—or *seem* to have in common—which might explain their *simultaneous* popularity in the 1890s and the early twentieth century?" Another suggestion, from Jonnie Guerra, is to assign several of Helen Hunt Jackson's poems together with thematically similar ones by Dickinson and then ask students to write an essay that explores why Higginson preferred Jackson's poetry to Dickinson's. In one more variation on the theme of comparison or contrast, Maryanne Garbowsky asks students to describe an imaginary meeting between Dickinson and Whitman.

Research on Dickinson's themes, life, family, or cultural background figures in many assignments. Among the topics suggested are Dickinson's reading, nineteenth-century housekeeping books or popular women's magazines, the Civil War in Massachusetts, religious revivalism in the 1840s, nineteenth-century games and how they enter into Dickinson's poetry, the poet's garden, and her eye problems. Some teachers observe that original research on Dickinson is possible for upper-level students and can have a strong motivating effect on them. Student research might involve textual study or comparisons of different versions of one poem, using Franklin's edition of the fascicles, the 1890s texts, or the variorum edition. Finally, in the category of research assignments, we received recommendations for engaging students with Dickinson criticism. One method is to ask students to read summarize, and evaluate a single scholarly article. Another requires students to summarize and evaluate several interpretations of a single poem, using Joseph Duchac's annotated guide to criticism and *American Literary Scholarship* to locate articles.

In addition to these assignments, a "miscellaneous" category is also of interest. We list these in no special order:

> Survey the teaching of Dickinson in local high schools.
> Write an introduction to one poem, in the context of others similar to it.
> Write an introduction to one of the fascicles.
> Analyze some published translations of Dickinson poems.
> Choose a poem that a fictional character (e.g., Daisy Miller, Edna Pontellier) might profit from reading, and discuss.
> Analyze a play or other work based on the life or work of Dickinson.

Other projects depart from the conventional paper assignment. Students have set poems to music and have written poems in Dickinson's style. (See Paula Uruburu's description of the latter in the appendix.) Another instructor gives students the option of writing a poem on an emotion akin to one that Dickinson treats.

Keeping a journal encourages students to study selected poems over a period of time; the journal can also provide the basis for additional assignments, as Joanne Feit Diehl explains:

> One approach that has seemed to work especially well is to ask the students to select two or three Dickinson poems and make these the core of a journal which they keep for . . . two or three weeks. Each day, or every few days . . . I ask my students to read their poems, chosen by them on the basis of intrigue, mystery, or affinity, and to write a few notes on the poems. At the end of the time allotted, I ask both that the students hand in their journals, a cumulative reading of the Dickinson texts, and that they present to the other class participants a brief summary of their progress in understanding the poems. As a final assignment in this progression, I require that the students write brief papers on one of the poems to which they have formulated their responses over time.
>
> What I have found . . . is that the students reflect upon their own reading as well as upon the poem; that they come to realize the importance of a sustained, concentrated act of attention, and that they begin to appreciate the complexities of reading Dickinson—how much a reader brings to the poems and how her experiences from day to day can affect interpretation. My students have enjoyed this particular assignment, and, in my estimation, profited from it in ways that make them better readers not only of Dickinson but more generally of literature and at times, one hopes, of themselves.

The journal-based report is one of several kinds of student presentations suggested. In one seminar, students write short weekly papers, analyzing things like diction or syntax in a single poem; the papers, read in class, form the basis for discussion. (See Barbara Packer's assignment for such a paper in the appendix.) Inez and Willis Wager, who describe their class as "a group of colleagues joined together in a common enterprise," circulate the students' writing among class members in mimeographed booklets: "The purpose is to facilitate the exchange of ideas and observations on a more extensive scale than is possible by oral means. Reading and thinking about what is conveyed is as much a part of the class activity as the more conventional form of lecture and recitation." In other courses students present oral reports on individual poems; Lynne P. Shackelford groups students and assigns each group to teach one poem to the rest of the class. Finally, in Cheryl Walker's seminar, students have a group oral exam on Dickinson criticism (see her description in the appendix).

Aids to Teaching

Supplementary material—even facts of her life and various interpretations of her poetry—are secondary. Students should be encouraged to read and reread the poems themselves. If the teacher can convince that he/she is interested in the reactions and interpretations of the students, a real step has been taken. What I think today may be deepened tomorrow. What you think today may color the teacher's reading. If the poem has just one meaning—is it poetry? How a tenyear-old boy who loves to hunt reacts to "A wounded deer leaps highest" may be more relevant than the reactions of a city-bred Ph.D. of sixty.

Inez Wager and Willis Wager

Many of our respondents echo the Wagers' sentiments. They repeatedly stress the need to focus on the poems and frequently suggest that reading each poem aloud can lead to a clearer understanding not only of Dickinson's structures but of her meanings as well. Several respondents mention Franklin's manuscript books as a way to introduce students to Dickinson's process of creation and what Franklin calls her "continuing workshop" (*Manuscript Books of Emily Dickinson*). Johnson's variants, even with the imposed orderliness of print, can be used to similar purpose. Other critical and historical works mentioned in response to our query about supplementary material for students include *Emily Dickinson's Reading* by Jack Capps, *The Years and Hours of Emily Dickinson* by Jay Leyda, *The Voice of the Poet* by Brita Lindberg-Seyersted, *Emily Dickinson and Her Culture* by Barton Levi St. Armand, and *The Madwoman in the Attic* by Sandra Gilbert and Susan Gubar. (A number of other books mentioned appeared more often in response to our related queries about reference, background, biographical, and critical works, and that information is included in the "Instructor's Library" section.)

The use of audiovisual materials in the classroom is, not surprisingly, related to the type of course being taught. Most survey classes focus attention primarily on the poetry, giving some attention to biographical and historical background and possibly to criticism as well. But many of our respondents do offer suggestions about material they have used to enhance their presentations of Dickinson and her work. Cited most frequently is William Luce's play, *The Belle of Amherst*. In addition to the text itself, the play is available on record, film, and videotape, and several respondents mention local productions as well. Most comments about it include a strong caveat, however; as one writer phrases it, "[The play] helps bring the poet 'alive' for beginning students, but they must recognize that it is highly interpretive." Another states that she includes it "mostly to suggest the limitations of that view." Several people mention the short (29-min.) film *Emily Dickinson: A Certain Slant of Light*, by Jean Mudge and Bayley Silleck, and another names a filmstrip, *The World of Emily Dickinson*, produced by Guidance Associates. A new film, *Emily Dickinson*, produced by the New York Center for Visual History, is notable for its inclusion of commentary by Adrienne Rich and Richard B. Sewall.

Recordings of Dickinson's work by Nancy Wickwire and Julie Harris are noted by several respondents. Also mentioned are Virginia Terris's presentation, *Emily Dickinson as a Woman Poet;* an informal panel by Dickinson scholars at the 1980 Emily Dickinson conference in Amherst as part of the recording *Four Generations of Women Poets*; and American composer Aaron Copland's *Twelve Poems of Emily Dickinson*. Another musical setting of poems by Dickinson is Elam Sprenkle's *Six Songs for Mezzo-Soprano and Brass Quintet*. One writer suggests recordings of nineteenth-century hymn tunes for an understanding of Dickinson's stanzaic form: after singing the hymn, teacher and students can sing a Dickinson poem to the tune, a device that may show how the form itself can be ironic.

Other literary material that can shed light on Dickinson and her work includes poetry by Anne Bradstreet ("The Prologue," "The Author to Her Book," love poems), Walt Whitman (*Drum Taps*, "Out of the Cradle Endlessly Rocking," "A Noiseless Patient Spider"), Christina Rossetti ("Goblin Market," "Monna Innominata," and other love poems), and Elizabeth Barrett Browning ("Sonnets from the Portuguese," *Aurora Leigh*). Besides his poetry, some of Emerson's essays are recommended: "Circles" can be paired with Dickinson's poems on circumference, and "Compensation" with her poems on that subject. Selections from Thoreau's *Walden* might provide an interesting comparison with Dickinson's treatment of nature, solitude, and other issues. Hawthorne's tales are suggested as are Melville's short stories: "Bartleby the Scrivener" might be of particular interest. Also recommended are Mary E. Wilkins Freeman's story "A New England Nun" and James's *Bostonians*. Books on domesticity and the home by Catherine Beecher and Harriet Beecher Stowe might give students insights into Dickinson's environment. Popular poetry of the era, such as that in Rufus Griswold's *Female Poets of America* and that reprinted in Richard Sewall's biography, show, "by contrast, the audacity of [Dickinson's] undertaking," notes one writer. Poems about Dickinson by poets writing today, such as Adrienne Rich and Sandra Gilbert, may also illuminate students' understanding of Dickinson's impact on American poetry.

Materials from Dickinson's life that respondents find useful include, besides Franklin's *Manuscript Books*, Dickinson's letters, T. W. Higginson's "Letter to a Young Contributor," and early editions of Webster's dictionary.

Among the miscellaneous aids mentioned by our respondents are paintings by artists of the Hudson River school; material about the popular religious culture of the nineteenth century, including gravestone art; photographs of Dickinson, her home, and important figures in her life; a gravestone rubbing of Dickinson's marker; and a lithograph of the ruby-throated hummingbird (for poems 500 and 1463). We would recommend, too, the New York Graphic Society volume, *Acts of Light,* a collection of Dickinson's poetry illustrated by artist Nancy Ekholm Burkert, with an appreciation by Jane Langton. The book includes notes by the artist about the Dickinson material that inspired her paintings.

The Instructor's Library

We asked respondents to recommend works in two categories, reference and background (historical, cultural), and biography and criticism; we use the same divisions here. Such a distinction, however, is not always true to the works themselves; many contain valuable material in both categories. Most notably, Richard Sewall's *Life of Emily Dickinson* is cited frequently in both. The survey that follows is by no means exhaustive; in choosing items to include, we have been guided largely by the frequency with which they are mentioned by our respondents. Our main purpose is to bring to your attention texts that have been most useful to these experienced teachers of Dickinson. While we sometimes identify major concerns of the works, we do not, in general, summarize and evaluate them. In many of the essays that follow, instructors mention these books and others in more specific terms.

Primarily because of space restrictions, but also because few respondents mentioned journal articles, this survey is, with a few exceptions, limited to books. Several sources of information on current and past articles on Dickinson are readily available. The annual *MLA Bibliography* has the most comprehensive listing of each year's scholarship. The annual

American Literary Scholarship (published by the American Literature Division of the MLA) regularly summarizes and evaluates the year's work on Dickinson. The most up-to-date source, though it is still more limited in scope, is the selected annotated list of current articles published regularly in *American Literature*. Two bibliographies devoted to Dickinson are extremely useful. Willis J. Buckingham's *Emily Dickinson: An Annotated Bibliography* "aims to provide a comprehensive list of published materials" on Dickinson: it covers the years 1850 to 1968 and emphasizes scholarship and criticism in English and other languages. Joseph Duchac's *Poems of Emily Dickinson: An Annotated Guide to Commentary Published in English, 1890–1977* lists and briefly quotes all critical references to each poem. In addition, issues of *Dickinson Studies* frequently include a current bibliography. *ESQ: A Journal of the American Renaissance* also publishes many articles on Dickinson.

Reference Works

Biographies of Dickinson are discussed below; an easily accessible source, widely cited by her biographers, is Jay Leyda's two-volume *Years and Hours of Emily Dickinson*, which chronologically details the daily life of the poet and her community.

If Leyda's book is as close as most instructors can get to the material records of Dickinson's life, the work of Thomas Johnson and Ralph W. Franklin brings them closest to the texts of her poetry. In 1955 Johnson published, in three volumes, *The Poems of Emily Dickinson, Including Variant Readings Critically Compared with All Known Manuscripts*. The descriptions of manuscripts; the variant words, stanzas, and poems; and the publication history make this text an invaluable resource. Likewise indispensable, Franklin's two-volume *Manuscript Books of Emily Dickinson* reorders, according to Dickinson's design, and reproduces all the manuscripts that she bound into booklets or fascicles. Indeed, Franklin's edition reminds us of the limits of even as meticulous and exhaustive a work as Johnson's. Thus Susan Howe, in *My Emily Dickinson*, adopts Johnson's method of presenting the variants for each poem she quotes, but she also points out the absence, in Dickinson's fascicle manuscripts, of things like numbers for the poems and regular print, as well as differences between Johnson's and Dickinson's line breaks (23, 35).

"For several years, my Lexicon was my only companion," Dickinson wrote to T. W. Higginson (*Letters* 2: 404). Her lexicon was Noah Webster's 1844 *American Dictionary of the English Language*. According to Buckingham, the 1841 and 1845 editions of the same title were essentially the same ("Dictionary"). For information on Dickinson's other reading, Jack L.

Capps's *Emily Dickinson's Reading, 1836–1886* is comprehensive; Capps lists the family library's contents and Dickinson's references to her own reading, describes marginal notations, and suggests connections between individual readings and poems. Sewall's *Life* and George Frisbie Whicher's *This Was a Poet* both have useful chapters on the poet's reading. Another useful tool for study of the poems is S. P. Rosenbaum's *Concordance to the Poems of Emily Dickinson.*

Background Materials

Many teachers recommend reading Dickinson's contemporaries and forebears, literary and nonliterary. Most suggest, in particular, American writers of the nineteenth century, chiefly Emerson. The other American Romantics, including Margaret Fuller, are also suggested. The poetry of Dickinson's major contemporaries is easily accessible; Whicher's anthology, *Poetry of the New England Renaissance, 1790–1890* (out of print), includes substantial selections of major and less well known poets, and an appendix in Sewall's *Life* contains samples of the newspaper verse Dickinson read. Other recommended works that contributed to, or are representative of, the poet's religious inheritance are the poetry of Anne Bradstreet and Edward Taylor, the hymns of Isaac Watts, and the sermons of Jonathan Edwards. The influence of the King James Version of the Bible is apparent in Dickinson's letters as well as in the poems. British writers (Shakespeare and the Romantic poets) are mentioned; a fuller list of contemporaries who contributed to Dickinson's literary environment would of course include the Brownings, the Brontës, and George Eliot. Directly related to Dickinson's writing career is Higginson's "Letter to a Young Contributor," in response to which Dickinson initiated their correspondence.

Finally, in the view of many instructors, Dickinson's own letters are indispensable to the study of her poetry. Edited by Thomas Johnson and Theodora Ward, the letters are available complete in three volumes, and in part in the one-volume *Selected Letters.* Though most instructors will probably not use the "Master" letters directly in their teaching, they may find it enlightening to examine Franklin's edition of *The Master Letters of Emily Dickinson.* Again, this work reminds us how provisional are some of the texts on which interpretations of Dickinson's life and poetry have been based.

Several works of literary history are recommended. F. O. Matthiessen's classic *American Renaissance: Art and Expression in the Age of Emerson and Whitman* provides solid analyses of some of Dickinson's major contemporaries (though Dickinson is mentioned only in passing). Hyatt Waggoner, in *American Poets from the Puritans to the Present*, and Roy Harvey

Pearce, in *The Continuity of American Poetry*, each devote a chapter to Dickinson. Waggoner emphasizes her rejection of orthodoxy and the influence of Emerson and the Bible on her; Pearce considers the centrality of the self in her poetry and differences between her and Emerson. Among works devoted to woman writers, Gilbert and Gubar's *Madwoman in the Attic*, which discusses Dickinson in the context of a primarily British tradition, is frequently cited. Emily Stipes Watts, in *The Poetry of American Women from 1632 to 1945*, surveys similarities between the poetry of Dickinson's and that of other American women poets. In *The Nightingale's Burden: Women Poets and American Culture before 1900*, Cheryl Walker discusses in greater depth Dickinson's use of thematic and role conventions of the nineteenth-century "poetesses."

Works of social and cultural history can also illuminate Dickinson's background and situation. Recommended texts fall into two groups: those that emphasize the Protestant religious inheritance and those that concern some aspects of female experience. In the first category, the work of Perry Miller stands out: *The New England Mind: The Seventeenth Century*, *The New England Mind: From Colony to Province*, and *Nature's Nation*. Also important is Sacvan Bercovitch, *The Puritan Origins of the American Self*. Among works that emphasize female experience, *The Feminization of American Culture*, by Ann Douglas, is useful for its analysis of women's role in religious culture. Nancy F. Cott's *Bonds of Womanhood: "Woman's Sphere" in New England, 1780–1835*, studies the social background of the mid–nineteenth century cult of domesticity. Barbara Welter's *Dimity Convictions: The American Woman in the Nineteenth Century* includes essays on varied topics. Lillian Faderman's history of romantic friendship and love between women, *Surpassing the Love of Men*, offers an alternative to the most common approach to Dickinson's love poetry, the search for the male lover. Carroll Smith-Rosenberg's essay "The Female World of Love and Ritual: Relations between Women in Nineteenth-Century America" also suggests another context for understanding some of the friendships documented in Dickinson's letters.

Finally, several works devoted to Dickinson concentrate on her relation to her times or to continuing literary tradition. Karl Keller's *Only Kangaroo among the Beauty: Emily Dickinson and America*, discusses Dickinson's affinities with writers from Anne Bradstreet to Robert Frost. Barton Levi St. Armand, in *Emily Dickinson and Her Culture*, uses an interdisciplinary approach to relate Dickinson to aspects of American culture as varied as folk art and painters of the Hudson River school. Shira Wolosky, in *Emily Dickinson: A Voice of War*, analyzes Dickinson's response to the Civil War and to the rhetoric that surrounded it. Karen Dandurand, in "New Dickinson Civil War Publication," also considers the poet's response to the war, while calling into question some well-established assumptions about her attitudes toward publishing.

Biography

If you could read only one book about Emily Dickinson, it should be Richard B. Sewall's *Life of Emily Dickinson*. Almost universally recommended by respondents, it describes in exhaustive detail not only Dickinson's life but her family history, her Amherst and New England milieu, and the lives of her associates, and it is informed throughout by a thorough familiarity with the poetry. Many respondents also recommend either Thomas Johnson's *Emily Dickinson: An Interpretive Biography* or George F. Whicher's *This Was a Poet*. The usefulness of Whicher's book is seriously limited because the author did not have access to all the poems or to reliable versions of those he did have; nonetheless, his description of Dickinson's New England background is among the best we have read. Johnson, too, sheds light on Dickinson's relation to her Connecticut Valley environment. Another useful study is Albert Gelpi's *Emily Dickinson: The Mind of the Poet*.

Dickinson's life has always incited speculation, biographical interpretation of the poems, and controversy. Two noteworthy examples, each cited by several correspondents, are John Cody's *After Great Pain: The Inner Life of Emily Dickinson* and William H. Shurr's *Marriage of Emily Dickinson*. Cody's generally orthodox Freudian interpretation has inspired numerous critics to propose alternate readings. Feminism has produced some of the most interesting recent work on Dickinson; two such studies that make significant contributions to our understanding of Dickinson's life as a woman are Adrienne Rich's classic essay "Vesuvius at Home: The Power of Emily Dickinson" and Barbara A. C. Mossberg's *Emily Dickinson: When a Writer Is a Daughter*. Finally, we note the new biography by Cynthia Griffin Wolff, *Emily Dickinson*, which promises to contribute to many of the debates surrounding the poet.

Criticism

Dickinson scholars have written and continue to produce an impressive volume of solid and useful criticism, only a fraction of which we can mention here. As before, we have been guided in large part by the responses to our survey. Some of the best of Dickinson scholarship is cited here, but much that is excellent is not, because of limited space and the nature of this series. Again, we hope you will use this introduction as a starting point for your own investigations of Dickinson studies.

The critical book most often recommended by instructors is Charles Anderson's *Emily Dickinson's Poetry: Stairway of Surprise*. This excellent study takes a thematic approach, beginning with art, then moving through nature and the inner world to death and immortality.

Dickinson's development as a poet is explored in David Porter's *Art of Emily Dickinson's Early Poetry*; the book has a wider interest than its title might suggest. Notable among studies that treat Dickinson in relation to Romanticism are Robert Weisbuch's *Emily Dickinson's Poetry*, especially valuable for its analysis of her analogical poetics, and Joanne Feit Diehl's *Dickinson and the Romantic Imagination*, which explores Dickinson's necessary subversion of the tradition of Wordsworth, Shelley, Keats, and Emerson.

Contrasting analyses of Dickinson's poetry of interior experience are offered by Clark Griffith, in *The Long Shadow: Emily Dickinson's Tragic Poetry*, who sees dread of ambiguity and fear as dominant, and Suzanne Juhasz, in *The Undiscovered Continent: Emily Dickinson and the Space Within*, who argues that for Dickinson, living in the mind was a positive solution to the problem of how to be a poet. In contrast, Christopher Benfey, in *Emily Dickinson and the Problem of Others*, treats Dickinson as a thinker responsive to skepticism and emphasizes her interest in reciprocal relation with the world. Helen McNeil, too, in *Emily Dickinson*, emphasizes Dickinson's intellectual concerns, calling her a heuristic poet, who elaborates an epistemology of feeling and difference.

Wendy Martin, in *An American Triptych*, combines biography and criticism in her study of the evolution of a female counterpoetic in the poetry of Bradstreet, Dickinson, and Rich.

Ruth Miller, in *The Poetry of Emily Dickinson*, argues that a common dramatic principle underlies the structures of the fascicles.

Numerous studies have illuminated Dickinson's language and other aspects of her style. Brita Lindberg-Seyersted's *Voice of the Poet: Aspects of Style in the Poetry of Emily Dickinson* and Roland Hagenbüchle's "Precision and Indeterminancy in the Poetry of Emily Dickinson" are both helpful. Rebecca Patterson's *Emily Dickinson's Imagery* analyzes the poetry's imagery in relation to its eroticism. David Porter, in *Dickinson: The Modern Idiom*, draws on a study of the manuscripts to analyze Dickinson's relation to modernism. In *Lyric Time: Dickinson and the Limits of Genre*, Sharon Cameron treats Dickinson's language in her analysis of the problematic issues of temporality in the poetry. Margaret Homans, in *Women Writers and Poetic Identity*, uses poststructuralist and feminist approaches to analyze Dickinson's exploration of the nature and power of language. In *Emily Dickinson: A Poet's Grammar*, Cristanne Miller analyzes the poet's language use, which she argues can be accounted for by recent speculative descriptions of women's writing.

Recommended for students and helpful for the beginning instructor are three introductory works: Denis Donoghue's *Emily Dickinson*; Paul J. Ferlazzo's *Emily Dickinson*; and John B. Pickard's *Emily Dickinson: An Introduction and Interpretation.*

A number of critical anthologies usefully collect varied articles on Dickinson. *The Recognition of Emily Dickinson* (Blake and Wells), *Emily Dickinson: A Collection of Critical Essays* (Sewall), and *Critical Essays on Emily Dickinson* (Ferlazzo) all include Allen Tate's "New England Culture and Emily Dickinson" (titled "Emily Dickinson" in the Sewall anthology) and Yvor Winters's "Emily Dickinson and the Limits of Judgment." Sewall's anthology also contains Richard Wilbur's "Sumptuous Destitution," Louise Bogan's "A Mystical Poet," and Archibald MacLeish's "The Private World" (a similar essay by MacLeish appears in Blake and Wells). *The Recognition of Emily Dickinson* and *Critical Essays on Emily Dickinson* both offer numerous early reviews of the poetry, among them essays by Higginson, Thomas Bailey Aldrich, and William Dean Howells. *Critical Essays on Emily Dickinson* includes a number of quite recent articles, such as Rich's "Vesuvius at Home," Rebecca Patterson's "Emily Dickinson's 'Double' Tim: Masculine Identification," and essays by Sharon Cameron, Jane Donahue Eberwein, and Barbara Mossberg. An anthology that emphasizes recent criticism is *Feminist Critics Read Emily Dickinson* (Juhasz), with essays by Margaret Homans, Adalaide Morris, Cristanne Miller, Karl Keller, Sandra Gilbert, Barbara Mossberg, Joanne Dobson, and Joanne Feit Diehl.

Instructors will find a history of Dickinson's reception in Britain and the United States from 1862 to 1962 in Klaus Lubbers's *Emily Dickinson: The Critical Revolution.* In *Emily Dickinson in Europe*, Ann Lilliedahl surveys Dickinson's reception in Scandinavia, Germany, France, and French-speaking Switzerland.

Having paid a great deal of attention to the difficulties Dickinson can pose for the student and having described some responses to them, we end this section by repeating what many of our colleagues have written to us, confirming our own experiences: students like Dickinson. Some are instantly captivated, despite (or because of?) the bafflement. And many others, once they see how to begin approaching her poetry, are equally delighted and intrigued. Still perplexed, yes, but when they realize that perplexity is part of her program, that theirs is shared by others, including sometimes their teachers, they rise to the challenge and often go on to become adventurous and insightful readers—more confident, perhaps, of the value of poetry and, surely, of their own abilities. Darryl Hattenhauer reports that his students "like to write on Dickinson more than on any other American poet." Wendy Bean Barker, explaining her choice of the *Complete Poems* as a text, writes, "I find that whenever Dickinson is the focus of our reading and discussion, as many as half of the students will read the complete poems all the way through. They become 'hooked.' "

Most of their teachers are already hooked. William Shullenberger undoubtedly speaks for many when he says that "her lyrical and syntactic difficulties are the very things that make Dickinson most fun to teach. She teaches herself in a way, because the students are bound to question the text, and the questions both open the poem and rebound back on the students." Barbara L. Packer, too, speaks for many: "I find her an absolute delight to teach. The students love her, too. She's almost a self-enclosed course in how to read poetry. . . . " As these observations suggest, and the essays that follow demonstrate, Dickinson offers teachers and students a compelling opportunity for the kind of dialogue that produces both instruction and delight.

Part Two

APPROACHES

INTRODUCTION

The twenty essays that follow explore approaches to Emily Dickinson's poetry and her life that have been used successfully in undergraduate classes throughout the United States. In some introductory courses, students may read as few as five or six poems, while those in an upper-division seminar might well read them all. All our contributors, however, as their essays make clear, are committed to conveying Dickinson's range, her complexity, and her poetic power regardless of the limitations a particular course may impose on them.

The essays are organized into four groups. The first and second describe ways to introduce Dickinson and her poetry and ways to read the poems in class. The essays introducing the poetry address concerns shared by teachers at all levels; approaches similar to those described here may even be useful in graduate seminars. The essays in the third section propose ways of grouping the poems for study and draw attention to different aspects of Dickinson's art. While the approaches in this section evolve from contexts that poems and poet create, those described in the fourth section place the poetry in larger contexts that are illuminated but not created by the poems themselves. The essays in each section address pedagogical concerns involved in teaching Dickinson in any situation: presenting the poetry to new readers, reading individual poems, considering relations among the poems themselves, and exploring the relations between Dickinson's work and the world. Readers will quickly realize, however, that the essays address more issues than those identified by the section headings. Dickinson's treatment of death, the epistemological questions her poems raise, and the implications of gender are just three examples of topics that arise frequently and in varied contexts.

Richard B. Sewall begins our first section with a discussion of ways to present Dickinson to first-time readers; his essay is enriched by insights gleaned from his nearly fifty years as a teacher and scholar. John Mann then describes how he uses Dickinson's first five letters to Thomas Wentworth Higginson to introduce some of the biographical, aesthetic, and epistemological questions raised by the poetry. The next three essayists write about introducing Dickinson in distinctive contexts. Mary L. Morton uses Dickinson to teach freshmen how to read poetry, Katharine M. Rogers teaches Dickinson in an introductory literature survey required for all students in an urban public college, and Alice Hall Petry describes the special challenges of teaching the poetry to fine-arts students. The final essay in this section provides a bridge into the following ones: Rowena Revis Jones describes the use of small groups for teaching Dickinson in composition classes and then explains how this method can be adapted for advanced literature classes.

The second group of essays concentrates on reading the poems, with the first two emphasizing Dickinson's poetic practices. James Guthrie discusses a poetic device, near rhyme, familiar to teachers if not to students. Cristanne Miller analyzes some of the distinctive linguistic and grammatical habits that characterize Dickinson's poetry and often perplex teachers and students alike. The other two essays in this group examine the process of reading. Suzanne Juhasz describes a line-by-line approach and stresses the effect of gender on Dickinson's multiple meanings. William Shullenberger outlines a strategy of collaborative reading that responds to the disconcerting effects of the poetry's indeterminacy.

Writers in the third section consider Dickinson's poetry in some of the contexts it creates. In Nancy Walker's and William Galperin's essays, the contexts are thematic. Walker discusses Dickinson's treatment of love and shows how poems on this theme can illuminate the poet's range of imagery and personae. Galperin uses the insights of feminism and posthumanism to explore the development of the poetic subject's powers of self-definition and autonomy. Dorothy Huff Oberhaus places Dickinson's poetry in a generic context in her Comedy, Wit, and Humor and American Humor courses. Douglas Novich Leonard describes an approach to teaching the poems in the fascicles created by Dickinson and suggests how her lyrical sequences can be taught with Whitman's long poems.

The writers in the fourth section approach the poetry in the contexts of Dickinson's life, the world she lived in (variously defined), and literary relations. Frank D. Rashid discusses the uses and limitations of biography in teaching Dickinson's poetry. Taking a feminist perspective, Cheryl

Walker answers frequently asked questions about Dickinson's life and poetry in terms of the poet's experience as a woman. Charlotte Nekola uses
Dickinson's letters and recent historical scholarship to examine the poet's
relation to nineteenth-century ideas about issues such as the "separate
spheres" of men and women, marriage, and religious conversion. Barton
Levi St. Armand uses an interdisciplinary approach to discuss her treatment of death and bereavement, placing her in the context of nineteenth-
century popular culture. In an American literature survey class, on the
other hand, Elissa Greenwald considers Dickinson in relation to literary
realism. Finally, Mary Loeffelholz, from a feminist and posthumanist perspective, discusses how Dickinson's relations to historical constructions of
the female self and the poet can be explored in women's studies and English classes.

While all the essays necessarily incorporate both interpretation and pedagogy, their underlying assumptions often differ strikingly. Indeed, our
contributors and their essays implicitly argue with one another on issues
central to Dickinson's poetry. For example, different answers to the question of how Dickinson is to be related to her culture might be detected in
Cheryl Walker's and St. Armand's interpretations of her famous white
dress. Significant tensions may also be discovered underlying several readings of the same poem, for instance, the discussions of "There's a certain
Slant of light" (258) in the essays of Shullenberger, Leonard, and Greenwald. And contrasting assessments of the "smallness" of Dickinson's poems
lead Sewall, Morton, and Petry to differing pedagogical assumptions and
practices.

Our contributors differ, too, on the role biography should play in the
study of the poetry—an unavoidable question, since students commonly
bring one or more of the Dickinson myths to class with them. Rashid,
recognizing the fascination the myths can hold for students, proposes that
teachers use the life as an entry to the poems but feels that we need to
guard against overemphasizing biography and shortchanging the poems.
Guthrie, though, prefers to begin with style, which he uses as "an antidote
to the sensation of strangeness" that Dickinson's life produces for students.
Petry takes an opposite approach, beginning her unit on Dickinson with
discussion of the myths and their implications.

Of concern to all readers and teachers of Dickinson is how we can find
meaning in her poems. Some find the poems characterized by an indeterminacy that finally defeats our efforts to interpret them definitively. Others assume that the poems have meanings that can be found, solutions that
careful analysis will yield. Some might take these to be irreconcilable assumptions. Yet Juhasz describes a way to treat multiplicity as meaning, and
even those who argue most strongly for indeterminacy acknowledge that

for teachers and students a meaning-implying activity like grouping the poems thematically may be a necessity. A related question concerns the unity, or lack of it, of Dickinson's oeuvre. Sewall finds that the motifs of pilgrimage and experiment serve as unifying threads. Leonard argues that the fascicles reveal structural and thematic unities that illuminate the meanings of individual poems. Galperin, on the other hand, contends that Dickinson's poetry resists any kind of "totalizing structure."

Related to questions about decipherable meanings is the issue of the reader's relation to poet and poems. Can we assume that some element of universality, of familiarity grounded in our common humanity, inheres in the poems? Should we invite students to respond to the poetry in terms of their own experiences? Some of our contributors explicitly address these issues; others' assumptions are implicit in their discussions. A dilemma may attend these questions, in our recognition that emphasizing the "common" or "universal" has often effectively denied real differences, while validating the perceptions and experiences of the privileged. (This recognition is basic to contemporary discussions of canon formation in American literature.) Dickinson seems to insist on difference, on the disconcerting, on discontinuity. Yet she also addresses us. And can we respond to what we cannot recognize at all, on any level? As teachers, especially, we need ways to mediate this perhaps ultimately unresolvable tension. Miller seems to suggest one way, when she asks students to "imagine more than one kind of experience that might prompt the writing of a poem like 'It was not Death' (510) and then to let the remembered or imagined experience drop while they focus just on the feeling 'it' created or the multiple responses they have to 'it' that Dickinson provides evidence for in the poem."

These essays are by teachers of diverse backgrounds and inclinations, who bring to their writing the experiences of teaching students of even greater diversity, at schools of every sort. In concert, they make an unusual but, we hope, a pleasing music. Most readers will probably recognize tunes they have sung or played themselves. Yet the arrangements, as well as the counterpoints, may be unfamiliar. In the essays' dissonances and harmonies we can hear many of the questions—some old, some new—that currently engage academics and theorists. That contention may sometimes lie not far below the surface is not, then, surprising. We hope that our readers will find the symphonic plentitude both intellectually challenging and emotionally engaging.

For the appendix, to illustrate the rich variety of responses to the initial survey and to suggest in some detail the range of possibilities for undergraduate assignments, we have selected three very different explication assignments from William Galperin, Barbara Packer, and Lynne Shackelford;

two assignments that particularly encourage creative responses to Dickinson's poetry from Paula Uruburu; and the questions for an oral group examination given by Cheryl Walker.

All quotations from the poems are from Thomas Johnson, *The Complete Poems of Emily Dickinson*; they are identified by first lines and by the numbers assigned in that text. We have omitted end-of-line punctuation when first lines serve as titles and when final dashes or other marks would complicate sentence punctuation. Unless otherwise noted, references to Dickinson's letters (*L*) are to *The Letters of Emily Dickinson*, edited by Johnson and Ward. For clarity and ease of reference, we give the volume number followed by the page number, rather than the letter number.

RRF and CMG

INTRODUCING EMILY DICKINSON

Teaching Dickinson:
Testimony of a Veteran

Richard B. Sewall

I have taught the poetry of Emily Dickinson, off and on, since 1938, and I am still searching for the best way. I find that I do it a little differently every year—to fit the nature of the class, the temper of the times, and my own changing perspective (one does a lot of living—and reading—in a year). As with Shakespeare, there are many routes to the center; only, with Dickinson, the country is curiously uncharted, quite unlike the fine familiar territories of the great ones. We feel secure with Chaucer and Milton and Pope or (to come closer to Dickinson's world) Keats, Shelley, the Brownings, and Whitman or (to move on to the poets of our own time who strike me as easy going compared with Dickinson) Eliot, Frost, Stevens, and Yeats. Eliot? He's their (the students') man; they respond immediately to the early satires and are easily persuaded to press on. Frost? The tone is steady, the voice (pure New England) clear as a bell, and the form (as I heard him describe one of his short pieces) "neat as a pin." Stevens takes some doing (they all do, for that matter); but he has written and talked about his poetry a good deal; he is a public figure; we know where he is. In 1938 Brooks and Warren, in *Understanding Poetry*, opened up Yeats for me, and he has been an unfailing resource. None of these poets presents the problems of those 1,775 short, tense, disparate pieces (finished, unfinished, some mere fragments) that Emily Dickinson left in her bureau drawer, undated, untitled and, save for a tiny handful, unpublished (and those anonymously). In short—and this is important to keep in mind—she left us her workshop. When a selection from it was published in 1890, four years after her death, the first reviewer, Arlo Bates, called the poems "half barbaric."

And yet he liked them. For a late nineteenth-century ear conditioned by mellifluous Tennysonian (and sub-Tennysonian) cadences, this approval was an achievement. "Hardly a line," he wrote, "fails to throw out some gleam of genuine original power, of imagination, and of real emotional thought" (Blake and Wells 13). "Emotional thought"? A paradox? Or was Bates groping for a quality that has been seen in Dostoyevski: "ideas-as-lived"—that is, ideas felt on the pulses, in the bloodstream. If so, he was getting at something close to the center, an "existential" quality that links Dickinson to a powerful movement of our times. At any rate, Bates forgave the technical "barbarisms" (the approximate rhyming, the metrical eccentricities, the strained syntax, the grammatical oddities) in the delight of discovering what he called "a new species of art." Although the responses of most students to Dickinson's poetry will hardly be on so sophisticated a level, they will contain, I've found, much of the same element of surprise, even shock.

The question is, how to induce in students, most of whom come to lyric poetry either de novo or with well-developed prejudices, an experience of discovery—and delight—similar to that of Arlo Bates? Some few will have no difficulty in identifying (as they say) with Emily Dickinson—she is their woman from the first. But set a class loose on *The Complete Poems* (this is often my first assignment), and almost everyone will find something that rings a bell. Even those who are inclined to balk at lyric poetry will find something, somewhere, that interests them to the point of wanting to talk or even write about it (and sometimes these students turn out to be the most enthusiastic). I stress *The Complete Poems*: avoid anthologies if at all possible. They remove the element of discovery—an experience that even I, a fifty-year veteran, often enjoy as I leaf through the poems for the hundredth time and come upon one that hits me as if I'd never read it before, an exciting rediscovery. Anthologies take the fun away. "Here are the poems you are supposed to like," they seem to say. And I can hear the skeptical student say, "What? Those puzzling little snippets?"

Snippets, of course, is my word. It doesn't sound undergraduate. But it stresses my point about anthologies—a mostly psychological point but important: the element of size. Chaucer, Spenser, Shakespeare, Milton, the great novelists have size; they offer many handholds; even *Paradise Lost* has a story. Students unused to reading poems of such intense brevity as Dickinson's, packed with energy like so many supercharged storage batteries, may well zip through the dozen or so poems the average anthology gives to the poet, think they have done the lesson, and pass on unmoved. But confront them with 1,775 of those poems and it's hard to see how even the casual students can fail, even if bewildered, to be impressed. If at the same time you can bring the three volumes of her letters into the picture, half the battle may be won in the first engagement. Students, I've found, like to read things they can get their teeth into. They may get only a fraction of *King Lear* or *Moby-Dick*, but they can't shrug off the experience of reading them. Confronting students with the entire Dickinson canon is only the first answer to the problem of size. The next—indeed, the ultimate—is giving shape to that size—shape, and meaning, and power.

It can be done. I have had failures—but never complete ones, and I have learned how to do better next time. Dickinson has never entirely let me down, and I include classes from high school to graduate school; from classes of twenty freshmen to upper-class seminars to continuing-education lectures. The reason is not far to seek. She may be difficult, often puzzling (she liked riddles), hard to pin down. She defies easy classification. At first, one is struck by the *dis*unity of the canon, the disparity of the parts. We hear many voices—joy, sorrow; pleasure, pain; faith, doubt; the voice of innocence, the voice of experience; and many more. Which is Emily Dickinson's? With most other lyric poets, we can follow the developmental line or the thematic. But with Dickinson, almost all dating is problematic; the poems in the early pages of *The Complete Poems* are very much like those in the final pages. As to theme, the first editors in the 1890s divided the poems into four categories—Life, Love, Nature, Time and Eternity,— but ever since then those distinctions have been breaking down as we become more sensitive to the implications of her metaphoric way of thinking. (In a single poem, she may be directing her thought toward all four.) In spite of such roadblocks to a conventional approach, the reassuring fact remains: she is a popular poet who speaks to our common humanity just as surely, and with comparable power, as do the great ones. She is no longer a cult figure, cherished by the elite; but, thanks to the work of editors, scholars, critics, and a steadily growing number of teachers, her work is within the reach of everyone. For many undergraduates, still cherishing prejudices about poetry (and about Dickinson), her availability may be news; and even those who accept her readily will need help in understanding the nature, in its range and depth, of what it is they are accepting. This book is full of suggestions about how to do it. Let me lay out a few principles that seem pertinent.

First, I think it's important that anyone who undertakes to teach Dickinson should know at least enough about her life to avoid the clichés that have dogged her since the poems were first published: the Frustrated Lover, the New England Nun, the Moth of Amherst, the Woman in White, and (latterly) the Neurotic. It's good to know something about Amherst and its place in the Connecticut Valley culture: the town, Emily's schooling (Amherst Academy and Mount Holyoke), the college, the church with its late-Puritan preaching, the Dickinson family and Emily's daily routine, the books and periodicals at hand in her house (especially the *Springfield Daily Republican*, which she seldom missed). Such matters require no specialist's knowledge or formal introductory lectures. Enough can be conveyed—and perhaps best conveyed—as the class proceeds in the discussion of specific poems that require some sense of context.

Take, for instance, that fine poem, "I think I was enchanted" (593). Coming to Dickinson cold, how would a student know that it was her tribute to Elizabeth Barrett Browning and how, without some help, would even a sophisticated student sense the importance of the poem in the context of Dickinson's literary career? Only recently has David Porter shown the poem to be not only a moving tribute but a vivid account of Dickinson's first awareness of her own poetic mission, the birth of the poet in her (*Modern Idiom* 204).

From such contextual matters flow many others: Dickinson's literary affinities, especially with the other great women writers of her century, the Brontës and George Eliot, a matter that has been under much discussion recently; her relation to the great English Romantic poets, Wordsworth, Shelley, Keats, who have left us similarly vivid accounts of their call to be poets; and finally what we learn from this poem about Dickinson's sense of what poetry is and why she wrote it: poetry as revelation, poetry as "epiphanic." (As an antidote to the tendency to get too far out in such discussions, I have often had students compare Browning's lovely, flowing "How do I love thee? let me count the ways" with Dickinson's pert, saucy, staccato " 'Why do I love' You, sir?" [480]. The contrast is an admirable way of showing the vast difference between her style and the reigning nineteenth-century mode. No wonder that, except for those few anonymous pieces, Dickinson was never published. And yet it was Elizabeth Barrett Browning who, according to 593, first inspired her.)

As the clichés are pared away—a gradual process, I suggest—the outlines of Dickinson as a major literary figure should come into the clear. I have found it best to proceed inductively, poem by poem. That first assignment, a three-hundred-word paper on a poem of the student's choice, tells me a lot. I can see what the complaints are: Why are the rhymes so careless? Couldn't she do it right? (In time, students can be made to see that Dickinson's ear, far from insensitive, was very subtle, that she packed much meaning into her approximations—e.g., 842, a trifling poem save for the fine satiric touch of the "tell"-"dull" rhyme of the concluding stanza.) But mainly the complaints stem from bewilderment: What is she saying? That first paper usually reveals the source of bewilderment—her capricious punctuation and capitalization; a pronoun whose referent is not clear; a subject whose predicate doesn't show up till five or six lines later; a metaphor whose implications are lost on the student; a bit of playfulness missed (her humor often eludes even sophisticated readers); or some confusing syntax (remember, what appears so orderly on the printed page may be an unrevised bit from the workshop). Sometimes the major thrust of a poem is lost on students through failure to respond to a proper noun, the name of a well-known place or person. In an upper-class seminar recently, a student was stumped by the word "Calvary" (313): "What's Calvary?" And as to "Sabachthani" and "The Reefs—in old Gethsemane" (same poem), he was utterly mystified. Indeed, as students run across more and more of those proper nouns (and learn to look them up), they will come to respect the sheer range of Dickinson's knowledge. (What could they possibly make of 140 if they did not know something about Nicodemus?)

With those first papers in, duly corrected and annotated (I never said this would be easy), the first class discussion seldom lacks animation. Students like to defend their readings. Usually, even the most wayward readings contain enough truth to be the basis of creative development. Though sometimes it's a matter of plain error or ignorance, the process is usually not one of "I am right and you are wrong." The whole truth (if that is ever obtainable) emerges gradually, often with many students offering suggestions. By the end of the first class, perhaps a half-dozen poems will have been scrutinized and, it is to be hoped, illuminated. Always, each poem, after analysis, should be put together again in a sustained reading, perhaps by a student who is good at it but mostly by the teacher, who by training and practice has achieved sensitivity to that important element in Dickinson: tone. My earnest plea is to avoid at all costs the plaintive, smiles-through-the-tears tone of much of the reading one hears in the media. Beware of sentimentalizing Dickinson, of evoking pity. And read slowly enough to catch the nuances, the wit, the play of the words, the sonorities. In the teaching of Dickinson, much depends on the quality of the intonation.

She speaks, as I said, in many voices. Sometimes it's the child's voice, timorous or pleading or confused (196, 111); sometimes the midcareer satirist's (401); sometimes that of the anguished spirit (502); sometimes the voice of seasoned skepticism (1770); and so on and on, an almost

Shakespearean range. And within each poem that can be so tagged, the voice may change its tone abruptly, often at the end and with an unexpected twist. For instance, 111 ("The Bee is not afraid of me"): the first six lines might be Goldilocks in the woods—all is serene and beautiful, nature smiles on her, she has nothing to fear. Then in the last two lines the tone changes. She is weeping and asks why. We ask, too, both teachers and students. That no answer is completely right may be a revelation to many students who look for a simple yea or nay. Poem 556 ("The Brain, within its Groove") speaks, in the first two lines, with the voice, say, of a lecturer on mental disorders. The last six bespeak the terror of irreversible madness—the same lecturer, perhaps, but what a different tone! Many poems, after depicting action or turbulence of spirit, end with a reflective summing-up that involves an abrupt change of tone. The much-debated 754 ("My Life had stood—a Loaded Gun") is a striking example; 772, shorter, less complicated, is another: the last line produces one of Dickinson's characteristic reflective apothegms, "All—is the price of All." The reader must be constantly alert to such changes. Often they breathe life into the poem, which may live or die according to the reader's sensitivity to tone. A good assignment is a paper in which tone is the major focus. Let the students search for their own examples.

Students (and teachers, too) will wonder about her strange punctuation (especially the dashes) and her capitalization. An interesting session, or at least a good part of one, may be spent on the problem. For this reason, I recommend the Harvard edition of the poems, edited by Thomas Johnson, the first to contain Dickinson's own usages, eccentric as they are, reflected as accurately as modern editorial practice allows. The capitalization follows no strict law; often it seems entirely whimsical. One of the rhetoric books she used at school recommended the use of capitals for emphasis, but often Dickinson capitalized words that need no such treatment. At least this can be said: it is often difficult to tell from her handwriting whether she meant a given letter to be capitalized or not. There was no editor to demand clearer copy. Johnson and his colleagues had to do considerable guessing. Also, remember this: Emily Dickinson studied German, where every noun is capitalized. If there is any consistent principle behind the capitalization, it probably should be stated in terms of her high regard for the individual word, its dignity, even its sanctity. She began a poem (about poetry, 1651) with a quotation from the Gospel of John, "A Word made Flesh. . . . " Once she wrote a friend about words: "We used to think, Joseph, that words were cheap and weak. Now I don't know of anything so mighty. There are those to which I lift my hat when I see them sitting princelike among their peers on the page. Sometimes I write one, and look at his outlines till he glows as no sapphire" (Sewall, *Lyman Letters*

78). With such a high regard for words, she might have capitalized them not only to give them emphasis but to do them homage.

Her use of dashes has been the subject of much speculation. In the manuscripts, they differ in length, some hardly more than exaggerated dots. Some turn slightly up, some down—leading to the theory that they are elocutionary guides. It is more likely that she was following the advice in one of the rhetoric texts in her school: "[the dash] is employed as a substitute for almost all of the other marks; being used sometimes for a comma, semicolon, or period; sometimes for a question or an exclamation, and sometimes for crochets and brackets to enclose a parenthesis" (Parker 45). Austin and Lavinia, Emily's brother and sister, used the dash profusely in their letters; it was in style. Emily used it as a sensitive instrument to regulate rhythm and gain emphasis. A remarkable instance in her letters is the sentence, "I often wonder how the love of Christ, is done—when that—below—holds—so—" (L 2: 406). And note the fine control of rhythm in the last line of "After great pain" (341). The dashes slow the pace to enact, rhythmically, the process of freezing to death: "First—Chill—then Stupor—then the letting go." (Another good assignment: a paper on the use of dashes in a few other Dickinson poems. Successful? Unsuccessful? And why? A few exercises like this would soon dispose of the notion that she did not know what she was doing.)

Her metrical subtleties are a source of endless discussion and discovery. Only occasionally does the hymn form—the common meter, "8s and 6s"—betray her into singsong; the wonder is the skill with which she makes something new and exciting out of that supposedly limited form, invents new forms when she finds need of them, and varies the basic iambic beat so sensitively as to avoid monotony. There are metrical surprises everywhere. Let the student inclined to smile at "I'm Nobody! Who are you?" (288) do a metrical analysis of the poem, with special attention to the control of pace. Or, if that fails to convince, try the next poem, "I know some lonely Houses off the Road" (289). "After great pain" (341), one of her few poems in iambic pentameter, is one of her great metrical accomplishments. (There should be no argument after that.) I have never lingered long on such matters—there is always so much else to say—but enough, I hope, to show, again, how a highly conscious artist goes to work. For students who find her music hard to hear, I have often put that gnomic bit "Experiment escorts us last" (1770) to good use. It seems at first glance little more than an aphorism put metrically. But sing it to the tune of "O God our help in ages past" and see how expertly, and delicately, the hymn meter is used. The gnomic bit becomes a poem.

Of all the elements in Dickinson's poetic equipment, none is more essential than metaphor—and none, perhaps, presents a greater obstacle to the resistant student. Emily herself anticipated the resistance in a playful letter (a Valentine) to a young man in Amherst when she was nineteen. In asking her friend for what we would call a date—a perfect meeting—she wrote, "I am Judith of the Apocrypha, and you the orator of Ephesus." Then, should he think she was talking nonsense, she added, "That's what they call a metaphor in our country. Don't be afraid of it, sir, it won't bite." (*L* 1: 92). Her remark was, in a sense, prophetic. Her young (and predictably obtuse?) friend could stand for a whole generation of readers who found her an enigma and a puzzle. They were unable or unwilling to follow her metaphoric trail till it opened into a clearing. (Even Thomas Wentworth Higginson, one of her first editors and an experienced man of letters, admitted his difficulty in penetrating what he called the "fiery mist" with which she surrounded herself [Sewall, *Life* 1: 5].) Her letters, which, unlike the poems, can be dated fairly precisely, show a steady development toward the economy and suggestiveness of metaphor. The poems, on the other hand, are metaphoric from beginning to end. For instance: the garden of poem 2 is the love and warmth and brightness of home compared with the "darkness" of her brother Austin's life in far-off Boston. In 1774, happiness ("Too happy Time") is sugar dissolving in water, that is, fleeting; while "Anguish" is a bird without feathers or too heavy to fly: it stays. Many poems are nothing but sustained metaphors, like 1463 ("A Route of Evanescence"), which, perhaps to be sure that it would not be mistaken, she sent to Mabel Loomis Todd with the remark, " . . . please accept a hummingbird" (*L* 3: 740). Similarly, she made sure that Mrs. Todd would understand that the "minor Nation" of 1068 was crickets. (Question: what does she make of them *metaphorically*?)

The subject of metaphor is, of course, immense. The thousands of metaphors in the Dickinson canon are rich in meanings, suggestions, hints, challenges to the imagination, incitements to thought—which means, for pedagogical purposes, endless subjects for discussion, written and oral. (I favor as many written exercises as possible; students usually do better thinking when they have to commit it to paper.) The understanding and the enjoyment of Dickinson depend largely on the ability to respond to metaphoric thought, to see what she is saying by her hummingbirds and crickets and sunsets and winter landscapes. To become familiar with her way of thinking, to become (as we would say) comfortable with it, is to gain access to the world of poetry in general, and hence marks a milestone in a student's education. One is tempted to say that after her, the rest is easy. But I have heard students say it; and, with notable exceptions, I think they speak truly.

Finally, the synthesis. How to put it all together? Is there any principle or controlling idea that gives unity to the often contradictory parts? Teachers approaching Emily Dickinson should have some sense of where they're coming out, else the whole exercise will fritter away in fragments. Here are a few gleanings from my experience:

First, do not ask her to be what she was not. She did not write plays or novels or epic poems. She was a lyric poet; and, as Kenneth Burke has reminded us, lyric poets are under no obligation to see life steadily and see it whole. Consistency, system, *programme* or *projet* need not be their concern. What we ask of them is precision, insight, vividness in the parts, relevance to our common humanity. In values such as these, Dickinson has few peers.

Second, inconsistency, contradiction need not mean welter or confusion. In an early letter, Emily Dickinson spoke of "this wilderness life of mine" (L 1: 99); shortly after, she wrote, "I wish I were somebody else" (L 1: 103); and, a few years later, "I wonder how long we shall wonder; how early we shall *know*" (L 2: 336). But in her full maturity, the wilderness became a "Matchless Earth" (L 2: 478); she saw life as (possibly) "the thrilling preface to supremer things" (L 3: 683); and she is recorded as telling a friend, "There is always one thing to be grateful for—that one is one's self and not somebody else" (L 2: 519). These are not so much inconsistencies and contradictions as they are records of the stages of a pilgrimage, a lifelong struggle to achieve what she called a "Columnar Self" (789) and in the process to penetrate the mysteries of existence as far as the human mind is able. The metaphor of the pilgrim is frequent in her poetry (35, 101, 132, 143, 773). Several remarks in her letters (e.g., L 2: 357) apply it to herself.

Third, if the idea of pilgrimage fails to stir the student pulse, perhaps the idea of that gnomic quatrain, "Experiment escorts us last," will. She was an experimenter of the spirit, and her probings took her through almost the entire range of experience we humans are heir to. She illuminated all she touched, from the experience of hearing a bird sing at dawn (1084) or the sound of the wind in the tress (321), to the nature of worship (564), love (917), despair (258). She garnered much wisdom along the way, savored everything savorable, gave ceaseless thanks for the gift of life. "All pity for Miss Dickinson's 'starved life' is misdirected," wrote Allen Tate in 1932. "Her life was one of the richest and deepest ever lived on this continent" (Sewall, *Collection* 19–20). And the evidence for this statement is in the poetry.

Dickinson's Letters to Higginson

John Mann

Emily Dickinson once told a friend that "there is always one thing to be grateful for—that one is one's self & not somebody else" (*L* 2: 519). And in 1866, lamenting the death of her beloved dog, Carlo, in a letter to the same friend, Thomas Wentworth Higginson, she nominated Immortality her "Flood subject" and called herself a "Finless Mind," whose exploring should advisedly be done from the safety of the river "Bank" (*L* 2: 454). After fifteen years of reading and teaching Dickinson, I can report that her capacity to be herself and no one else—her capacity to surprise—remains undiminished. Encountering her powerful individuality still stuns, and much about her life and art continues to be mysterious. Truly her mind steered without fin, and her explorations of complex inner realms seem unlimited by time, place, or circumstance. Those inner journeys strike my students like seismic shocks, and as a teacher of Dickinson's poems, I must contend with an immediate impression of overwhelming power matched by a style of strange and wonderful difficulty.

It is fun to remind students that a famous editor seemed equally mystified when Emily Dickinson wrote him in 1862, enclosing several of her poems. In fact, it is a useful strategy to present the poet's first five letters to Higginson as a revelation of her sensibility, her style, and the inner crises that produced her poetry. The five letters to Higginson are short enough to be mimeographed and handed out to the class. On the first Dickinson day I talk briefly about her family, her life in the Connecticut Valley during the 1830s and 1840s, and her year at Mount Holyoke in 1847–48, with its religious crisis. I base my remarks on material in the Whicher and Sewall biographies. I mention that apparent change in her life in her late twenties, when she began to record her poems in fair copies in the fascicles. (Students are fascinated by these threaded packets, accumulating for years in her dresser drawer.) I point out that by the time of her first letter to Higginson, she was almost thirty-two years old, had not married, and was living, as she would for her whole life, in her father's house in the small western Massachusetts town of Amherst. The United States, I add, was already a year into the agony of the Civil War.

I spend the rest of this initial day on Dickinson in a kind of close reading of the letters to Higginson. These arresting documents unfailingly elicit questions from students about the meaning of key words and cryptic phrases and sentences. Such initial questions can be very helpful in launching a difficult poet: students who raise their hands here often prove more willing the next hour to tackle the poems collectively. As an early reviewer pointed out, Dickinson's letters "deepen the impression made by

Miss Dickinson's poems, and they afford material for the study of an extraordinary style" (Jordan 57).

The Higginson letters particularly introduce students to the remarkable compression of Dickinson's style, the chief technical feature of the poems. The letters, moreover, offer students a dramatic immersion in this poet's sensibility, turning their attention especially to her inner life, which was increasingly becoming her primary reality in the early 1860s. Study of the five letters uncovers special strategies, modes of secrecy and revelation by which the poet met the world and Higginson, the public man of letters. These strategies often point to analogous strategies in the poems. The letters develop luminous words and metaphors that also electrify the poems. And the letters pivot on a crisis of the poet's life and work: Did Emily Dickinson want to publish her poems? Would she be able to do so? I often end the hour with the chilling, inescapable fact about Dickinson's writing life—that she wrote nearly 1,800 poems but only ten are known to have been published in her lifetime.

Higginson's "Letter to a Young Contributor" appeared in the *Atlantic Monthly* in April 1862, and one can mention this document as the invitation that impelled the poet to send her famous first letter on 15 April 1862 (*L* 2: 403; Dickinson clearly read Higginson's article with close attention, chose him as her "Preceptor," and then made a number of shrewd references to the "Letter" in her own letters.) Students are intrigued by the appearance of Dickinson's letter in typescript, with its dashes and six single sentences, each a tiny paragraph, and its signature displaced from the bottom of the page to a card in a separate, smaller envelope. (For photographs of holographs of Dickinson's letters, including part of a letter to Higginson, see *L* 2, following p. 582.)

The first sentence carves its own memorable appeal: "Are you too deeply occupied to say if my Verse is alive?" It is helpful to point out to students that this sentence and the third one—"Should you think it breathed"—construct a metaphor of living, breathing life that Dickinson always attached to poetry and developed in several specific poems; such a conception makes Higginson's "surgery" on her poems graphic and physical, even bloody. Dickinson's second sentence—"The Mind is so near itself—it cannot see, distinctly—and I have none to ask"—directly appeals to Higginson's judgment but also suggests how hard it was for the poet to evaluate her work objectively. Later, in an arrogant rejection of other minds' judgments, she will declare, "I have no Tribunal" (*L* 2: 409). But "Mind," here a capitalized abstraction, will become a complex metaphor for the inner life (mind–Emily Dickinson–eye–perception–poetry) that animates many poems. She invites Higginson to criticize, to correct "the mistake," and encloses her name on a card, asking him "to tell me what is true."

Students can sense something of the density of these letters, and both the seriousness of the poet's appeal and her wit, if one reminds them that she may have been thinking of Pilate's query to Jesus in John 18.38: "What is truth?" Two major questions, then, energize this first letter: one about the nature and worth of her inner life, her poetry, and one about the nature of external reality. The mention of her fear of betrayal in the last sentence, the appeal to Higginson's sense of honor, and the shielding of her name in its own envelope can suggest her profound shyness, her state of tension about her work, her peculiar modes of secrecy. Higginson's "Honor" concludes the letter on a note of plaintive entreaty that also flatters Higginson's character. Dickinson enclosed four poems with this letter, one of which—"Safe in Their Alabaster Chambers" (216)—became in our century an acknowledged masterpiece.

Higginson apparently answered her letter quickly and kindly, though he was at the moment busy in Worcester raising the first black regiment to fight in the Civil War. His private opinion about her verse, however, appears in a letter he wrote to his *Atlantic* editor, James T. Fields, the day after receiving her first: "I foresee that 'Young Contributors' will send me worse things than ever now. Two such specimens of verse as came yesterday & day before—fortunately *not* to be forwarded for publication!" (Sewall, *Life* 2: 544). That *not*, one might argue, seems crucial to the subsequent course of Dickinson's career. Since Emily Dickinson's sister, Lavinia, burned all the letters to the poet she found after Dickinson's death in 1886, students must infer Higginson's response from her second letter to him (*L* 2: 404–05; 25 Apr. 1862). Obviously her first letter contained a direct appeal for help: is my poetry any good? she asks. Her second letter responds "from my pillow," as if to say her illness was brought on by his initial reply to her poems. Higginson seems to have requested personal information about the poet and her life, and Dickinson answers him, but with a barrage of delightful metaphor, indirection, concealment, and sometimes downright misstatement.

A part of the interest for students in this second letter—indeed, in the whole series—lies in sensing its combination of pathos (Higginson's "surgery" on her poems, his criticism, must have been more painful than he imagined) and pride in her poems' achievements ("I bring you others— as you ask—though they might not differ"). Much longer than the first, this letter envelops us in an increasing number of serious, though cryptic, statements about her art and her motivation for writing. Again, she cries out for help in evaluation, using a clothing metaphor Higginson had developed in "Young Contributor": "While my thought is undressed—I can make the distinction, but when I put them in the Gown—they look alike and numb." Robert Weisbuch notes that "self-distancing" was unavailable to Dickinson's voice, "for her fiction stresses that the self which criticizes lives intimately with the self which acts" (149). For Dickinson, inner life and action were wedded, were one. "Numb" in this context can be either adjective or verb; "Thought" confirms and continues the complex designation of "mind" begun in the previous letter.

I suggest to my students that Dickinson's fourth paragraph—"You asked how old I was? I made no verse—but one or two—until this winter— Sir"—consciously deceives: she was at this moment thirty-one years old and had copied in fascicles at least three hundred poems. (A lively discussion can ensue here about why she would want or need to deceive.) Her pose as child, or "little girl," or "dutiful daughter" had already become a defining feature of her writing, and teachers interested in the consequences of this pose can consult several recent critics (notably Mossberg, *When a Writer Is a Daughter* 83–87, and Juhasz, *Undiscovered Continent* 5–7). It may well have been part of a conscious strategy of "self-diminution" to conceal ambition when approaching Higginson (Martin 31). There follows the famous "terror—since September—I could tell to none," which has been variously interpreted as erotic bereavement (the Reverend Charles Wadsworth's leaving for California [Whicher 105]), fear of impending blindness (Sewall, *Lyman Letters* 73–77), even fear of pregnancy (Shurr 195–96). Students can understand, however, that Dickinson's poetry erupts from inner necessity and that those compelling imperatives— "terror," the tensions of a too-powerful inner life—might well have been too much for the poet to handle. (Can one ever name such things? This is one of those times a literature course can demonstrate what we all sense about poetry—that for poets the stakes in writing are high, even a matter of life and death.) She goes on to undervalue her education; students are interested in how women were educated in the 1830s and 1840s, and Dickinson's education was actually a very fine one, though vastly different from her brother Austin's. The "friend, who taught me immortality," now dead, can elicit a brief discussion of Dickinson's "Flood subject." Students find the poet's seeming obsession with death gripping but appalling, and an initial consideration of her "Immortality," as it appears in the letters, can help the class explore a difficult subject.

The next long paragraph, dealing with "Companions," parents, and her brother and sister, apparently responds to Higginson's request for information about her family and friends. It is one of my favorite sections in the series, in part because the opening naming of her central "Companions"— "Hills," the "Sundown," her "Dog"—identifies the overwhelming response of this New England poet to nature, a passion reflected in easily half her poems. Her comment that these natural things "are better than Beings— because they know—but do not tell," discloses her shyness and secrecy and offers a revealing analogy to her "presentation" of herself to Higginson. She rejects her mother, who "does not care for thought," and she humorously characterizes her father as a lawyer "too busy with his Briefs" to notice the children. All address another "Father" each morning, whom Dickinson describes as an "Eclipse," thereby presenting herself to Higginson as a religious rebel and, more important, underscoring the profound skepticism that would infect all her mature poems. Her final question, "Could you tell me how to grow . . . ?" expresses, perhaps, her fundamental need and may explain much about her motivation in writing Higginson.

Dickinson closes this letter by telling Higginson with no little pride that two "Editors" had requested poems before, an effective reminder to him (and to us) that she could publish, and by referring again to her difficulty of evaluation and her stark sense of diminished size. This time she signs her name, adding "Your friend." Higginson's response to her second letter must have been complimentary, since Dickinson's third thanks him, shrewdly pointing out it was not the first occasion her work had been praised: "I tasted Rum before" (*L* 2: 408–09; 7 June). The second, cryptic paragraph talks again about a "dying Tutor," but students can locate a source for her poetry in nature ("a sudden light on Orchards") and in inner emotional pressure ("I felt a palsy, here—the Verses just relieve"). Recalling Higginson's criticism in his first letter, she humorously declares she will not change—she "could not drop the Bells whose jingling cooled my Tramp." Jane Donahue Eberwein makes the fascinating conjecture that Higginson had perhaps suggested that Dickinson experiment with free verse (130). More emphatic, and defensive, are the following two paragraphs in response to Higginson's suggestion that she "delay 'to publish' ": she calls that "foreign to my thought, as Firmament to Fin" and tells him "My Barefoot—Rank is better." Dickinson's pride and anger spill out into the next two famous sentences answering specific criticisms: "I am in danger—sir—" and "I have no Tribunal." But as if to restore her reiterated sense of smallness and humility, the letter goes on to thank Higginson profoundly for his help and to invite him to be "my Preceptor."

This is the appropriate time in class to face squarely a central question in Dickinson's life and work—why she did not publish more. To many of us it has seemed impossible to understand the letters to Higginson except as a request not only for criticism but for aid in publishing her work. Thus the tremendous sense of crisis, even agony, in her facing in these letters the recognition that her work might never find an audience. Yet a controversy surrounds this question. Recent writers, notably David Porter (*Modern Idiom* 111–12) and Karen Dandurand ("New Dickinson" 17 and "Why Dickinson Did Not Publish"), argue that Dickinson never intended to publish her poems and did not write Higginson for this reason. Perhaps Vivian R. Pollak offers the most balanced appraisal when she writes:

> Although there is some reason to believe that if Higginson had hailed her at the beginning of a great career and urged her not to "delay 'to publish' " Dickinson might have been prevailed upon to yield up some of her least obviously autobiographical poems to public view, there is more reason to believe that no external pressure, even of a favorable sort, could have persuaded her to take up the public vocation of poet. (228)

What will finally be compelling to students is that Dickinson elected to be a private poet, with the result that one of our two greatest nineteenth-century poets wrote for thirty years without any certainty that her work would reach an audience. A momentous inner dialogue between public and private is everywhere in these letters.

Dickinson opens her fourth letter with a humorous self-description offered in place of a requested photograph (L 2: 411–12; dated by Higginson July 1862). Two paragraphs, especially, offer students further glimpses of Dickinson's "poetic" and her specific need of Higginson. She asks for continued criticism, returning to the medical metaphor of the second letter: "Men do not call the surgeon, to commend—the Bone, but to set it, Sir, and fracture within, is more critical." Sharon Cameron remarks that "for Emily Dickinson . . . there was a powerful discrepancy between what was 'inner than the Bone—' (321) and what could be acknowledged" (26). Students can find interior fracture in major Dickinson poems they will later be reading ("There's a certain Slant of light" [258] and "After great pain a formal feeling comes" [341] are often anthologized). But her "fracture within" graphically demonstrates the agonized tone of these letters, caught between revelation and the need to sustain and protect her inner life.

She then follows with the famous "My Business is Circumference" and "Myself the only Kangaroo among the Beauty." According to Porter, the first phrase "reflects need without a definable goal" and points to her problem of trying to structure poems without a definable center (*Modern Idiom* 105). Yet students like the magical abstraction "Circumference" and can understand the appeal of powerfully expanding centers to a poet who would quest for the infinite. It still "afflicts me," the poet writes in her fourth letter—again, the inner compulsion. Near the end of the letter Dickinson hastens to warn Higginson about too-easy autobiographical inferences: she is a "supposed person" in her poems. This can profitably introduce students to the multiple personae her poems generate, to their complexities of voice. She signs this letter "Your Scholar."

Her fifth letter (*L* 2: 414–15; Aug. 1862), remarkable for its references to explosions and power, reminds us that a sense of overwhelming force, welling up from within and barely controlled, often erupts in the poems she wrote during the 1860s. After humorously offering more poems ("Are these more orderly?"), she speaks of this problem of control: "I had no Monarch in my life, and cannot rule myself, and when I try to organize— my little Force explodes—and leaves me bare and charred." Such was her need of Higginson—not for the "Orthography" but for "the Ignorance out of sight." She responds to his concern that she is "shunning Men and Women" by speaking cryptically of the "Chestnut Tree," the "Skies . . . in Blossom," and the "noiseless noise in the Orchard," later writing an Emersonian paragraph about "Goblins" becoming "Angels" in the woods. The two correspondents have begun, apparently, to speak of a Higginson visit, though this was not to occur until long after the Civil War. And she responds to his apparent mystification with her work ("You say 'Beyond your knowledge' ") by lamenting "All men say 'What' to me, but I thought it a fashion." This comment can reassure students who read a Dickinson poem in complete bewilderment, but it can also return the class to the fundamental problem of a poet who wrote out of sometimes incomprehensible inner necessities but who at some point wished to be read by others.

By the time the class hour ends, students who have attended closely to these letters should have sufficient familiarity with Dickinson's life and style to begin to read her poems. Deriving a coherent aesthetic from such a tangle of metaphor and cryptic phrasing, however, is a more difficult matter. One critic finds such meaning or "life action" in the fourth letter:

> The July 1862 letter to Higginson serves as a paradigm of this larger metaphor that invested her poetry and even the details of her quiet life with astonishing significance and with an overriding unity. The design of her life was a process of movement from her smallness, a haunting sense of primal inadequacy, to circumference or the point of ultimate boundary between the finite and the infinite, the known and the mysterious, the human and the divine. (Eberwein 16)

Most readers of these letters will not find such a coherent poetic program. The letters present themselves, rather, as a shimmering veil of indirection and oblique commentary. The poet, writing out of severe private need, invites Higginson and us to consider the contours of her inner life—but only so far. Much is kept secret: "what she requires above all is that something about her, or *in* her, remain hidden from the view of others. It is the terrible exposure of existence that appalls her" (Benfey 62).

All this, one hopes, will convince students that Emily Dickinson was a poet compelled to define what no one had defined, to name what could not be named. Suzanne Juhasz calls the letters to Higginson "acts of seduction," designed to interest a public man of letters in the work of an ambitious, but private, poet ("Reading" 172). Ultimately, the seduction these letters arrange is of her readers, among them our students, who turn eagerly from the letters' riveting, perplexing language to the larger feast of the poems themselves.

How Language Works:
Learning with Dickinson

Mary L. Morton

In 1929 I. A. Richards's *Practical Criticism* revealed that even Cambridge students reading for an honors degree in English were mostly inept when they interpreted and evaluated poetry by unidentified authors, an act that cut them adrift from the judgments and generalities they had been taught to mouth. In our era of declining reading skills, how much more inept are our future accountants, physical education majors, and even language majors enrolled in introduction-to-literature courses. In twenty years, the best model I have found to teach students to read a poem is the poetry of Emily Dickinson. They cannot depend on the speaker to announce the meaning, or on a couplet to summarize, but are, rather, forced to unravel the riddles themselves by considering the connotations, the images, the sound, the comparisons. In addition, they learn something about language, the importance of words in context, and the limits of ambiguity. Perhaps more than any other poet, Dickinson shows the novice "How lovely are the wiles of Words" (qtd. in Wolff 65).

To begin, of course, students must be invited by the work. Dickinson's poems, invitingly brief, look interesting: short, irregular lines; dashes; random capitalization. A struggling freshman may empathize with the truth of "Your thoughts don't have words every day" (1452), trying to explain the metaphysics to the teacher who ostensibly does not understand or sympathize. Dickinson's phrasing, moreover, reminds us of song lyrics and student slogans that short-circuit the language of the business world.

There are other reasons more students try harder with Dickinson. One is the immediacy of the problem: the lines are not just there but pose a question demanding an answer. Students identify with the emotions of fear, wonder, depression, and pain. Another possible reason is the affinity her poetry has with film, though students recognize this only subconsciously.[1] While at the freshman level my students and I do not explore the relation of montage in poetry and in film, we do approach her poetry as riddles to be explored. Puns, riddles, jokes appeal to all. When students solve a riddle by Dickinson, they have a feeling of success—one they usually do not associate with reading a poem. The methods used to examine the riddles develop close reading skills and thus enable students to analyze all poetry, freeing them from the anxiety or boredom induced by having someone tell them what the poem is "about" and from the necessity of mouthing clichés based on hazy notions of English teachers' expectations. Moreover, although we examine evidence leading to solutions of poetic riddles, we eventually must conclude with our poet that "This

timid life of Evidence / Keeps pleading—'I don't know' " (696). Because
students generally suspect interpretation ("I never get what the teacher
gets out of the poem" is a typical comment), studying Dickinson's poetry
affords a direct experience with what can be deduced and what cannot be
deduced on the basis of evidence in the poem.

We begin with "I like to see it lap the Miles" (585) and "A narrow Fellow in the Grass" (986). Both require students to make inferences based on
evidence in the poem, the basic technique to be mastered. Even if some
students immediately know what "it" and "narrow Fellow" are, we still
(either in groups or as one group) draw up classifications for proof, having
as an object to see how we know what we know. Then, when we are not
sure whether or not we know, we can retrace the process. The classifications are of shapes and forms with their modifiers: verbs describing the
object's actions, verbs whose subject is the speaker, "I." The sum of the
thought can be ascertained by looking at the parts. In 986, "spotted shaft,"
"Whip lash" give a visual picture, along with the motion of "wrinkl[ing],"
"upbraiding." The speaker knows, feels, meets. For most of the locomotive
poem (585), the object's identity derives from its action: "lap," "lick,"
"stop."

Connotations associated with the shapes and their modifiers, the verbs,
are named and discussed, with alternatives suggested—like *slides* for
rides—occasioning, along with some fun, some nice observations about
subtle variations in meaning and effect. Then connotations of sound are
asked for. The *s* hiss of the "narrow Fellow" is readily discerned, but because trains are not as familiar as snakes, the locomotive needs more work.
An exaggerated sounding of the l-k-l-p-k-huh sounds seems to help. Although I do not believe in any absolute onomatopoetics, sound certainly
suggests meaning, a simple enough concept often ignored by students who
slide their eyes once quickly over the page. Moreover, discussion of the
effects of sounds helps students to identify actively with words and what
they do, to see the personalities of words often regarded as dull gray squig-
gles to be endured rather than enjoyed.

The discussions may run vertically, as here described, or horizontally, or
simultaneously in enthusiastic groups. But another step is to examine the
comparisons. Using first the classifications they have made of shapes and
verbs, and then any others they may draw up, students compose statements of what is compared to what. Our main concern is metaphor, for
similes, with their markers of *like, as, than*, are easy enough. Metaphor is
a problem because the definition students come armed with—a comparison of two unlike objects for a particular purpose—is inadequate. The primary metaphors in Dickinson's poems are comparisons not of objects but
of her feelings with some object—or with some objectification of her feel-

ing. Any student needs practice in thinking about the ways we, poets and all, try to express emotions that "don't have words every day."

Another reason the standard high school definition of metaphor confuses the student and prevents understanding is that often one part of the comparison is missing, look for it where one will. Reading Dickinson's poetry, students can learn to infer the missing part because most of the poems we study deal with familiar emotions. Reassured by their success in identifying the snake and the locomotive on the basis of metaphorical descriptions, students are willing to tackle the emotive metaphor of the line "I feel for [Nature's People] a transport / Of cordiality." Here Dickinson compares a feeling to an act or condition, with all its ramifications. This is also a good place to contrast a literal rendition like "I feel for them / Cordiality" because to think of what a metaphor is helps to define what it is. Moreover, distinctions between literal and figurative language are important to meaning. The phrase "Zero at the Bone" affords a good discussion of paradox; of absence being stronger than presence, especially in contrast with "Transport of Cordiality." The resounding *o* assonance in the "Zero . . . Bone" provokes additional connections among sound, expression, and all the connotations thereof. Thus, from one of Dickinson's easiest riddles is conveyed an understanding of how to abstract comparisons; to infer from the clues; to articulate the connotations implied; to group according to function and similarities; then to synthesize the parts and identify not only what is spoken about but how the speaker feels about it.

Sometimes students are upset because they find the locomotive compared to a devouring monster in the first three stanzas and then to a docile horse in the concluding lines. Their discomfort affords a meaningful exercise in flexibility and a lesson about procrustean beds that need not be made. The speaker's point of view is so immediate that her surprise at the obedience of the powerful machine becomes the reader's.

After our cooperative efforts with the snake and the locomotive, students are asked to apply the same methods to "It was not Death, for I stood up" (510), to find out what *it* is. Obviously we are moving into finding names for abstractions, which leads into an area of greater ambiguity, but an area essential for honest interpretation. With "It was not Death," students have the additional practice of noting comparisons to what the feeling is *not* as well as of putting things in groups under time and space headings, orienting themselves to fundamental comparisons between seasons and the human condition. Sometimes we take the fourth stanza, where the speaker expresses her feeling that her life is a door, as the basis for an essay, introducing all possible reasons, connotations, and clichés about "doors." Usually the assignment is a success. Although I do not mention biography at the freshman level unless specifically asked, the students recognize and are intrigued by the speaker's evident depression.

Another poem the students deal with successfully is "After great pain, a formal feeling comes" (341). They are asked to classify the "forms" the "feeling" takes and to find any parallels they can between the movement of the stanzas and the last line: "First—Chill—then Stupor—then the letting go." After the perusal of shapes, verbs, connotations, sounds, and comparisons, the students are asked to furnish possible identifications of the "great pain," giving evidence not only from the poem but from their own experiences. They name a variety, ranging from kinds of physical, mental, and emotional pain. In discussion it is generally agreed what the pain could be and what it could not be. Thus, while the figures and connotations furnish irrefutable evidence of the sensations, the cause of the original pain can only be surmised. Students are encouraged to find plausible causes for such agony.

Even at the freshman level a study of Dickinson's language proves the "undeveloped Freight / Of a delivered syllable" (1409) and leads students to a consciousness of how language works. In this exploration, many students will lose their notion that a poem can mean only what the teacher or book says it means or that it can mean anything anyone says—as Humpty-Dumpty asserts, in *Alice through the Looking Glass*. Careful examination, arrangement into groups, specific articulation of comparisons—all are methods to find answers to Dickinson's riddles. The answers are worth finding because they usually make vivid states of the mind and heart familiar to the reader, whether of depression or love ("Wild Nights" [249]). Dickinson's linguistic riddles mirror riddles of existence.

I have taught too long to pretend that any approach is effective all the time, but I have been encouraged by reports of students saying, "She'll teach you how to read a poem. Man, I never thought I could." Some of my peers say the approach is too cut-and-dried; but Ezra Pound observed that "[p]oetry is a sort of inspired mathematics, which gives us . . . equations for the human emotions" (14). Dickinson's poetry proves a paradigm of that definition. In addition, Richards's admonition in *Practical Criticism* has perhaps not been heeded often enough in its sixty-year history:

> Most descriptions of feelings, and nearly all subtle descriptions, are metaphorical and of the combined type [sense metaphor and emotive metaphor]. The power to analyze explicitly the ground of the transference is not widely possessed in any high degree, and it is less exercised both in school-training and in general discussion than might be desired. (212)

NOTE

[1] I had played "Guess what it is" and "How did you come to say that?" many years before reading Dolores Dyer Lucas's fine book *Emily Dickinson and Riddle*, which includes a nice discussion of Dickinson and film technique (122–26).

Introducing Dickinson in a Basic Literature Course

Katharine M. Rogers

I teach Emily Dickinson's poetry in Landmarks of Literature, the literature course in our core curriculum at Brooklyn College. This introductory course has a crowded syllabus, in which lyric poetry is represented by a British and an American Romantic poet. I choose Dickinson for the American, partly for the sake of including a woman author. Since I organize the course generically—going from drama to fiction to lyric poetry—I can lay the groundwork for understanding figurative language and the poetic approach to truth as we read Shakespearean tragedy and Chaucerian narrative. In the section on lyric, I work more intensively on precise discrimination of language (What exactly are the authors saying? Why did they choose this word instead of that?) and on interpretation of metaphors and other poetic figures.

Since few of my students are humanities majors, my first task in the course is to persuade them that reading great literature is worth the effort it requires. They are particularly wary of lyric poetry, which is usually hard for them to understand and does not offer the character and plot interest of, say, a Shakespearean play. Moreover, previous experience with studying poetry has left many of them believing that the lyric poet writes in code, which they must wait for the teacher to decipher. By supplying a context of poetic conventions and by prodding my students to recognize experience that they share with the poet, I try to persuade them that they can interpret Dickinson themselves. Once they are engaged with the poetry, they can begin to appreciate the artistry with which she conveys her sensory impressions and emotions.

At the beginning of my unit on lyric poetry, which runs about two weeks, I state explicitly that written assignments will be only a few pages long to allow for especially careful reading, because of the greater concentration and complexity of poetry. I expect students to work on understanding the figurative language and, at the very least, to look up every word they do not know. If time permits, I divide the class into groups of five or six (taking care to include one good student or more in each set), give each group responsibility for one poem in the assignment, and have them discuss their poem among themselves for ten minutes so that they can organize their thinking before presentation to the class.

Dickinson's compressed, idiosyncratic style and her apparent remoteness from the concerns and experience of my students make her a difficult poet. So I take pains to prepare for her beforehand, as well as to choose poems that express widely recognizable sense impressions and feelings. We come to Dickinson from Blake (*Songs of Innocence* and *Songs of Experience*). Our English Romantic poet is more accessible in theme and subject but similar in poetic technique. Both write with brevity and intensity, use deceptively simple meters, and rely heavily on metaphor. And they offer interesting contrasts, partly related to their differing genders. Blake is often concerned with public issues, Dickinson largely with the private mind; both Romantic poets glorify individuality and subjective experience, but Dickinson is less positive because she was constrained by the traditional strictures on confident self-assertion in women.

By this time, the students should have some understanding of poetic language and a clear idea of what a lyric poem aims to do, and we are ready to spend a week reading Dickinson. We approach her through poems of physical description, which are comparatively easy to grasp because they concern experiences students can share. These must be carefully chosen, though: my urban students do not recognize the "flower that Bees prefer" and have seen "A narrow Fellow" not "in the Grass" but in a cage at the zoo. Many of them do have pet cats, however, and can respond with delight to "She sights a Bird—she chuckles" (507). They are happy to discover that they can figure out the antecedent of "She," even though it is not named until the eighth line. We go on to explore the beautiful precision of the diction—"chuckles" for the subdued, deep-throated sound a predatory cat makes, "flattens" for her hunting attitude. We note how the poet uses exaggeration to convey the cat's barely contained excitement— "Her Teeth can hardly stand." The last stanza offers some particularly good examples of the way figurative language operates. Obviously "Hopes" cannot be "juicy"—then what is? What is the physiological process referred to in line 9? What does Dickinson gain by fusing emotional with physiological description? Does the "Bliss" of line 11 belong to the cat or the bird or both? How does this ambiguity enrich the poem? In what sense are the bird's wings "disclosed"? How can Dickinson call two wings "a hundred"? This poem invites comparison with Blake's poem "The Tiger," where, too, the poet's vision makes us see better.

We move from Dickinson's descriptions of physical objects to her descriptions of mental states, still focusing on animation of language and truth to experience. In reading "It dropped so low—in my Regard" (747), we start with the antecedent of "It," considered literally and figuratively. How do we know that Dickinson is talking about something more significant than a broken vessel? What does she gain by describing a mental event in physical terms? Can the antecedent of "It" be identified? Does it matter? What are the advantages of a relatively open symbol? The second stanza provides a good exercise in getting the author's precise meaning: Who does she blame for her disillusionment? What is the psychological difference between being betrayed by another and realizing that one has duped oneself by overestimating someone? Why might the second discovery be more painful?

In "Remorse—is Memory—awake" (744) we ask what Dickinson means by calling memory "awake." How is waking different from the usual condition of memory? Why is this state appropriate to remorse? We analyze the effectiveness of the metaphors—in what ways does the surrounded house convey the misery of remorse? What, finally, is the relation between remorse and hell? " 'Hope' is the thing with feathers" (254) is another good example of Dickinson's concrete presentation of an abstract psychological state. We concentrate on the organizing metaphor: In what ways does hope, as she describes it, act like a bird? Do birds, in fact, sing in bad weather? Why does hope sing "the tune without the words"? What is meant by saying hope never "asked a crumb—of Me"? What emotions does Dickinson generate by comparing hope to a bird? Why does she introduce the bird as a "thing with feathers"? In discussing these poems, my students come to appreciate the poet's insight into psychological states common to all of us. A young man who lost his mother, for example, found some consolation in this poetic assertion of the strength of hope.

Having established this common ground, we move to a particular circumstance of the poet, her gender. We close in on her presentation of an area of experience that, though certainly not peculiar to her, is characteristic of her life: that is, response to restriction. I sketch the circumstances of her life and draw from the class what they know about the lives of nineteenth-century women in general. Then we are ready to see how Dickinson dealt with her situation—sometimes rebelling against limitations and sometimes making a rich life for herself within them. We look at "I never hear the word 'escape' " (77) and analyze the speaker's situation and her attitude toward it. How do the phrases "quicker blood" and "sudden expectation" convey the intensity of her feeling? What is the comparison behind "flying attitude," and why does it imply inevitable frustration? What is the difference between the prisons of line 5 and the restrictions on the speaker? Why does she see herself as childish?

Dickinson turns the same situation and metaphor positively in "They shut me up in Prose" (613), where we note the repressiveness of a nineteenth-century girl's upbringing and the triumphant assertion of mental power to resist it, so well expressed by the absurdity of imprisoning a bird in a roofless enclosure. Her metaphorical use of "Prose" affords a good opportunity to review and elaborate on the difference between the approach of poetry and that of prose, which I have been developing all semester. In "Superiority to Fate" (1081), which expresses a more sober triumph, we pay particular attention to vocabulary. What words in the poem link with "earn"? What realm of experience is suggested by "earn," "pittance," "strict economy," "subsist"? Are these the kind of words we would expect in a poem about spiritual experience? Why are they an effective choice? How do they express Dickinson's concept of spiritual achievement and her attitude toward it? Words such as these—unusual if not unique in a poet's vocabulary—can be related both to her Puritan New England background and to her role as a woman, since women have traditionally been charged with conserving the household property and income.

We conclude with a poem that deals specifically with constraints that affect women. "She rose to His Requirement—dropt" (732) comes as close as Dickinson ever did to direct comment on a social institution. We take pains to formulate precisely the speaker's evaluation of marriage—how she builds up and reduces by alternating positive and negative words, how she suggests rather than states in the second and third stanzas. In the first line, for example, the woman "rose"—but, then, a "requirement" is generally thought of as something that ties one down, and, besides, it is "His" requirement—and at the end of the line, she "dropt." (I make the point here that a poet, unlike a prose writer, has the expressive resource of line divisions, so that "dropt" gets particular emphasis.) On the other hand, playthings should be dropped when one grows up, and a wife's work is honorable. We note the poet's speculative tone about what the wife has given up ("If aught She missed"), her purposely abstract diction ("Amplitude," "Awe"), and the ambivalence of her concluding simile (the sea develops "Pearl, and Weed"). We come out with a wonderfully precise evaluation of the positive and negative aspects of marriage for a woman. Finally, again relating Dickinson's poetry to life as we experience it, we compare her evaluation with contemporary feminist critiques of marriage and ask ourselves whether it holds true today.

Since this is an introductory course that allows only a week for Dickinson's poetry, I avoid her more difficult poems, those that use idiosyncratic symbols and those that are concerned with her conflicts as a woman poet. I focus not on the nineteenth-century recluse, the rural New Englander who was frightened by Calvinist sermons, the consciously dedicated poet but, rather, on the woman who expressed feelings we share. When we have finished discussing Dickinson's poems, I hope my students will recognize sensations and mental experiences that they themselves know but had never before perceived so vividly.

Teaching Dickinson to the Fine Arts Major

Alice Hall Petry

I happen to teach American literature at an art college. And even though this college—widely regarded as one of the foremost schools of the fine arts, architecture, and design in the nation—enjoys the luxury of unusually high admissions standards, the fact remains that I face the kinds of problems faced by most people who seek to teach English to budding artists. My students, having channeled much time and energy during their secondary school years into exploring and refining their artistic talent, often have very limited knowledge of major authors, major works, literary genres, or literary technique. For many of them, English classes were an unwelcome distraction from art during their high school years, and that attitude is often firmly ingrained by the time they arrive at college to begin intensive work on their bachelor of fine arts and bachelor of architecture degrees. Further, they have frequently had so little practice in reading that they find it difficult to respond to texts in a thoughtful, sensitive, critical fashion—a problem that of course plagues students even in the nation's finest liberal arts institutions, but that is perhaps especially acute with art students, a startlingly large percentage of whom suffer from reading disorders such as dyslexia. Finally, our college library is an art library: it has justly famous collections of fine art prints, drawings, slides, and art books, but neither the resources nor the space for extensive holdings in English and American literature—let alone a particular author. Despite these far-from-ideal conditions, I have managed to have much success in teaching Emily Dickinson. Partly by trial and error and partly by conscious strategy, I have over the last decade developed a series of approaches to Dickinson's poetry that captures my students' imaginations and makes my work in the classroom a pleasure. In fact, in many ways Dickinson has proved to be an ideal literary figure to teach to art majors.

Perhaps surprisingly, I have found that most of my students—even the foreign students, who constitute slightly more than ten percent of the student body—are already familiar with Emily Dickinson. This familiarity is, however, both limited and distorted. I can count on most of my students' having read in high school a handful of much-anthologized poems such as "I'm Nobody! Who are you?" (288), "Much Madness is divinest Sense" (435), and "There is no Frigate like a Book" (1263), but their understanding of these poems is limited essentially to theme. The technical aspects of the poems, Dickinson's innovations, her place in literary history—in short, the reasons they are asked to study Dickinson's poetry—are quite unknown to them. A more serious situation is that my students come to college knowing a few provocative details of Dickinson's personal life, and this knowledge—which can be summed up as "She was a crazy woman who wore all white and hid in her house in Massachusetts writing poems"—far outweighs what little genuine interest they may have in Dickinson's poetry. Under these circumstances, the temptation for a teacher is to refuse to discuss Dickinson's intriguing personal life and to focus instead on a New Critical analysis of the poems; but in fact this is impossible and quite likely counterproductive. There simply is no denying that my students do know a few misguided details about Dickinson's private life and that they find them fascinating, so I take full advantage of the situation. I customarily devote an entire class (usually 90 minutes) to my introduction to Dickinson, trying to put the popularly known details of her life into proper perspective. I start by asking students to tell me the "facts" they know about Dickinson, and I list these on the board. Since the list is rather predictable ("She was really small," "She never went anyplace," "She avoided men"), I am ready with the information needed to qualify each "fact": that Dickinson was five feet five inches tall and hence rather statuesque for a nineteenth-century woman; that her famed seclusion did not begin until after she had written over half of her poems, before which she had traveled to such cities as Boston, Philadelphia, and Washington, DC; that she was close to several men, including Benjamin Franklin Newton, Judge Otis Lord, and the Reverend Charles Wadsworth—gentlemen whom high school teachers apparently never mention. This teaching strategy imparts the truth, but at the same time it makes students question the reliability of "popular knowledge" and probe the possible sources of the misinformation. For example, what is there about Dickinson's poetry which suggests that this tall woman was short? For that matter, why is it that even a contemporary like Thomas Wentworth Higginson, who actually met her, reacted to her as if she were a child, a "little person," as he wrote in the *Atlantic Monthly* in describing their 1870 interview? (Eberwein examines these paradoxes in *Dickinson: Strategies of Limitation*.) As budding artists, my students are deeply concerned about the impressions of *themselves* that they convey in their own work. They worry that, years from now, the public will use their art to infer things about their personalities and life-styles that will be gross distortions of reality. Concomitantly, they find both intriguing and horrifying the idea that the artist's private life can command more attention than his or her art. So the "personal life" approach to Dickinson is decidedly relevant for art students, and it generates a desire to see what her poems really say.

At the same time that I try to put Dickinson's life into perspective, I try to place her in the proper historical and cultural context—a sort of American-studies approach greatly facilitated by Barton Levi St. Armand's *Emily Dickinson and Her Culture*. Clearly there is not enough time in any literature course (at an art college or elsewhere) to trace quickly what was happening in religion, technology, art, demography, economics, and so on in nineteenth-century America. But I do select poems for study that will illuminate what was happening in Dickinson's world and how she was responding to it. We analyze "I heard a Fly buzz" (465) with an eye to the poem's place in a society where "watching" at a deathbed was not a morbid act but a carryover from the Puritan era when attendance at a death was a spiritually healthy activity. We study "I like to see it lap the Miles" (585) in the light of the nineteenth-century attitude toward trains as exciting technical achievements that were integrated readily into a pastoral landscape (see Marx). We look at "I taste a liquor never brewed" (214) for its satire on transcendental thought. Students are invariably amazed that Dickinson had a healthy interest in the ideas and technology of America and Europe; they are surprised that she had the perceptiveness and humor requisite for satire; and they are especially stunned to learn that she read a great deal— including the wide-ranging *Atlantic Monthly*, cover to cover, every month, as well as a variety of other magazines, newspapers, and books (see Capps). For most of my students, who have little time or inclination to read and who tend to see "book knowledge" as somehow antithetical to creativity, Dickinson's reading is an absolute revelation, and I build on it by discussing briefly the specific books that she used in her writing. In our analyses of her snake poems, for example, I provide a synopsis of Oliver Wendell Holmes's 1861 "medicated novel," *Elsie Venner*, which Dickinson apparently read in its serialized version in the *Atlantic Monthly*. This psychological study of a genetic aberration recounts how a pregnant woman, attacked in her home by a rattlesnake, gives birth to a child with ophidian characteristics. Its use in the poem "In Winter in my Room" (1670) confirms that Dickinson did use specific literary sources in her poetry (see Petry). Likewise, valuable secondary source for exploring this aspect of Dickinson is George Monteiro and Barton St. Armand's underappreciated study "The Experienced Emblem." It traces how specific poems in the Dickinson canon (e.g., "Faith—is the Pierless Bridge" [915]) were directly inspired by the illustrations and poems in a popular nineteenth-century book, *Emblems and Allegories* by William Homes and John W. Barber. Dickinson of course is an extremely visual poet, but many of her poems, such as " 'Hope' is the thing with feathers" (254), are all but impossible to picture in the mind's eye; even my highly imaginative art students admit that they cannot visualize—and hence could not sketch— some of her poems' central images. Monteiro and St. Armand's study clarifies the sources of these less-tangible poems while suggesting the power of book illustrations to inspire—something of great interest to my art students, many of whom are majoring in illustration. At the same time, approaching Dickinson's poetry through her reading raises a hot issue: to

what extent can Dickinson—or any artist—be regarded as truly original
when inspiration comes (consciously or otherwise) from an outside source?
There are no easy answers to such a question, but the lively discussion it
generates clearly encourages my students to reconsider what they mean by
"originality" and "creativity," whether in Dickinson's work or their own.

Discussions like this help break down what I have found to be a serious
barrier to art students' appreciation of literature: a tendency to differentiate between "writers" and "real artists." My first- and second-year students in particular resist thinking of poets as artists, perhaps because they
see only the finished products: polished poems on a printed page.
Whereas my students know firsthand the challenges of creating their own
paintings, sculpture, and jewelry, they tend to assume that writers produce poems *ex tempore*. This notion applies especially to Dickinson's
poems: her preference for familiar words and for quatrains is much
appreciated by dyslexic students, who find her poetry mercifully easy to
read; but for many other students there is an assumption that these poems
were ridiculously easy to write—and hence not worthy of the label "art"
or, for that matter, of anything but a cursory glance. I counter this attitude
by distributing photocopies of the holograph rough drafts of several Dickinson poems that are available in Ralph W. Franklin's *Editing of Emily
Dickinson*. Initially students are overwhelmed by the appearance of the
draft of, say, "Two Butterflies went out at Noon" (533), and I give them
several minutes to try to decipher what Dickinson has written. The labor
and uncertainty that are so palpable in the rough draft tend to nullify the
idea that Dickinson jotted down little poems off the top of her head between baking batches of cookies. But what really engrosses my students is
the two-fold next phase of this exercise: examining copies of the typed
transcript of the rough draft and comparing both the holograph rough draft
and the typed transcript of the poem to the version of the poem presented
by Thomas H. Johnson in *The Complete Poems*. Students are impressed
that (as the typed transcript in Franklin reveals) Dickinson struggled with
"Two Butterflies," undecided whether the word "pushed" in the line
"Until a Zephyr pushed them" should be replaced by "chased," "flung,"
"spurned," or "scourged"; and in studying the transcripts and speculating
why she discarded each of those words, students acquire a respect for her
conscious artistry, for the importance of revision to a creative writer, and
for that most basic of poetic elements, word choice. But, at the same time,
they are taken aback to see the version of "Two Butterflies went out at
Noon" that appears in the Johnson edition. They feel it has little discern-
ible relation to the poem Dickinson was creating and wish to know the
justification for editorial emendation. I find this controversy vital to our
study of Dickinson. My explanation of the "improvements" in word choice

and punctuation made in her poems by the editors of the *Springfield Republican*, for example, leads into a discussion of editorial prerogatives while illuminating some of the problems faced by unknown women writers in the nineteenth century. More important, it demonstrates far more clearly than a dry lecture how startlingly innovative Dickinson's poetry was for her time. Suddenly her slant rhymes and dashes seem fresh and daring and important to my students: they find themselves respecting Dickinson as an original artist, rather than dismissing her as a reclusive neurotic with a facile talent for writing little poems about insects and friendship. But the comparison of the rough drafts with the Johnson versions generates the most emotional class discussions; and those emotions are only intensified when I distribute copies of Robert N. Linscott's versions (*Selected Poems and Letters*), which seem even more corrupt—gone are the famed Dickinson dashes and selective capitalization—than Johnson's. My students are protective, even defensive, about their art; they vehemently oppose the idea of an outside hand, of the present or future, trying to "improve" their creations. And so our discussions of editorial practices make a strong impact—so strong, in fact, that one student or two will question whether it is even legitimate to speak of an "Emily Dickinson poem" instead of a "Dickinson-Johnson" or "Dickinson-Johnson-Linscott" poem. It is essential to emphasize that "Two Butterflies" is an extreme case: many of Dickinson's best-known poems are from fair copies, and editorial changes have been minimal. Once students understand this fact, they are eager to study the poems as works by Dickinson herself.

These discussions of editorial prerogatives lead to a fresh appreciation of Dickinson's thematic and technical achievements. As noted, the examination of rough drafts generates a genuine respect for Dickinson's word choice, and much of our class time is devoted to a careful reading of individual poems. We look at the slant rhymes and dashes, of course, but also at the internal rhyme, the use of sound, line length, stanzaic divisions, tone, and so on, always returning to one basic question: Why did Dickinson choose to do it *this* way? Once students begin to internalize that question, their appreciation of her improves exponentially; and I have found it worthwhile to assign at least one paper that is essentially an explication de texte of an unfamiliar poem. I have received particularly thoughtful papers on "Our lives are Swiss" (80) and "I asked no other thing" (621).

At the end of our study of Dickinson, there invariably arises the question of Dickinson's current fame and the likelihood of her reputation enduring. As one can imagine, my students are concerned about their own reputations as artists, both in their lifetimes and posthumously, so they are intrigued by the situation of Dickinson—an unknown who became a major author only after her death and whose *Poems* (1890) was more a popular success than a critical one, at least initially. By probing the sources of her lasting fame (her technical innovations, her universal themes, and, yes, even the rather distorted details of her personal life), students come to a greater understanding of artistic celebrity.

Obviously I cannot pursue all these strategies in every course in which I teach Dickinson. In my freshman-level survey course entitled Introduction to Poetry, I have the time to teach perhaps only six Dickinson poems, so the emphasis is on explication. But for my upper-class students, especially in a course such as American Women Writers in which one-fourth of the semester is devoted to Dickinson, I incorporate a number of these strategies. I assign some three dozen poems, along with her letters: the text here would be Linscott, supplemented by copies of selected poems from Franklin (*Editing of Emily Dickinson*) and Johnson, and as much class time as possible is spent studying individual poems. But always in teaching Dickinson, I make it a point to assign "The Spider as an Artist" (1275) for either class discussion or an outside paper: the poem is decidedly relevant for art students, who come to feel that they, like the spider, have taken Emily Dickinson "by the Hand."

I do not feel that any English professor, especially one at an art school, should try to turn undergraduates into literary critics. I do feel, however, that it is important, even urgent, to help students understand that works of literature are work of art. As such, they are the products of a variety of factors—writers' knowledge of their cultures; their training in literary technique; their emotional states, personal situations, sensitivity, and responses to their worlds—interacting in ways that even their creators might never fully comprehend. Works of literature are thus mysterious entities that raise far more questions than can ever be answered. This uncertainty should not intimidate us, for if literary works are destined to endure, it is because the questions they raise are worthy of being asked. The Dickinson canon, those seemingly simple poems that so move and often perplex us a century after their creation, admirably illustrates this principle.

Group Work as an Approach
to Teaching Dickinson

Rowena Revis Jones

Emily Dickinson's preoccupation with the inner life, apparent in the subjectivity of her poems, lends itself especially well to an inductive teaching approach. Among critics at every level, her wide range of responses invites such a latitude of interpretation that students of her poetry will feel a particular need to arrive at valid conclusions on the basis of evidence within the texts themselves. While you as the instructor should supply textual and contextual information at the start, guide with questions, and provide feedback on their work, students must arrive finally at their own interpretations. Working together with other students in small groups offers useful interchange and a supportive setting in which to achieve this. Likewise, composition students will sharpen their abilities as writers as well as their appreciation of poetry by distinguishing among the elements of Dickinson's style in company with their peers. Using the settings of a beginning writing class and an advanced literature section, this essay illustrates the use of group work as a method of reading Dickinson with undergraduates.

Careful planning is of course a major key to successful group work. Goals must be well defined and related closely to the nature and level of the class. Questions or directives must be phrased precisely, appropriate poems for study selected, and tools and references identified. Taking into account the makeup of the individual class, you must decide how the students are to be grouped, how the groups are to function, what your role should be, and how each group's results will be shared with the rest of the class.

Introducing Dickinson's poetry in an initial writing course, especially one the students may not have elected, requires an explicit statement of purpose. My own chief reason for including Dickinson's poems in any writing course is that they provide an excellent resource for increasing clarity and vigor in the student's diction. The specific goal of group study, then, could well be to examine the poet's word choices for elements such as economy, precision, concreteness, and connotation. Students will benefit from noting the extreme care with which Dickinson discriminated among words and from examining the differences that the "right" words make within particular poems.

Either preparatory to the actual group work or as a follow-up, the instructor may emphasize the importance Dickinson herself attached to her "lexicon" and the care with which she selected words. Unless variants are available for the actual poem or poems being studied in student groups, it would help at this point to project or duplicate from the 1955 variorum edition one or two illustrations of alternate word choices that Dickinson considered before making what have been judged her "final" choices. Nothing as elaborate as the successive drafts of "Safe in their Alabaster Chambers" is necessary, although this poem could be cited in passing as a classic example of extensive revision. Noting a few substitutions such as "softly" for "swiftly" in line 11 of "These are the days when Birds come back" (130), or "Otter's window" for "kitchen window" in "Blazing in Gold and quenching in Purple" (228), would demonstrate the point adequately. The worksheet draft of a brief poem such as "Summer laid her simple Hat" (1363) also illustrates the poet's process well. Changes in diction made by editors, as in "I heard a Fly buzz—when I died" (465), could further illustrate the deliberateness with which the writer chose her own words. The class as a whole might then discuss the effect of such changes.

On the assumption that many, if not most, college freshmen are not well acquainted with Dickinson's poetry, I prefer to select myself the poems to be read in class. Also, in a freshman class I generally have all the groups consider the same poem at one time, to encourage dialogue when they reconvene. I may introduce it with a motivational device—perhaps a question dealing with the students' own experiences of the subject the poem will address or with their own attempts at some point to apply an effective turn of expression to a given feeling, thought, or event.

As copies of a poem are distributed, grouping should take place casually. In introductory classes, to avoid the appearance of structure or prejudgment, I allow groups to form naturally, according to where students have already chosen to seat themselves for the course. For maximum participation, clusters of no more than five students each work best.

It is important for you to move about and be an active listener as students begin breaking the ice and sharing insights among themselves. In addition to ensuring that conversations keep on course, you will pick up points and differences that invite a nod or brief comment on the spot or that will help you guide later discussion in class.

Written instructions are a helpful complement to your oral explanation of expectations. Directions to the groups could include some or all of the following: (1) Select a scribe to record and later represent the group's observations to the rest of the class. (2) After carefully reading through the poem two or three times, silently and also aloud, compose a one-paragraph paraphrase. Use complete sentences. This should be a composite of individual drafts. The scribe, however, should also record any alternative readings on which the group does not reach consensus. Although your principal objective now is to discover what responses you have in common, you will want to be aware at the same time that the poem may offer more than one possible interpretation. (3) Once you have agreed on what this brief paraphrase should include, return to the text and examine it more intensively, line by line and word by word. Make note of any points at which the writer's arrangement of words contributes to your reading. Are there any reversals of "normal" word order? Any unexpected juxtapositions? If so, what effects do you think Dickinson intended? (4) Suggest words that Dickinson has omitted from her lines that you ordinarily would expect to see supplied. (5) Agree on no more than a half dozen words in the poem that impress you as most effective, or striking, within their particular contexts. Classify these as verbs, nouns, or modifiers. (6) Underline all words and phrases that appeal directly to any of the physical senses, particularly those that achieve visual exactness.

Additional directions may follow if the students appear perceptive and sufficiently prepared: (7) Analyze any use Dickinson has made of figurative language, as in a stated or unstated comparison. By this time, you probably will have repeated some of the same words or phrases at least once. (8) Cross through all words that you can agree are emotionally neutral, that make little or no appeal to feeling. In reverse, agree if you can on two or three that evoke the strongest subjective responses. (9) Identify words that appear to have been selected at least partly for their sound, perhaps because they revolve around or repeat certain letters or combinations of letters, or contribute to the length or stress of syllables. (10) Note any word that you believe would be better understood were its historical roots known. A member of the group could volunteer to look up such a word in the *Oxford English Dictionary* and report back at the following session.

Depending on class time available and the groups' apparent progress, you may have the students pause at any number of points and compare their findings as a class. After representatives have read aloud the prose paraphrase, for instance, class interchange that you direct should recognize likenesses and differences among group readings. Even though you may want to recognize multiple possibilities, you would do well to open the study of Dickinson in a freshman class by emphasizing what the students can discover in common during the first reading of a poem. An initial brief paraphrase is intended not only to encourage beginning students to pay careful attention to the syntax but also to assure them that there can be some agreement regarding the overall tone and theme of the poem. I find that beginning readers of Dickinson need the confidence that can come from first achieving a degree of peer consensus within a small-group setting. Once persuaded that they are at least headed in the same general direction, they can proceed more boldly to examine the poem part by part and to scrutinize its diction more closely. When the process is complete, the contrast between the paraphrase and the poem itself will help them to appreciate Dickinson's artistry.

Looking first at the poem as a whole will emphasize that the meaning of words lies largely in their context, in their relation to other words. It will also increase students' awareness of the importance of arranging words purposefully. At the same time, noting omissions and isolating words that carry particular weight will highlight Dickinson's method of cutting through to the essentials of language and thus enhancing the vitality of her verse. As representatives go on to cite omissions and nominate words that their groups consider especially well chosen, you must press for reasons for those selections. Wide participation should occur now, as group members elaborate on their representatives' reports. You should also extend the focus on effective word choice by calling attention to the energy and clarity of the verbs selected, the concreteness of certain nouns, and the size and precision contributed by adjectives or adverbs. At this point you will find opportunities to underline how the parts of speech work together to create a vital whole.

The possibilities inherent in words sensitively selected are barely touched until imagery and connotation, features central to Dickinson's style, are explored. Like some aspects of sound, however, these elements may not be familiar to all freshmen. Through small-group work, though, more hesitant students especially may be encouraged to try their hand at addressing the more difficult directives. If they do reach this stage, of course, their appreciation of the range of possibilities in a Dickinson poem will be enhanced significantly beyond the level of the initial paraphrase.

An alternative or additional group device designed to highlight the clarity and vigor of Dickinson's language at this time requires that you prepare for each group in advance an overhead transparency of a poem, inserting parentheses around a few key words. If the exercise is a continuation of group work as already outlined, the words will be those selected earlier by the students. Enough space must be provided on the transparencies for the groups to write in one synonym or two for each of the words in parentheses. As each group completes and projects its transparency, the class can review a variety of word substitutions. The opportunity to test their vocabularies, and especially to see that in the end no two words are identical, makes this project instructive as well as fun. Groups will enjoy comparing results, and the entire class will be helped to realize the distinctiveness of Dickinson's diction.

Writing instructors, or course, have a vast array of poems from which to choose samples for group study. "A narrow Fellow in the Grass" (986) makes an excellent poem with which to begin because of its familiar tone and narrative, which students quickly relate to, and because of its visual exactness ("The Grass divides as with a Comb," "spotted shaft," "Whip-lash/Unbraiding in the Sun," "wrinkled") and the shiver communicated by the concluding phrase ("Zero at the Bone"). Two others that I find particularly successful at an introductory level are "Blazing in Gold and quenching in Purple" and "I heard a Fly buzz—when I died," both alluded to earlier. Dickinson's selection and arrangement of words in these poems strikingly demonstrate her effective use of language. Examining "Blazing in Gold," students will note the delayed subject ("Juggler") at the end, the progressive movement from light to darkness, and the key positioning of verbals to carry the action and lock together the lines. They also will enjoy the figurative language ("Leopard" in a "Bonnet"); the connotations of power ("Blazing," "quenching," "Leaping"), of glory ("Gold," "Purple"), and of gentleness ("Touching," "tinting," "Kissing"); as well as the repetitions of certain consonants and vowels: *l, s, t, a, e, i* or *y,* and *o.* "I heard a Fly buzz" will startle even the most skeptical with its precise rendering of intense silence and diminished sight. "Eyes" and "breaths" will evoke responses by their very impersonality, as they grow "dry" and "firm." The "last Onset," the "King," and the signing of a will become irrelevant, set against the sense impressions and alliterative play in a "Blue, uncertain stumbling Buzz."

Using group work in an advanced literature class also helps students discover and develop their abilities within a supportive setting; at the same time, it introduces a competitive element by stimulating them to sharpen and defend interpretations intended to convince their peers. Consensus is much less a key here than among freshman. With students who have elected an advanced literature class, far more than with those in a required composition course, you can anticipate legitimate differences of interpretation both within and among groups. Given their greater motivation and better reading skills, these students should be ready to use the group setting primarily to test their varied responses. While beginning readers may also introduce insights that differ from those of the group as a whole, these more experienced students naturally will be much better prepared to discover and to defend their individual explications. You as leader will want to encourage them specifically to appreciate multiple meanings wherever they can support these with a logical application of internal evidence.

At this level, organization is especially important if students are to read on their own, yet receive necessary direction. An initial consideration is the point at which group work will occur within the total Dickinson course unit. Less structure naturally is involved when students form groups at the very end of the unit in order to share with one another papers they have prepared individually. In this situation I group students according to the approaches they have used or the poems they already have chosen on their own. I look for common denominators among their papers that predict mutual interest and understanding within small groups. The benefit lies in the students' having an audience other than the instructor. The rest of the group should have read each poem as well as each of the papers in advance. Students may have the opportunity to revise their papers after the presentation, if they believe group feedback has helped them to do so. You grade the final drafts.

Another method puts greater responsibility on you to select representative poems for study but still leaves room for student preferences. Following a general introduction and some practice reading Dickinson poems together as a class, you choose clusters of poems relating to various aspects of a Dickinson theme or to certain leading characteristics of the poet's style. By preference, or by seating or alphabetical arrangement, students form groups focusing on one of these clusters. The aim of the small group study will be to identify and analyze the central theme or characteristic common to the poems and explain its development or use to the rest of the class. The class presentation will include a detailed explication of one or more of the poems. Interest will increase if each group comes to the front of the class as a panel in which various members assist the leader. A panel format will also open more possibilities of interpretation among these advanced literature students than a single representative from the group would be likely to provide.

When making up the clusters of poems, you will need to determine a balance between a survey of Dickinson's major themes and techniques and an opportunity for close reading within a restricted range. A single major subject or characteristic per group offers ample scope and can be directed toward both ends. Many poems on death, for example, can be grouped loosely according to the finality of death's physical presence and the impenetrability of the dead (for example, "How many times these low feet staggered" [187], "A clock stopped" [287]); death's democratic dignity and its suggestion of fulfillment ("One dignity delays for all" [98], "This World is not Conclusion" [501], "Ample make this Bed" [829]); or the fearful uncertainty of the persona, mounting even to terror ("That after Horror—that 'twas us" [286], "It's coming—the postponeless Creature" [390], "Death is the supple Suitor" [1445]). Dickinson's argument that suffering best defines its opposite ("Success is counted sweetest" [67], "For each ecstatic instant" [125], "Tho' I get home how late—how late" [207]); her predilection for extreme, piercing situations ("Essential Oils—are wrung" [675], "Through the strait pass of suffering" [792], "A nearness to Tremendousness" [963]); the sanctifying, elevating effect of suffering ("I should have been too glad, I see" [313], "Dare you see a Soul *at the White Heat?*" [365], "The hallowing of Pain" [772]); or the spiritual paralysis suffering can produce ("I felt a Funeral, in my Brain" [280], "After great pain, a formal feeling comes" [341], "The Soul has Bandaged moments"

[512])—each of these aspects of Dickinson's portrayal of suffering and pain can be examined in depth by one group of students, in poems that the instructor has chosen carefully in advance for that purpose.

Responses to nature likewise invite a variety of groupings, as do its separate phenomena. Another classification could be dominant images and allusions, as natural ("Of Bronze—and Blaze" [290], "He fumbles at your Soul" [315], "As imperceptibly as Grief" [1540]); domestic ("I like a look of Agony" [241], "If you were coming in the Fall" [511], "The Bustle in a house" [1078]); or religious ("There came a Day at Summer's Full" [322], "Mine—by the Right of the White Election" [528], "One Crucifixion is recorded—only" [553]). The possibilities for forming such clusters within the Dickinson canon are exceptionally large; you will need to be guided by your knowledge of the typical and the significant and by your particular goal. While groups reconvene and report what they have discovered through a rather intensive study of an important and well-focused topic, the entire class receives a desirable breadth of exposure.

You may need to point out even to these advanced students that categories drawn for the sake of study and discussion are intended only to indicate some of Dickinson's major emphases and do not begin to account for the full canon, that the classifications are by no means mutually exclusive, and that few if any are absolute. "There's a certain Slant of light" (258), for example, can be read as a poem about nature's effect on the spirit, or as a poem primarily about death.

The development of library skills can be nicely incorporated into the goals of such group work. Students can be asked to locate a number of explications of the poem under consideration. Such research will press them to discriminate among interpretations that differ or even conflict and to test these against the internal evidence of the text itself. While research certainly can feed into papers students write on their own and then share, it can also be incorporated into analyses produced by the group working together. Each member can write a précis of a published explication of one poem being studied by the entire group and evaluate the explication on the basis of his or her examination of the poem itself. The précis and evaluation are then handed in for grading. After this preparation by all the members, the group can attempt a joint explication to present orally to the rest of the class. Where readings differ significantly, however, individual members should be invited to explain or support their positions as well. If time allows, you as instructor could encourage still wider involvement to give students further opportunity to test their conclusions. Depending on the general reception that interpretations receive, this could be an especially appropriate time for students to be cautioned against relying overmuch on personal impressions and private associations. Peers provide a useful forum for testing the soundness of an interpretation, and advanced literature students with expertise and self-confidence are not likely to let unsupported generalizations pass unchallenged. Using an inductive approach, of course, does not imply opening the door to whatever private reading a student proposes. Likewise, emphasizing the importance of tone and connotation in Dickinson's poetry need not encourage excessive subjectivity. The point to be reinforced is that close reading involves informed reflection and the sound application of reason to elements within the poem.

The library exercise need not be time-consuming. Students should be referred to Joseph Duchac, *The Poems of Emily Dickinson: An Annotated Guide to Commentary . . . 1890–1977*, and to *American Literary Scholarship* since 1977. You may need to remind students that the explications they have read are intended to stimulate their own thinking. Students are to support, modify, or reject the conclusions of these writers. Where they agree or differ, they need to explain why, reflecting what the critic has said and providing specific evidence from the poem itself to justify their positions. Students will, of course, document all references.

Because interchange is richer if a variety of viewpoints is explored, it helps if group members consult one another and agree to use different explications. Also, if you are at all familiar with the books and articles located in Duchac or *ALS*, you can help group members select divergent approaches or interpretations. If a group focuses on a poem such as "Because I could not stop for Death" (712) or "Further in Summer than the Birds" (130), for which commentary has become a growth industry, you should be prepared to make some recommendations.

While essay questions may provide useful evaluations of the students' grasp of Dickinson, in the advanced literature class I invariably assign an independent poetry explication as the final instrument for the unit. If they understand from the start that a poem they have not seen before is to be distributed for them to analyze in the final class period, groups and individuals will concentrate throughout their study on developing their skills. With the support of peer groups guided by the instructor, they should emerge with not only an appreciation and understanding of Dickinson but also a sense of accomplishment, pride in their ability to interpret a poem, and the desire to make a lifelong habit of reading and discussing good writing.

READING EMILY DICKINSON

Near Rhymes and Reason:
Style and Personality in Dickinson's Poetry

James Guthrie

For many high school and college teachers the average student's response to Emily Dickinson and her poetry is discouragingly predictable: she was, at the very least, a highly unusual lady and her poems were universally morbid. Some of the more outlandish aspects of her personality become so firmly set in the students' memory that they blot out much of the poetry itself. Although my approach to teaching American authors is usually biographical and historical, with Dickinson I make an exception. By starting with her style, I hope to provide an antidote to the sensation of strangeness her life evokes in most students.

One element of Dickinson's style that I have found particularly useful for stimulating student interest is her use of near rhyme. Many students fail to notice any rhyme in some of Dickinson's better-known poems, although most of her poems do have regular rhyme schemes. I discuss near rhyme as an alternative to exact rhyme, asking students whether they consider exact rhymes a criterion of poetic excellence, whether exact rhyme is intrinsically more satisfying, and if they think a poet who uses near rhyme has a tin ear. Then, after having them flip through the Dickinson poems in their anthologies, I ask what percentage of the poems employ near rhyme. The findings usually surprise students; in fact, no other poet of her generation used near rhyme so frequently. As we look at some additional poems reproduced on overhead transparency sheets, I pose the following questions: Why might Dickinson have avoided using exact rhymes exclusively? Can we find regular patterns in her alternations from near rhyme to exact rhyme? Does the presence of near rhyme help underscore the meanings of her poems? Could her use of near rhyme have been an integral part of her perception of herself as a poet?

Near rhyme benefits the poet by reducing the amount of time spent searching for an exact rhyme, a search that can become especially frustrating in rhyme-poor English. Also, poets who are not fastidious about finding exact rhymes do not have to trim their meanings so often to fit the rhyme scheme, and can hence articulate their themes more precisely. Finally, near rhyme can achieve musical effects whose subtlety equals or exceeds that produced by exact rhyme. Taken as a whole, rhyme can be regarded as a scale ranging from no rhyme at all to exact rhyme, with dozens of gradations in between that poets can employ to modulate their sound—and even to create a system of dynamics analogous to that in music. Typically, Dickinson used a network of related sounds to hold her poems together, combining assonance, consonance, and near and exact rhyme. That network is tightly woven in the following poem, which she sent to her mentor, T. W. Higginson:

> The Mind lives on the Heart
> Like any Parasite—
> If that is full of Meat
> The Mind is fat.
>
> But if the Heart omit
> Emaciate the Wit—
> The Aliment of it
> So absolute.   (1355)

Every line in this poem rhymes, if we consider all the final words ending in *t* as rhyming. But the same consonant haunts the rest of the poem in "that," "Emaciate," and "Aliment," a pattern complemented in the first stanza by the long *i* assonance in "Mind," "Like," and "Parasite" and in the second stanza by the long *o* in "omit," "so," and "absolute." A glance at the semifinal pencil draft of the poem, in Johnson's variorum edition, reveals that Dickinson intended to create this pattern of related phonemes from the start. Although the first stanza survived virtually intact, her second originally read:

> But, if the Heart be lean
> The boldest mind will pine

> Throw not to the divine
> Like Dog a Bone

After picking out the patterns of assonance and consonance in this version, students may be asked why it is inferior and whether the poem would sound better to them had it been written in exact rhymes.

A peculiar psychological reaction ensues when a near rhyme occurs where an exact one was expected. We may feel a slight twinge of disappointment or a sense of imbalance. Dickinson used this sensitivity to the presence or absence of rhyme to her advantage, inserting near rhyme at the ends of lines describing feelings of uncertainty, apprehension, disappointment, or shock. On the other hand, as many experienced poets and readers of poetry point out, exact rhymes tend to connote confidence, satisfaction, certainty, or a sense of order, and Dickinson often reserved them for lines in which her poetic personae regain their mental equilibrium. Critics disagree, however, on just how intentional her selection of near or exact rhymes to fit the situation was. George F. Whicher, for instance, says he doesn't see Dickinson resorting to near rhymes in lines signifying "doubt and dismay" exclusively, for they are quite as likely to appear in lines expressing ecstatic joy (*Critical Biography* 248). Nevertheless, patterns that exploit the psychological connotations of rhyme and near rhyme turn up repeatedly in Dickinson's poetry. One strategy she adopted was to begin and end her poems with exact rhymes and to use near rhyme for the intervening stanzas. In this way she could match her rhyme to the shift in her poetic persona's mood from confidence to uncertainty, then back to reassurance. A good example to show students is "Don't put up my Thread and Needle," a poem that may describe her anxiety about her eyesight during an illness in 1863:

> Don't put up my Thread and Needle—
> I'll begin to Sew
> When the Birds begin to whistle—
> Better Stitches—so—
>
> These were bent—my sight got crooked—
> When my mind—is plain
> I'll do seams—a Queen's endeavor
> Would not blush to own—
>
> Hems—too fine for Lady's tracing
> To the sightless Knot—
> Tucks—of dainty interspersion—
> Like a dotted Dot—

> Leave my Needle in the furrow—
> Where I put it down—
> I can make the zigzag stitches
> Straight—when I am strong—
>
> Till then—dreaming I am sewing
> Fetch the seam I missed—
> Closer—so I—at my sleeping—
> Still surmise I stitch—   (617)

An exact rhyme occupies the poem's center at "Knot" / "Dot," as if the poem itself had a well-placed stitch sewn through its middle; otherwise, except for the opening stanza, near rhyme predominates. The first stanza's *abab* rhyme scheme reappears after three intervening *abcb* stanzas, the dissimilarity of "missed" and "stitch" notwithstanding, for consonance and assonance strongly suggest the absent rhyme. The "incompleteness" of this final stanza corresponds to the uncertain state of the narrator's health, as if the "crookedness" of Dickinson's evanescent rhyme scheme might be straightened out once she recovered her health. Ironically, her near rhymes and her irregular rhyme scheme permit her to achieve effects here that might have been impossible using regular, exact rhyme.

Another rhyming pattern prominent in Dickinson's poetry is a gradual movement either away from or toward exact rhyme. In this way her rhyme could function as a diminuendo or a crescendo, depending on whether she wished to build suspense or indicate a recovery from some traumatic event. Some of her better-known poems can show students how Dickinson turned this strategy to her advantage. "I felt a Funeral, in my Brain" (280), for example, employs full rhymes in its first four stanzas (including the initial stanza's "fro" / "through," which may have constituted an exact rhyme in nineteenth-century New England dialect), but "down" / "then" in its final stanza, as the narrator breaks through the barrier separating imagination from reality. "A Mien to Move a Queen" (283) also merits a closer look, but one famous poem in particular demonstrates the way Dickinson used rhyme to achieve a crescendo:

> A narrow Fellow in the Grass
> Occasionally rides—
> You may have met Him—did you not
> His notice sudden is—
>
> The Grass divides as with a Comb—
> A spotted shaft is seen—

> And then it closes at your feet
> And opens further on—
>
> He likes a Boggy Acre
> A Floor too cool for Corn—
> Yet when a Boy, and Barefoot—
> I more than once at Noon
>
> Have passed, I thought, a Whip lash
> Unbraiding in the Sun
> When stooping to secure it
> It wrinkled, and was gone—
>
> Several of Nature's People
> I know, and they know me—
> I feel for them a transport
> Of cordiality—
>
> But never met this Fellow
> Attended, or alone,
> Without a tighter breathing
> And Zero at the Bone— (986)

In the first stanza little similarity exists between "rides" and "is." The succeeding three stanzas' near rhymes end with *n*, in "seen" / "on," "Corn" / "Noon," and finally "Sun" / "gone," which approaches exact rhyme; this trend culminates in "me" / "Cordiality" and "alone" / "Bone," a strong rhyme that recapitulates the *n* rhyme deferred in the penultimate stanza. This intensification of Dickinson's rhyme corresponds neatly with the process of recognition, by both reader and narrator. First, although the word *snake* is never mentioned, we become increasingly certain (prompted, perhaps, by sibilance in the first stanza) that this is indeed the answer to Dickinson's riddle. Second, initial curiosity is replaced by horror when, thinking it's a buggy whip, the narrator reaches for the snake. The fifth stanza's reassurance, expressed with exact rhymes, is a feint; the long *o* of the final rhyme, as well as in "Fellow" and "Zero," mimics the narrator's indrawn breath of shock and realization.

Although I encourage my students to examine the rhyme scheme of any Dickinson poem they read to see if the rhymes complement the poem's meaning, I caution them against attributing all Dickinson's rhyme choices to subtle planning and an elaborate system of poetics. Her use of near rhyme simply isn't methodical enough to permit us to say she was always conscious of why she elected to use a particular rhyme. Sometimes she caroms from exact rhyme to near rhyme to no rhyme without apparent reason. At other times, however, her use of near rhyme seems so deliberate as to be self-referential, as if the slightly dissonant chord her near rhymes strike were a signature for her eccentric personality. Take, for instance, poem 526:

> To hear an Oriole sing
> May be a common thing
> Or only a divine.
>
> It is not of the Bird
> Who sings the same, unheard,
> As unto Crowd—
>
> The Fashion of the Ear
> Attireth that it hear
> In Dun, or fair—
>
> So whether it be Rune,
> Or whether it be none
> Is of within.
>
> The "Tune is in the Tree—"
> The Skeptic—showeth me—
> "No Sir! In Thee!"

To see how cleverly her rhymes reinforce the poet's point, we must first consider that Dickinson, influenced by her reading of Emerson, is using this poem to assert the existence of a connection or correspondence between humanity and nature. When she says that the oriole's song may be a common experience or "only a divine," her gentle sarcasm provokes us to question the division we habitually make between the two. This conflation of the mundane with the divine (a perennial theme in Dickinson's poems) is echoed by the teasing similarity between the rhymes and the near rhymes, for, as students will notice, the third line in each of the first four stanzas is a near rhyme for the two lines preceding it, except in the final stanza, where scrupulously exact rhymes emphasize her certainty. But Dickinson's transcendental observation is accompanied by an aesthetic judgment that could be applied to her own poetry: like the birdsong's banality or divinity, the beauty of the poet's song can be decided only subjectively. If we think the poem has meaning or underlying order—if it is a "Rune"—we feel it is beautiful; if not, it is simply "Dun." The "Fashion of the Ear" determines which.

Dickinson's poems about birds provide some tantalizing insights into her opinions about her poetic style as well as into her feelings about being a poet. Because we have so little hard biographical information about her, much less a poetic manifesto, such insights are important. My students frequently express dismay over Dickinson's shyness and her notorious reluctance to publish, and her obsessive insistence on privacy does seem evidence of neurosis. But privacy and reticence can, like near rhyme, offer a poet certain advantages. On being asked what some of those advantages might be, my students mention several. First, such a poet needn't face the disappointment of rejection. Second, a poet who lives out of the public eye, having no one else to please, needn't be a conformist. Third, a poet without literary ambitions won't develop a swelled head; style won't fall victim to vanity. The relation between ambition and vanity is quite possibly the subject of the following, fairly early poem:

> For every Bird a Nest—
> Wherefore in timid quest
> Some little Wren goes seeking round—
>
> Wherefore when boughs are free—
> Households in every tree—
> Pilgrim be found?
>
> Perhaps a home too high—
> Ah Aristocracy!
> The little Wren desires—
>
> Perhaps of twig so fine—
> Of twine e'en superfine,
> Her pride aspires—
>
> The Lark is not ashamed
> To build upon the ground
> Her modest house—
>
> Yet who of all the throng
> Dancing around the sun
> Does so rejoice?   (143)

I ask my students to look carefully at this poem's rhyme scheme. They soon see that Dickinson characterizes the wren with exact rhymes (including "high" / "Aristocracy") and the lark with near rhymes. Dickinson's exact rhymes seem to underscore the wren's overfinicky delicacy as she builds her nest with "twine . . . superfine," while near rhymes are more in keeping with the lark's modesty. Pretensions to aristocracy turn the inherently humble wren into a striving perfectionist, while the lark, who builds her nest on the ground, has the leisure to "rejoice" in song. I believe Dickinson is admonishing herself in this poem not to cater to vanity by pursuing literary ambitions for their own sake, while at the same time reassuring herself that her idiosyncratic rhyming style is the most appropriate and satisfactory for her. She may even be expressing a hope here that she can have her cake and eat it too, for the lark does indeed achieve artistic prominence, despite her modest home.

Students put off by Dickinson's strangeness may come to appreciate her more if the initial approach to teaching her poetry involves a study of her style. Her rhymes, meter, metaphors, imagery—all these may be used to stimulate a discussion of her technical ability as a poet. Afterward, the genuinely peculiar facets of her personality may be brought to light, especially as they relate to the content of her poems. I ask my students to consider Buffon's observation that "the style is the man," and I encourage them to ask themselves what new things they have learned about Dickinson the woman from studying Dickinson the poet. Sometimes they respond that behavior which might at first seem highly unusual can come to look, in retrospect, highly original.

Dickinson's Language:
Interpreting Truth Told Slant

Cristanne Miller

My students often remain silent at the beginning of a unit on Dickinson if I ask questions about a poem's subject, but they volunteer any number of practical questions about how to understand the language in the poems. Why does she use so many dashes? Why does she use the root forms of verbs instead of their appropriate conjugations? Why does she write in incomplete sentences? Why does she use adjectives as nouns or nouns as adjectives? And so on. Even more of a hindrance to understanding a poem than these irregularities, however, is the beginning reader's lack of a feeling for the kind of interpretation possible in a poem that contains such language. Since I teach relatively small discussion courses only, analysis of individual poems always consumes a major part of a Dickinson unit, and it is the backbone of my Dickinson seminar. From my experience teaching such classes, I have become increasingly convinced that learning to read Dickinson's poetry is partly a matter of learning what we can expect in the way of clarity from her language. I now begin discussion of the poems by talking about what Dickinson leaves out and puts into her poems and about how her omissions and inclusions both expand and restrict the poems' meanings.

As I stress repeatedly in my classes, it would be equally ridiculous to think a poem can mean whatever the reader wants it to or to make fast rules for the interpretation of grammatical or technical peculiarities of language; a dash, for example, is not a blank space for us to fill with our private fantasies about the poem, nor do all dashes mean the same concrete thing. Meaning is contextual. On the other hand, I repeat with equal frequency, poems are built of words, and we do not begin to understand the poems until we think about why Dickinson has chosen to repeat certain ungrammatical or unusual patterns and how they operate in particular poems (an activity that requires some speculation). Understanding the characteristic patterns of her language use may, in turn, clarify the direction of Dickinson's intent in individual poems.

Dickinson's dashes provide an obvious starting point. Although nineteenth-century writers frequently used dashes, especially in informal writing, Dickinson generally used them more disruptively, more often, and in more various ways than her contemporaries did. Most often, Dickinson's dashes imitate the stops and starts of speech. In the middle of a sentence, for example, dashes may isolate words for emphasis or mark off sentence fragments, giving the effect of impulsiveness or strong emotion ("Of Course—I prayed— / And did God Care?" [376]); at other times the dash creates an effect of breathlessness or hesitation ("When—suddenly—

my Riches shrank— / A Goblin—drank my Dew—" [430]). A dash may usher in abrupt changes of subject or metaphor, as though Dickinson feels greater freedom to articulate the associative leaps of her thinking when she is not bound by conventional punctuation. When a dash occurs at the end of a sentence or poem, the statement seems to remain without definite closure; the poet has stopped but not necessarily concluded: in "Because I could not stop for Death—" (712), for example, the speaker finally surmises the "the Horses' Heads / Were toward Eternity—."

Apart from punctuation, the most obviously striking feature of Dickinson's poetry is its compression. By deleting words or phrases and devising elliptically compacted metaphors, Dickinson omits all that is not essential to her meaning. Such deletion causes no problems when the poet simply omits a pronoun, auxiliary verb, or introductory phrase that is implied by the rest of the poem; when Dickinson exclaims "The Wife—without the Sign!" in "Title divine—is mine!" (1072), we can be fairly certain she has only excluded "I am" or "I have become." We are familiar with omissions like these in the shortcuts of daily speech; their meanings are recoverable. Dickinson, however, also uses nonrecoverable deletions, or holes in meaning, that cannot be filled in by grammatical extension or the logic of a context;[1] replacing these deletions requires an interpretation of the poem. Although I typically divide my Dickinson unit (of from 3 to 8 classroom hours) into rough subject categories and discussion often focuses on these themes, much of the analysis of individual poems returns us repeatedly to the question of what we can and cannot know in a poem. What (I usually ask) does Dickinson make nonrecoverable, and how (students more often ask) do we know what are reasonable choices for filling these gaps? Within each subject category, I mark particular poems as being useful for talking about such deletions and then bring discussion around to them.

Nonrecoverable deletion takes several forms in Dickinson's poems. For example, Dickinson concludes the brief horror fantasy "He fumbles at your Soul" (315) with the lines "When Winds take Forests in their Paws— / The Universe—is still," but she does not explain how this epithet corresponds to the central event of the poem. The reader must determine whether his scalping "your naked Soul" and winds' taking forests in their paws are analogous or in contrast and how one event illuminates the other. Is the human realm of vulnerability or mixed anticipation and terror like the natural realm of winds and forests or different from it? Because there is no connecting phrase, we cannot be sure how these descriptions fit together. The deletion is nonrecoverable without recourse to interpretive explanation that the poem itself does not provide. Lack of clear reference may also be a form of nonrecoverable deletion. In this poem the reader must decide who or what combination of forces "He" is (God? poetry? a lover? patriarchy personified?) and what it means that "He scalps your naked Soul." As with the questions that nonrecoverable deletion raises in any poem, there is no right answer—just a reasonable sphere of speculation, given the immediate context of the poem and the concerns that reappear in Dickinson's poetry.

Dickinson's lack of inflectional markings for verbs similarly requires interpretation from the reader. In "There is a Zone whose even Years / No Solstice interrupt— / . . . Whose Summer set in Summer, till / . . . Consciousness—is Noon" (1056), the uninflected verbs "interrupt" and "set" do not confuse the syntax of the poem, but they create a sense of timelessness and indeterminacy. "Summer set in Summer" reads more like a description of a jewel fixed in its setting than like the grammatical attempts at reconstruction "Summer sets itself . . . " or "Summer will (repeatedly) set itself. . . . " The form of the verb implies more than its definition can account for—here the verb *set* seems to include a substantive, a temporal state of being. Greater ambiguity results from the uninflected verbs concluding "Further in Summer than the Birds" (1068). Here the "Loneliness" that the poet traces to the cricket's "Mass" is

> Antiquest felt at Noon
> When August burning low
> Arise this spectral Canticle
> Repose to typify
>
> Remit as yet no Grace
> No Furrow on the Glow
> Yet a Druidic Difference
> Enhances Nature now

Where "There is a Zone" describes a moment or place beyond time, "Further in Summer" describes a transitional instant of "Druidic Difference" between the end of summer and the beginning of fall. In each case, the action seems both suspended and continuing: the Canticle "arise"; [it?] "remit" no Grace. The verbs prevent place and time from being easily categorized.

A different type of ambiguity results from other deletions of words or forms marking voice, tense, and person of verbs. For example, Dickinson exclaims ambiguously that "To pile like Thunder to its close . . . would be Poetry—"

> Or Love—the two coeval come—
> We both and neither prove—

Experience either and consume—
For None see God and live—   (1247)

The penultimate line might read: "Experience either [poetry or love] and [you will] consume [both poetry and love]"—that is, you cannot taste either event partially; to experience them at all is to consume them totally. The verb can, however, just as logically be read in the passive voice: "Experience either [poetry or love] and [you will be] consume[d]." This reading implies the exact opposite of the previous one; now the reader or lover is overwhelmed by the experience instead of actively engulfing it. In either case, the actor has no choice but must consume or be consumed as an inevitable result of the first small experience. To fill the grammatical hole created by this, or any, uninflected verb, the reader must try out various interpretive reconstructions and may well find that more than one supports the context of the poem. For obvious reasons, this fact helps promote lively class discussion; even very bright students are more likely to talk when they see clearly for themselves that reasonable answers cannot be "wrong." Other poems with uninflected verbs or verbs that are ambiguously active or passive that I often discuss, or refer my students to, include numbers 379, 515, 700, 742, 765, 828, and 1206.

This same kind of active reading is required when Dickinson makes an unspecified object or event the subject of a poem or uses both masculine and feminine pronouns to refer to the same person. The most famous example of the former occurs in "It was not Death, for I stood up" (510), where the poet spends six stanzas telling us first what "it" is not (Death, Night, Frost, Fire), then what "it" is "like" (Death, Night, Frost, Fire, Midnight, and Chaos), and finally the effect "it" seems to produce (Despair), but never tells us what "it" is. Wherever she uses unspecified "it" ("I gained it so" [359], "It struck me—every Day" [362], "Ended, ere it begun" [1088]), the object or event must be provided by the reader's imaginative identification with the experience the speaker describes. With her lack of biographical reference, Dickinson creates a blank scene—"it" or "this" or "that"—which readers understand only by finding a comparable scene or experience in their own lives. This, too, is a good exercise for student readers: I ask them to imagine more than one kind of experience that might prompt the writing of a poem like "It was not Death" and then to let the remembered or imagined experience drop while they focus just on the feeling "it" created or the multiple responses they have to "it" that Dickinson provides evidence for in her poem.

In other poems, "it" may refer to an unspecified person or to the poet's self. "I cannot buy it—'tis not sold" ends with the speaker's wish "just to look it in the Eye— / 'Did'st thou?' 'Thou did'st not mean,' to say, / Then, turn my Face away" (840). The conclusion reveals that "it" is a person ("Thou"), but the impersonal pronoun metaphorically identifies him with the entire effect he has had on her—as though, for example, love or happiness and a person were the same, and both were tangible things. (As I tell my students when this question arises, as it inevitably does, I usually assume a nonspecific "Thou" is male because when Dickinson specifies gender, her antagonist is most often male.) In "Why make it doubt—it hurts it so" (462), the speaker apparently tries to distance herself from her suffering by referring to herself in the third person—perhaps partly out of self-protection and partly out of pride. The ruse, however, does not hold up, and the poem concludes, "Oh, Master, This is Misery." Dickinson uses indefinite pronouns without specifiable reference in several other poems; among my favorites for teaching are 448, 531, 577, 840, 921, 1110, 1113, and 1301.

Making reference ambiguous may undercut social norms as well as undercutting the expected distance between subject and perceiver. In "She rose to His Requirement—dropt / The Playthings of Her Life / To take the honorable Work / Of Woman, and of Wife" (732), Dickinson muses that if this wife becomes dissatisfied it will be known "only to Himself," as only the sea knows of "His" buried "Pearl, and Weed." The ambiguous reference of this masculine pronoun may suggest that only God knows of her discontent or that only her husband knows (a less likely interpretation, but one students inevitably bring up; I respond that it assumes the wife is unconscious of her state and so could not be dissatisfied). More likely, the pronoun refers to the woman herself, conferring masculine status on her to mark the oceanic depth, breadth, and wealth of the life she does not reveal. Associating masculinity with depth and power has a strong social precedent in mid–nineteenth-century America, where women were often regarded as being little more serious than children. Other poems where Dickinson collapses the distinctions between masculine and feminine roles and gender through pronoun shifts or ambiguous reference include 124, 190, 196, 429, 481, and 1748. Like other kinds of disruption, blurring or overturning gender distinctions forces a revaluation of the distinctions and of their effect on our perceptions, or our lives.

Omitting the suffix of an adjective or adverb—"more angel," (493), "They might as wise have lodged a bird" (613), "step lofty" (1183)—also disrupts assumptions that the world can be known and described. Hoping a soul will become "more angel" seems to give it substantive form, as though the soul is made up of proportions that can be readjusted; furthermore, where "angelic" tempers the association between angels and death, the ungrammatical adjective "angel" leaves that association fully intact: to be "more angel" is to be nearer death. Similarly, adding suffixes to adjectives, adverbs, or verbs or just adding an article may jiggle our sense of certainty in the word—for example, "the Overtakelessness" (1691) or "a blame" (299). Using a word of one grammatical class to function as another or using a word outside its normal semantic restrictions disguises a complex prediction. For example, we must decipher what "careless" might mean when "We talk in *careless*—and in *toss*— / A kind of *plummet* strain" (663): our talk is careless? or, we both assume the vocabulary of social nonchalance even though the occasion is not trivial? or, we feel the strain of keeping our speech frivolous, because the encounter is so momentous for us both? And none of these hypotheses takes account of the contrasting metaphorical connotations of *"toss"* or *"plummet."* The reader must unravel the relation between the words; and while the direction of meaning is clear, their nonstandard use of form prevents certain meaning. Dickinson's compressed, deceptively simple descriptions suggest, without spelling out, the complexity of an event. Her words resonate meaning partly because they have no obvious message.

The question of how to read Dickinson is always followed by the broader question of why she writes as she does, and many students who read this poet for the first time in college have ready answers: she never finished her poems; she was not a self-conscious artist; she kept changing her mind about what she thought; or she was unsystematic and incapable of sustained focus or consistency. In responding to these trivializing readings of the poet's work, I stress two areas; Dickinson creates language patterns that are disjunctive and unconventional or outright ungrammatical, first, because no other style of language would enable her to express her perception of the overlapping terrors, miracles, and complexities of everyday life and, second, because no other style would have enabled her to do so with less personal risk. The proof is in the poems themselves. Clarifying or tidying the poems generally results in their simplification; Dickinson cannot imply all that she does in so compressed a form without her stylistic peculiarities.

First and last, I reiterate that Dickinson's style arises from her deliberate choice, not from carelessness or a lack of sophistication or time. Her most frequently revised poems contain the same irregularities of punctuation, syntax, and word use as do her poems that exist in only one clean copy. Certainly the publication of her poems would have forced Dickinson to make temporary choices between the variant words and phrases that she writes below the line or at the bottom of her texts; for example, she would have to choose whether "The Firmaments" or "The Universe" is "still" in "He fumbles at your Soul" (315) and whether "He" prepares your "Substance" or your "Nature." Nonetheless, the poet would most likely have continued to vary those choices in the copies she sent to friends and maybe, like Marianne Moore in her lifelong revision of already published poems, even in the copies she submitted for republication. Furthermore, I argue, when a student is particularly recalcitrant on this point, to consider Dickinson's texts unfinished or inferior to those of other poets because of their irregularities and variants would be to treat them differently from the way we conventionally treat incomplete or questionable texts of other writers—for example, Shakespeare, who left us no text for several of his plays but whose work we do not hesitate to subject to serious analysis. There is no evidence that Dickinson considered her unusual word choice, punctuation, and fragmentary syntax as flawed or suitable for general emendation. For these reasons, reading Dickinson's poems should not be a matter of figuring out what she really wanted (but didn't quite manage) to say. Instead, reading Dickinson is a matter of understanding what the play of metaphor, analogy, and nonstandard language use *do* say in each poem, or understanding the possibilities of meaning that her extraordinary language provides.

NOTE

[1]I borrow the term *nonrecoverable deletion* from Samuel R. Levin, "The Analysis of Compression in Poetry," and the discussion between Eugene R. Kintgen, "Nonrecoverable Deletion and Compression in Poetry," and Levin, "Reply to Kintgen."

Reading Doubly:
Dickinson, Gender, and Multiple Meaning

Suzanne Juhasz

My classes on Dickinson tend to focus on reading the poems. Any generalizations we make about her as poet or person result primarily from, and are grounded in, her poems. Those poems are not self-evident. The minute one begins to read them carefully, they open up, flower, expand, so that suddenly all that may have seemed clear (oh, I know what this poem is about) becomes complicated, suggestive, dense, even downright contradictory.

In my recent teaching of Dickinson I have been concentrating on how to admit and accommodate the essential presence of multiple meanings in her texts. I do not believe that all responses to a poem are "right," nor do I believe that there is really no such thing as "meaning." So my students and I need to find ways to use the poetry's obscurity or actual doubleness as part of the poem's meaning. I am especially concerned with what effect gender, along with the woman poet's uneasy relation with patriarchal forms, has to do with Dickinson's language. For example, issues of gender, its poetics and politics, can help us understand the impulse toward simultaneous privateness and publicity, or the famous telling it slant, or even the making of alternative, contradictory, and simultaneous messages.

In the close-reading process that I have developed for Dickinson over the years, each line is experienced as it comes, as it helps to accumulate toward an interpretation; metaphors are initially taken "literally," their dramatic reality examined before their symbolic implications; and syntax is first understood as normal, so that embedded or elided syntax may more readily be recovered. This process provides a useful format for encountering and accommodating the significant presence of nonrecoverable or multiple meaning. Such multiplicity occurs at all levels of language in Dickinson's writing, from the definition of a single word through syntactic structures through theme or central idea. Consequently, reading Dickinson demands a technique, and a perspective, that can see doubly.

We should begin by asking why this multiplicity should exist at all. It is not enough to note its presence, as most readers of Dickinson are eventually forced to do, especially when they then proceed to phase it out of existence, to "solve" the problem it is seen to have created. Understanding its origin helps us to read it properly. One reason (there are no doubt others) derives from Dickinson's gender, her situation as a woman in a patriarchal culture. For in essence the ontological condition of what the anthropologists Shirley Ardener and Edwin Ardener call a "muted group" within a dominant culture is one of doubleness, since reality is experienced both from the dominant patriarchal perspective and from the muted female perspective (qtd. in Showalter 261–62). In culture as it is presently constituted, gender designates difference; yet expression of that difference is controlled by hegemonic structures. Language itself can be understood as such a structure; certainly, writing as a profession and as an art has been traditionally so regulated. When a woman writes at all, she speaks a difference customarily identified by its very silence. One way to grasp the contradictions, evasions, and ambiguities that characterize Dickinson's poetic language is to see that they derive from and textualize this profound doubleness, as her writing reveals both the abiding power of the patriarchal perspective and the manifold difference of the female perspective. Dickinson will accept a cultural given, enact it, challenge it, transform it, even deny that transformation—often in the same poem. In this way her language expresses not so much a system of overt and covert messages as her multiple experience of different yet simultaneous realities. Consequently, doubleness *is* the meaning; and the way the class reads her poems should release rather than simplify or suppress it.

Slowing down the analytic process helps, because it allows us to recapture, or re-create, the original reading experience, when the poem happens without much predetermination about pattern, or point, or meaning. Of course, the poem rarely exists for us in a total vacuum: we know who wrote it, we have read other poems by her, we have studied American literature. Nevertheless, the first time through, what happens next, and then next, comes as a surprise (especially in Dickinson), so that we are in a better position to permit the doubled perspective that the words so often initially engender, before we try to organize them better. Reading line by line, then, letting each line happen fully, discretely, like viewing a film frame by frame, is a way to be especially receptive to the experiential nature of the poem's creation of meaning. Clearly, we must fake it to an extent: first, because we have read the poem before, so we do have some sense of where things are heading, and, second, because we can never avoid this sense of direction, since the poem is always reaching past each individual moment to create an extended action in space and time. Nevertheless, the ploy, or technique, enables the now critical reader to give each word and phrase its due.

Dickinson herself establishes an environment of suspended animation in her poetry by her peculiar use of punctuation, in particular, the dash, that feature of Dickinson's style which most immediately catches students' attention and curiosity. Her dashes, both within individual lines and at the ends of them, imply both discreteness and connection. What the connection is, however, they do not, as do periods or semicolons, signify. When dashes control syntactic relation, as they do in Dickinson poems, they reinforce and promote doubleness.

Encouraging what my students think of as a "literal" reading of the poem's figurative language also contributes to this experiential method. I think of it, rather, as letting the metaphors exist as action in their own right, with their own reality, before being translated into something abstract and symbolic. For example, when Dickinson, in poem 789, speaks of a "Columnar Self," we experience a sense of possible overlap between columns and selves having to do with mass, weight, texture, direction, before we come up with some interpretation like "self-reliance" or "integrity." In fact, these abstract concepts are limited and limiting with reference to Dickinson's subject: they leave out information present in the metaphor, and thus, I maintain, should not be encouraged this early on in the reading. Translating or decoding in this way bypasses the poem as it is written—and, frequently, misses the meaning.

Finally, a word about syntax and Dickinson's private, idiosyncratic language, which is always the class's initial stumbling block to approaching her poetry. To some extent, this characterization of her language is true; Dickinson's solitude and isolation, as well as her genius, had something to do with the "shorthand" quality of her writing. And yet, at the same time, her messages were meant to be read, or heard, as reading the poems aloud instantly reveals. They sound not like another language but like a peculiar dialect of our own. From this perspective, we can understand that elisions are meant to be recovered, for the syntax is mostly normal, regular. Consequently, when it's not, those differences make sense because of the changes they ring. For example, in the second line of 789, "How ample to rely," replacing "amply" with "ample," or adverb with adjective, causes the amplitude to modify not only the act of relying but the columnar self, a doubling that is borne out later in the poem when the self becomes an "us," a "crowd."

Nevertheless, sometimes syntax is not recoverable, creating the confusion, or multiplicity, to which I have been referring. Double meanings can cancel each other out, or enrich each other, or provide a suggestive tension, or irony, or contradiction. For example, in the concluding stanza to 789, Dickinson defines the crowd constituted by the self as consisting of "Ourself—and Rectitude— / And that Assembly—not far off / From furthest Spirit—God." The dash between "furthest Spirit" and "God" makes it impossible to tell whether God is the furthest spirit or the assembly, which in turn offers two seemingly contradictory definitions of the self's relationship to God. In the first case, the self is everything but God; in the second, God, too, is included in the self's society. These alternative meanings may be seen as canceling each other out or, taken together, as expanding our understanding of the central concern of the poem, the nature of the self. The point of the poem is that the self relies on itself, not God, so that whether God is considered an aspect of self or as the only thing in the universe that isn't comprised by the self becomes secondary to an understanding of where power resides. Reading both possibilities as valid, the two together suggesting the whole meaning, helps us understand the central attitude of the poem. This way of seeing may be likened to the way plastic overlays in a medical textbook work. Individually, each means something in particular about the human body; taken together, they show a more complete meaning.

Taken all together, these elements of slow-motion reading permit the reader to sustain a double perspective: to allow more than one thing to happen at a time and to see what results when they do. As a more extended example of this process, I consider here poem 315, "He fumbles at your Soul."[1] Of necessity, I offer monologue instead of dialogue, but what I document are the stages and results of class discussion, normally elicited through question, answer, and comment.

I always begin by reading the poem aloud. Then I return to the beginning, to the first line. First lines in Dickinson are crucial, as we are constantly made aware when we have to use them, for want of anything else, as titles. In a certain sense, the first line *is* the poem. For Dickinson structures her poems by the principle of accrual. They are like snowballs that, from rolling in the snow, grow fatter but do not change in nature. Hence, apposition and parallelism—rarely narrative—organize development in her poems. Dickinson's ideas complicate themselves, but they begin with an announcement of subject and purpose. Almost always the first line is a definition, even when, as in 315, it describes an action. "He fumbles at your Soul" is an event, but the poem is going to be about what such an event means.

> He fumbles at your Soul
> As Players at the Keys
> Before they drop full Music on—
> He stuns you by degrees—
> Prepares your brittle Nature
> For the Ethereal Blow
> By fainter Hammers—further heard—
> Then nearer—Then so slow
> Your Breath has time to straighten
> Your Brain—to bubble Cool—
> Deals—One—imperial—Thunderbolt—
> That scalps your naked Soul—
>
> When Winds take Forests in their Paws—
> The Universe—is still—

Yet Dickinson's first lines are as problematic as they are explanatory. For every piece of information, there is usually a question, which is why we need the rest of the poem: to elucidate an enigmatic beginning. A "he" is acting on a "you," but who are these actors? We can't say, having only a sense of subject and object, and yet the customary correlation of these roles with active (subject) and passive (object) is curiously reversed. Because the "you" is the consciousness experiencing the event, "object" becomes "subject" here. And, since the active agent, "He," is identified by gender only, we might assume, especially since we do know the gender of the poem's author, that the "you" is female. Consequently, we may go on to surmise that in this poem the traditional object, the woman, speaks, thereby expressing her suppressed subjecthood in a poem that takes gender relationship as its subject.

"He" is encountered acting on your soul: something at the very heart of the person, its defining essence. (As I usually mention to students, Dickinson tends not to differentiate between words that define human essence, such as "heart," "soul," "brain," "consciousness.") What is he doing to this particular soul? Fumbling at it, as if it were a lock he is having trouble opening. To what end, we do not know. Here we are struck primarily by the sense of agency, of power being exercised on a resistant entity.

To understand this situation more clearly, we eagerly read on and encounter an analogy: "As Players at the Keys / Before they drop full Music on." Such a comparison gives tangible form to the situation, yet in terms not of interpersonal relationship but of artistic creativity. The "you" becomes "Keys," or a piano, while "He" is the "Players": the fingers, I think, of the pianist. Here metonymy provides a close-up: we see fingers at the keys; we understand music making. Now we begin to understand the action, "fumbling," better. Either this is a poor pianist, or the fumbling is meant as preparatory activity, awkward but transitional. It is a warming up for the real thing: the full music.

The analogy helps us as well to understand better the active/passive elements of the situation. For whereas the piano needs to be played to make music, the pianist can make no music without it. A double meaning therefore emerges from "Keys": the "ivories," surely, but also the means of gaining entrance, and even that which provides an explanation or solution.

Therefore, although it is too early in the poem to resolve the matter, we are faced with our first intimation of contradiction, or multiplicity of meaning. Ought we to take this experience of being acted on as invasion, implied by that fumbling at the soul, or as potential, implied by the piano analogy? Again, is the fumbling offensive or enticing in its awkward physicality? Statement plus analogy provides, not a simple conjunction, but a complementarity that complicates.

The following line, "He stuns you by degrees," is prefaced and concluded by dashes. Consequently, although in itself it is an independent
clause, restating the first line, it can be seen to refer both backward, sum-
ming up the first three lines, and forward, introducing the more complete
description of the same event that follows. The dashes, in other words, can
function as colons as well as periods. From one perspective, this hardly
matters, since the poem keeps repeating itself; from another, since the
repetition complicates and what is complicated is the "you's" experience of
the event, the syntactic overlapping underscores the way meaning in the
poem is created.

"He stuns you by degrees—" introduces the long verse sentence that
constitutes most of the poem, detailing the sequence of the central event.
The elements of this longer version are, however, the same as we find in
the opening summary: the aggressive albeit objectified outside agent,
characterized through verbs alone ("stuns," "prepares," "deals," "scalps"),
the consciousness of a receptive subject, an invasion of momentous proportions. Yet the event, now broken down into its components, has to be read
sequentially, as a process whose significance has everything to do with its
"degrees." Here the dashes, both breaking apart and releasing the lines of
verse, help to slow down, then quicken, the tempo to a climactic crescendo. Because students regularly want to hurry to some symbolic conclusion, I usually need to point out this process and bring them back to
the poem's own rhythms. First preparation, then the blow. He has no
existence other than his outward manifestations; she displays a complex
subjectivity.

Now analogy is replaced by metaphor: outer is inner, for this experience
is at once physical and spiritual. It is clearly a "Blow"; nevertheless, an
"Ethereal" one. Its effect on the recipient is to "stun" her, to deprive of
consciousness as a result of such violence, but also, perhaps, to astonish,
amaze.

The preparation is experienced as sound and pressure: "fainter Hammers" "further heard— / Then nearer—Then so slow." We comprehend a
growing volume and intensity, "Hammers" connoting violent blows, as well
as the striking of those musical keys referred to earlier, now as ominous as it
was artistic. Yet as we read, the steadily growing noise and pressure form a
background for the soul's response, as the "brittle Nature" (or "Substance,"
in another version) is seen to "straighten," then "bubble Cool." These are
comparative terms: straighten implies a previous crookedness; cool implies
an earlier heat. Inside the woman's outward passivity there is much activity, for, as in the relation between piano and pianist, this preparation is as
much the soul's work as it is "his." The straightness and coolness imply a
readiness, a calmness and a cognizance of what is to come.

The fainter blows have prepared for a climactic assault; it comes, finally, as "One—imperial—Thunderbolt— / That scalps your naked Soul." The last line of the stanza parallels the first line of the poem, while also exaggerating it. He is now entirely godlike and powerful; she is, conversely, entirely vulnerable, available. And if "fumbles" had seemed an act redeemed by its clumsy tentativeness, "scalps" leaves no doubt about its murderous brutality. And yet, at the same time, there is something as ecstatic as masochistic in the image of a blinding light, an electricity that, in striking, somehow purifies further a soul prepared, receptive, naked. A variant for "scalps" is "peels," reinforcing our sense of something both stripped, reduced to essence, and transformed. This is, we remember, an "Ethereal" blow, a stunning one at that. (Dickinson's variants themselves indicate her awareness—indeed, commitment—to doubleness in her writing, making them useful to class discussion. Her habit of providing alternative words, including them with even the so-called fair copies of many of the poems, shows her unwillingness to choose between them and suggests her proclivity for sustaining multiple meanings.)

This culminating moment occurs elsewhere in Dickinson's poetry. It is at this point in our reading that recourse to Dickinson's oeuvre seems relevant. For the poems as a whole define her major subjects by circling them, in a version of circumference that performs in macrocosm what individual poems do in microcosm, as their images and observations accrue to the opening line to create full meaning.

I point out to students that in poem 1581, for example, "The farthest Thunder that I heard," the image of a thunderbolt leads to a similar denouement. The speaker, struck by lightning, observes, "But I would not exchange the Bolt / For all the rest of Life." She goes on to compare her specialness to the condition of ordinary mortals, their "Indebtedness to Oxygen" to her "obligation / To Electricity." Again, in poem 974, the lightning image is used to explain the opening assertion that danger or calamity discloses "The Soul's distinct connection / With immortality." "Lightning on a Landscape," we are told, "Exhibits Sheets of Place— / Not yet suspected—but for Flash— / And Click—and Suddenness." Danger, in other words, as poem 1678 explains, "disintegrates Satiety," for it "Begets an awe / That searches Human Nature's creases / As clean as Fire." All these poems use the thunderbolt to represent the concurrence of danger and revelation, and they help us to see how, as in 315, the soul seeks out and benefits from this calamitous collision as well as is violated by it.

This is the crucial doubling at the heart of the poem. There is no way, at this point in the reading, to choose between or eliminate either of these attitudes. Nor can we come to a simple conclusion about the identity of participants in the drama or the exact nature of their relationship. We can say that he is aggressive, she is receptive, each thereby acting out traditional sex-role relationships; on the other hand, we note her subjecthood, his objectification. What is going on here "really?" the students are bound to ask. But it is not yet time to interpret, to translate in this way. For there remains another stanza to the poem.

After the detailed description of the encounter between "He" and "you" comes a couplet about winds and forests. What is its relation to the rest of the poem? The couplet takes the form of aphorism: "When Winds take Forests in their Paws— / The Universe—is still—," a truism that, because of its position at the conclusion of the poem, seems placed there to comment on and sum up the preceding events. But, both because it is preceded by the ambiguous dash and because the figurative vocabulary has altered—from thunderbolt to winds and forests—the connection is not readily clear. Still, we have to acknowledge that Dickinson has made this kind of switch before in the poem, first when she moved from the opening "fumbling at your Soul" to players and keys, then when she moved from the piano imagery to the thunderbolt sequence. In each case, however, the relationship between participants in the drama has stayed the same, and it remains so in the final couplet. "Winds" are aggressive, "Forests" receptive; the winds take (or "hold," in a variant) the forests in their paws, this further anthropomorphizing (winds like brutes—brutal) reinforcing our sense of violence. If this is the same situation once again, then the key line, because it describes result, becomes the final one. When this kind of event takes place, the universe (or "Firmaments," in a variant) is still. Everything, in other words, comes to a halt. What kind of halt, what kind of stillness? Death? Revelation? Transcendence? An end or a beginning? Not specifying becomes another kind of specification, because once again we are forced to entertain all the possible meanings for the word, for the idea. The stillness that is the result of winds' taking forests in their paws seems comparable to the scalped or peeled condition of the naked soul, which in turn is comparable to experiencing full music. Something utter, something ultimate. I am reminded of the concluding lines of poem 1247, "To pile like thunder to its close," which again uses thunder imagery to show how ultimate experience—here identified as poetry and love—results in what Dickinson calls consummation ("Experience either and consume"— consume something? be consumed? both?) and likens to the vision of God: "For none see God and live." Even as the poem implies that this not-living need not mean sheer death but could, rather, indicate a revelation that leads to transformation, so in 315 we get similar intimations, similar ambiguity.

Reading the poem this slowly forces us to encounter it on an experiential level. Consequently, we have a rather clear idea about what is in the poem and what is not, so that any interpretation we subsequently make can be firmly based on this information.

Let me begin with the nots. We do not find out who the actors are; we do not find out when this action is taking place; we do not find out the literal reference for the metaphors. But instead of trying to fill in by ourselves these so-called gaps (he's a lover; he's God; he's her father; this is sexual intercourse; this is religious conversion; etc.), we might better use these "omissions" as important information.

That is, if the "He" and the "you" are never specified, this may well be because they are not specific but general, or archetypal, representing, for example, something quintessential to maleness, femaleness. Dickinson thus projects her personal experience into more generic categories. The persistent present tense is informative in this regard, suggesting that the event is recurrent and typical, rather than one of a kind or once in a while. If the literal equivalent for this internal, psychological, and therefore metaphoric experience is not provided, we might understand that the event itself is conceived of as generic, indicative of the soul's encounter with an aggressive force that attacks, invades, transforms it. Sexual intercourse or religious conversion is, then, as much a metaphor for what is happening as is piano playing or storms. Because gender is explicitly associated with this occurrence, I would feel justified in reading it as a quintessential experiential pattern in a culture that is structured along gender divisions, and that would be the "conclusion" I would discuss at length with the class. The encounter of inner with outer, or receptive with aggressive, or reflective with projective may be more generally signified in terms of gender difference: female behavior/male behavior. If this statement is correct, Dickinson's poem both describes that kind of experience and evaluates it, in terms that are of a both/and, or double, nature. At once critiquing and participating in traditional gender arrangements, Dickinson reinterprets the meaning of these arrangements as well. She demonstrates how the female, even when she is behaving according to traditional norms, is nevertheless not object but subject, possessing, in fact, a subjectivity that is extremely complicated because it is usually not externalized. At the same time, Dickinson shows both how the kind of violence described here is oppressive and destructive and how there exists a need for endangering the self in just this way: putting oneself at the mercy of some force beyond one so that revelation and transformation might occur. Other poems less specifically gender-identified point to this same cultivation of a vulnerability that seeks out danger and benefits from it. This poem indicates how gender difference is linked to such critical situations.

Thus, poem 315 is a multifaceted analysis of the nature and uses of power itself. Even as it reveals the abuses of aggression, so it also shows why and under what circumstances it might be attractive. Demanding only one interpretation of this situation—for example, that Dickinson is attacking typical male-female interaction or, conversely, that she is submitting herself to it—denies the complex double reality to which this poem attests. Consequently, when we have finished reading a poem like 315, the class has experienced not only ways to think about the centrality of gender to Dickinson's language but—more crucial yet to an understanding of this poet—ways to respond to and work with her meanings as they are developed in the process of the poem.

NOTE

[1] I am especially indebted to Cristanne Miller's reading of this poem in *Emily Dickinson: A Poet's Grammar*, both for her discussion of the history of approaches to the poem and for her own interpretation—particularly its emphasis on the ongoing and typical nature of the events that the poem describes.

"My Class had stood—a Loaded Gun"

William Shullenberger

Because Emily Dickinson is such a trouble to the critic, she can be a great pleasure to teach. If the teacher is willing to risk the embarrassment of indeterminacy, willing to acknowledge that he or she can't claim particular mastery of what any of Dickinson's poems mean, working on Dickinson collaboratively in a seminar setting can be an exhilarating as well as unsettling experience. Dickinson teaches herself, in a way: the very lexical and syntactic difficulties of the poems provoke anxious and irritated questions, and the questions both open the text at the slant Dickinson encourages and open the students as they gradually discover their own need for a stability of meaning that Dickinson's poems withhold. Dickinson's poems, depending as they do on a "supposed person" for a narrator and erasing as they tend to do the cultural and historical and even personal contexts of their writing, provide training in the close reading and explication techniques of New Criticism, yet inevitably offer a great playground for poststructuralist reflection. Thus an extended approach to Dickinson can be the groundwork for training in critical theory and application. Whenever I teach an introductory-level course, I include six to eight class sessions on Dickinson, because she has so much to teach us about what is required of us when we read and about what we often unconsciously require of a poem. The following teaching approach, admittedly not particularly innovative in procedure, has worked well in introductory-level classes, but because Dickinson immediately breaks open our categories of thinking with her own mixture of primitivism, naïveté, and uncanny or canny rhetoric, the ideas might just as easily be adapted to upper-level classes.

As indicated above, I tend not to detail the cultural and historical background for Dickinson's work. I find it useful to remind students in a broad way of Dickinson's heritage of New England radical Puritanism, with its obligation of intense self-scrutiny, its sense of God's distance, and its recognition of the world as a plenitude of obscure spiritual signs. I also note the transcendental sidetracking of that tradition into a radical individualism and faith in the imagination's power either to make the universe or to make it fully human (Tate; P. Miller, *New England Mind: The Seventeenth Century*). But the broken traces of these intellectual heirlooms can be excavated from the poems themselves, and the pleasure that comes from discovering a linguistic or theological artifact in one of Dickinson's poems and then reconstructing its cultural origin should not be foreclosed by too early and emphatic a historicizing of the poems. Feminist critics properly attentive to Dickinson's linguistic strategies speculate in challenging ways on how much of her alienation as a writer is conditioned by her dependent status and her distance from the centers of political and literary power; her poetry, suspicious of authority, powerfully privatizing experience and hermetic in structure as well as meaning, is emphatically yet problematically a woman's work (Rich; Diehl; Dobson). The formal feeling of Dickinson's poetry, however, tends to conceal the features of its speakers and to universalize the experiences of dispossession and aphasia. Because the condition of metaphysical dread is difficult to gender-mark, the feminist treatment of Dickinson sometimes risks a disproportionate attention to her femininity (Pollak; Mossberg, "Nursery Rhymes"; C. Miller) and sometimes depends too much, as the older biographical criticism has done, on information about a life that Dickinson too successfully smoke-screened for too long a time to be relied on for interpretive guidance (Gilbert). That this dread, and the linguistic vacancies it opens in Dickinson's mature work, may have had its historical occasion in the catastrophe of the War between the States (Wolosky) serves to chasten the tidy New Critic or the vagrant deconstructor and to remind us that even Dickinson, the most hermetic of poets, creates her world elsewhere not ex nihilo but of the stuff that her neighbors and newspapers dump in her lap.

For all its value in the teacher's preparation, the historical, biographical, and ideological setting of Dickinson's work is something for our students to work toward, not work from. My stress in introducing Dickinson is to put the legends, the intellectual background, and the assumptions aside, to begin only with the assumption that Dickinson was a poet who took poetry very seriously, more seriously than anything else. Everything else in her life follows from that. Then we settle into the poems, as they curiously erase their own contexts and create about themselves as haunted a solitude as Dickinson created for herself in the twenty-odd years of her mature life as a writer. Wallace Stevens wrote, "the sublime comes down / To the spirit itself, / The spirit and space, / The empty spirit / In vacant space." This is what reading Dickinson with a class comes down to also: the spirit of the interpreter, emptied of its predispositions, the vacant haunted space of the poem.

Each of us consciously constructs a critical framework for working with Dickinson out of her scattered and fragmentary but suggestive commentary. From the interpretive framework Dickinson herself provides for the poems, the gnomic statements that figure most importantly for me include the following: "If I read a book and it makes my whole body so cold no fire ever can warm me I know that is poetry. If I feel physically as if the top of my head were taken off, I know that is poetry. These are the only ways I know it. Is there any other way" (L 2: 473–74). Her remark here to Higginson directs attention to the affective dimension of poetry, its profoundly unsettling impact on the reader as a measure of its success as poem. "Tell all the Truth but tell it slant— / Success in Circuit lies" (1129). This poem marks out Dickinson's strategy of indirection and suggests that her approach to meaning involves tracing the circumference of the poem, perhaps without ever reaching a center.

"Nature is a Haunted House—but Art—A House that tries to be haunted" (*L* 2: 554). I think Dickinson presents an enigmatic model of her aesthetic theory here. Art is a baffling mimetic structure that tries to re-create the haunted closure of Nature. That she conceives of nature as haunted house implies that she dwells in the aftermath of religious certainty, when the secure structure of a deity concerned with creation survives but only in decay, only in the reminder of a long-vanished presence. Art tries to summon to consciousness something of the effect of a having-been-dwelt-in, a moment of spiritual presence and indwelling full enough to leave a trace of it even in absence, yet the "trying" reminds us that the structure is only empty structure, a spatial closure built for a sense of recent absence that perhaps never arrives. "Renunciation—is a piercing Virtue— / The letting go / A Presence—for an Expectation—" (745). This poem articulates one of Dickinson's central themes, the discipline of willed loss that transvalues deprivation itself into a majestic fulfillment in the condition of poetic longing. It also suggests the peculiar condition of absence, of hauntedness, rendered in Dickinson's best poems: the distancing of the poetic voice from the object of its desire so that the space between them might be filled with a language that tries endlessly and epically to return to that object, yet by its very indirection, its very circumferencing, endlessly displaces it. "I work to drive the awe away, yet awe impels the work" (*L* 3: 817). Here we have the circuitous energy system of Dickinson's work, impelled by loss and by the look of death that it casts over the landscape, working to discharge the awe surrounding the loss, yet curiously like a cyclotron driving the energy of the loss and the awe to a new pitch of intensity by the very act of writing. For a more sophisticated class interested in theory, each of these statements can be used as an introductory koan to set the students' minds to work on particular aspects and sets of Dickinson's poems. What does she mean by this? What does this remark direct us to look for in the poems? Yet for an introductory-level class the statements might initially be reserved in order to gather or focus observations and confusions later during the discussion of the poem: can this remark help us to understand what's happening here?

Since Dickinson's poems seem to cancel time (Cameron; Poulet), it seems futile to arrange them in sequence for teaching purposes. An interesting possibility for advanced or graduate classes might be to study selections of fascicles, as reconstructed by Franklin, in order to explore Dickinson's original organizing intention. But for most undergraduate classes, thematic grouping seems handiest, although Dickinson's characteristic erosion of what we call "themes" makes this a very provisional enterprise. Such grouping also promises to reveal more about our concern with Dickinson than with her concerns in themselves. Nevertheless, for the sake of providing a controlled and somewhat developmental experience of reading the poems, I've mapped out thematic groups as follows, selecting out of each group target poems that the students can expect to discuss in class: Slants of Light (nature and consciousness): 258, 742, 1068, 1400, 321, 1084, 986, 328, 861, 348; the Missing All (God and self): 985, 338, 357, 315, 49, 724, 621, 303, 306, 745, 508, 1551; Alabaster Chambers (death): 712, 216, 449, 465, 389, 856, 860, 922, 943, 949; Formal Feeling (pain and aftermath): 341, 396, 280, 889, 875, 305, 301, 512, 686, 650, 443, 327, 792; the White Heat (creativity): 365, 1138, 1142, 1126, 448, 320, 569, 1651, 1261, 675, 883, 1129, 632; and the Loaded Gun (enigmas of self and other): 754, 1286, 594, 1072, 528, 461, 199, 463, 378. Anyone who examines these headings will discover that they offer an elastic boundary enclosing very diverse regions, like the borders of Canada. Students should be reminded to keep a dictionary handy when reading the poems, and they should be advised not to cancel eccentric or subordinate definitions but to keep them afloat in working out a reading of a given poem. If we're lucky and the students aren't sleepwalking, an hour's class might treat a single poem effectively; but it doesn't take long for the students to realize that Dickinson is not easily packed up and put aside.

One approach to handling the poems is to elicit questions and take them as they come; students are frank and can locate the moments of disturbance in a given text. Because it's difficult to anticipate where such a questioning might lead, it's useful to orchestrate the questions so that discussion works through the poem sequentially and to direct attention persistently to the syntactic, imagistic, and rhetorical events on the page. The more controlled approach to a given poem, which I tend to follow in the opening sessions on Dickinson, starts out with general questions to develop a context of understanding in which poetic details can be examined and tested. What kind of a poem is it—a definition, a landscape description, a tale or parable or allegory, a riddle, a request, a complaint, a confession, a prayer? Beginning here alerts students to the multiplicity of speech acts that can be called poems and prepares them to attend to the rhetorical and syntactic strategies Dickinson will use or subvert as she carries through the particular poem. What can we know about the speaker or the poem through the tone, the speaker's relation to the content of the poem, and the vocabulary the speaker employs? Questioning of this sort not only makes students concentrate on the speaking voice that haunts each poem but helps dispel the Dickinsonian monomyth of a morbidly self-absorbed spinster whose only concerns are death and loneliness. Students find instead a canny wordsmith continually revising and disguising the oblique angle of vision by which she approaches experience and the voice with which she enacts it. Sometimes it seems appropriate to ask the class for a preliminary assessment of the subject and the theme of a particular poem; although dragons may dwell in the creases of such questioning, such an investigation may provide some measure of intellectual security as the class proceeds from the general to the specific, stepping from plank to hazardous plank of word and trope, attempting to map the poem's erratic geography. A final general question can attune students to the affective pressure of the poem: what do you feel when you read this? The estrangement and confusion—the "haunted house" feeling—that Dickinson seems so often to induce can be both impetus and guide into the structure and rhetoric of the poem as we search to locate those strategies and those moments where the planks in reason break.

A look at two poems illustrates where such a teaching strategy might lead. I like to introduce Dickinson with 258, "There's a certain Slant of light," because of its firm development of a complex association between nature, God, consciousness, and pain. The poem offers a solemn yet steady gaze into the haunted house of nature and a precisely calibrated diagnosis of epiphany as pain and of the profound readjustment of the consciousness stunned into being by it. General questioning might evoke the description of the poem as a landscape poem, beginning with the phenomenon of late winter light and its impact on the consciousness. The speaker seems to talk out of personal experience, since "None may teach it—Any." Yet the authoritative exactness of the description, the relative impersonality and formal balance of the speech, the reportorial factuality of the indicative moods, and the universal "we" of the two middle stanzas—all suggest poise, control, a certain formal and detached feeling achieved by surviving the "imperial affliction" documented in the poem. An initial assessment of the subject might lead students to discuss divine visitation, the mysterious suddenness of the sense of a God beyond nature felt in the moment when a natural event breaks through the walls of our warmly insulated dull winter selves. Further, students challenged by Dickinson's radical doubt might develop the sense characteristic of Dickinson that revelation is painful, isolating, inducive to despair rather than religious confidence or bliss. The perplexing absence of a source for the "Heavenly Hurt" leaves the wound, the wakened and bruised consciousness, listening breathlessly for a consolation that never materializes out of the vacant aftermath of the light's sudden stroke. The reader's felt response to the poem tends to chime with such a thematic assessment: my students report feeling lost, depressed, dazed, filled with a negative kind of awe.

Directing those feelings toward their origin in the poem, students tend to discover the first dislocation in "oppresses," in the third line. Dickinson here inverts our semantic expectations, our inclination to associate darkness with oppression, and light, especially of the Jacob's-ladder sort implied in the first line, with the breaking through of divine mercy or wisdom. The third line initiates a sensory dislocation as well, for the visual categories of the first couplet are superseded by the increasingly tactile and potentially violent—"Heft," in Dickinson's dictionary, suggesting not simply weight but a beating (Alexander). Finally, the simile initiated with "like" turns the exterior of the landscape to the interior of the cathedral, preparing for the baffled interior experience of pain, despair, affliction reported in the middle stanzas. The simile completes the synaesthetic experience, as light felt as weight becomes audible in the suggested solemn cadences and resonances of cathedral tunes.

Although for the sake of economy I report these dislocations and dissolves as critical observations, my classes approach these observations as they respond to questions like "What happens here?" "Why does she turn the light into sound?" "How is an afternoon winter landscape like a cathedral interior?" The key connection students tend to discover is a pictoral one between late winter light and the shafts of light filtering down into cathedral gloom, but it is worth reminding them that the speaker gives us not cathedral light but cathedral sound. Although the simile manages a complex synaesthetic association, that association is discordant and intensifies the uneasiness begun with "oppresses." Like the unstable and shifting landscapes of De Chirico or Krazy Kat, Dickinson's poems tend to break down the familiar coordinations of space and time that provide our consciousness its security (Cameron; Alexander). The simile, which we expect to establish likeness, has a dislocating undertow characteristic of Dickinson's tropes; the sudden and intense fusion of the unlike terms of the comparison tends to heighten rather than dissolve their unlikeness, so that the reader's mind, afflicted with the internal difference, resists the momentum of the comparison even while being forced to assent to it in order to read on.

Attention to the diction and imagery of the middle stanzas will lead to the explication of the religious themes latent in the "Heft / Of Cathedral Tunes." Paraphrase may prove useful here, for it allows the students to articulate and discuss Dickinson's sense of the danger of religious experience, the possibility that divine attention may be felt as pain, wound, alienation, despair. Her radical challenge to piety of any denomination can have a salutary effect in a society where grace is cheap in a cultural bazaar that only guarantees brands of faith that feel good. But paraphrase is undermined by the strange disappearance of any location where the experience might be registered: "internal difference, / Where the Meanings, are" is as tantalizingly obscure a denomination of where the self feels itself changed as "imperial affliction / Sent us of the Air—" is evasive in its search for a point of the experience's origin. Students who have dangerously learned a little philosophy can probably run for hours through the mazes of selfhood and perception, objectivity and subjectivity to which these stanzas lead. Fortunately, the authority of the speaking voice and the measured firmness of the stanza structures contain such discussion and give it a point of return.

The landscape within and the landscape without, whose confusion began with that first simile and whose boundaries are eroded in the "interior" stanzas of the poem, merge at the poem's conclusion. Asked to discover and account for the figures of speech in the final stanza, students will note that the personified "Landscape" acts out the intensity of awe and breathless waiting appropriate to a human subject. The class might be led to relate this final, emotionally and sensorily vivid setting with the abstracted assertions of the middle stanzas: having there "lost" the self as the locus and center of feeling, the speaker seems to rediscover it in attending to the landscape without. Thus, like the initial simile, the personification implies a dislocation, and the "internal difference" of the apparently empty human subject from the landscape where the subject's own lost feeling expresses itself magnifies the sense of the newly desolate reality of a winter landscape that we all have thought we knew. The final simile is the final blow to intellectual security: "When it goes, 'tis like the Distance / On the look of Death." Asked what "it" and " 'tis" refer to, students are brought up against the recognition that "it" may still refer primarily to the "Slant of light" but that by now that slant signifies more—or less—than it did on its first appearance in the poem. The very pronoun *it*, which seems to provide the semantic stability that makes thematic paraphrase and interpretive proposition possible, seems to have lost its referent as it has wandered inward and outward at once in quest of meaning. What is "the Distance / On the look of Death"? In a strategy characteristic of the whole poem, the simile both activates and eludes our visual imagination; it also opens the frame of this very tightly rendered landscape upon infinite spacelessness. On the one hand, "Distance" and "look" seem to return us to the field of the visible; on the other, the image is strangely and irrevocably abstracted in such a way as to resist our making it familiar or recognizable (Porter, *Dickinson*). Does it direct our gaze across the now lifeless body of a landscape toward the infinite? Does it concentrate our attention on the strange vast silence that broods over the face of the dead? Does it ask us to imagine looking outward through the vacant eyes of the dead? All these suggestions, and others, have emerged from discussions that sometimes become desperate, as the students search for a semantic closure that the poem refuses: either they know less at the end of the poem than they did when they began it, or the truth that has come at such a slant leaves them deeply unsettled. If a visitation has been witnessed, it proves to be more death dealing than life giving. One student renders her sense of the weary awe of the concluding stanza quite beautifully:

> The light and the hurt have a lifeless silence to them. The final stanza seems like one last inhalation, as even the shadows hold in their breath, and one last exhalation as the light fades into infinity. The speaker reinforces this by comparing the disappearance of the light to the distance of the look of death. The look of death is generally a vacant stare into something infinitely far off. The death here seems to confirm the speaker's past perspective [of spiritual devastation]. It also refers to the dependency of life on light not only in a physical context but also in spiritual terms.   (Wasserman 3)

Poem 754, "My Life had stood—a Loaded Gun," provides as powerful a concluding discussion of Dickinson's work as 258 provides an unsettling beginning. The poem's lucid and self-contained simplicity of story and the cleverness of the euphemistic metaphors ("I speak for Him," "do I smile," "Vesuvian face") suggesting the cordiality of gunfire from the gun's point of view give students the pleasure of reading a fable and solving its riddles. One can ask the class to identify and answer the riddles implicit in the poem's figures of speech. One can also ask them to consider what it would feel like to be a gun and, abstracting from that by implication from the poem, in what way the explosion of violence can be pleasurable. Somehow, though, this level of discussion doesn't seem quite satisfying, because of the nagging inference that the poem is about something else. This inference is triggered by the metaphor of the opening line, which names the gun as a vehicle for the tenor of the speaker's life. The rest of the poem operates explicitly on the vehicular level; there is no reference back to the dimension of the tenor, the life, although the opening metaphor compels the reader to wonder about it. The poem as the extension of that metaphor has the self-contained, self-consistent complexity of an allegory, and even its most sophisticated readers attempt to excavate the "meaning" of the literal, or vehicular, story (Rich; Porter, *Modern Idiom*; Cameron).

In class this search for a coherent meaning takes shape around the question of how to identify the gun and the "Owner," who seem by the end of the poem not to be able to exist without each other. The dialectic between them takes shape in a series of suggestions that can be mapped out on the blackboard, as in figure 1. There is much to recommend each of these allegorical reconstructions, but testing them by returning to the vehicular level of the poem's facts will disclose the inconsistency if not the impossi-

Figure 1.

OWNER	GUN
God	human self
soul or mind	body
body	soul or mind
husband	wife
male	female
reason	passion
purpose	power
spirit	language

bility of each and undo any interpretive coherence they might establish. For instance, the idea that God uses human beings as instruments for his inscrutable and often violent intentions seems a properly heretical Dickinson premise; but it founders on the excruciating paradox of the concluding stanza, where the owner is declared to be mortal, and the gun, although deathless, is also lifeless on the owner's disappearance. The body-soul duality seems to speak to the symbiotic necessity of each for the other but founders on the same paradox, as the class's attempt to reverse the terms should indicate. At the very least, trying out these terms to account for the poem's meaning underscores the fragility and inadequacy of the philosophic commonplaces by which we try to understand ourselves. The poem then seems overdetermined; there are too many possibilities for what it means. Yet a careful examination of each possibility exposes it as underdetermined: not quite adequate or flexible enough to account consistently for the poem's "facts" (Cameron 65–69). Almost inevitably a student will cry, "Maybe the gun is just a gun." And the student will be right. Perhaps Dickinson is just playing with the writing-workshop exercise of telling a story from the point of view of an object. Yet the initial synapse opened by the primary metaphor can't be closed off; although the end of the poem forces us to confront the impossibility of retracing our steps across the synapse from the life of the gun back to the life to which it promises to refer, it also desperately insists that we can't stop attempting that passage. In effect the poem traps us in our quest for meaning, exposing to us a need for intelligibility to which the poem itself may be indifferent. Either we find ourselves confined to the innocent pleasure of reading a poem literally on its own terms and denied the poem's challenge of meaning, or we find ourselves guilty of interpretation, of "reading too much into" the poem; as Rilke describes "Les Saltimbanques," we are either trapped in the "pure too little" or lost in the "empty too much."

Perhaps the reading that makes the most sense is that the voice speaking in the poem is the breathless mouth of the poem itself (Yeats), waiting to be hailed and summoned into being by the purpose of the reader, content to be the cordial instrument through which the reader's fantasies of power and defensiveness can be realized, deathless yet without life unless called by the human need for meaning. Here I confess my own need for depth and for allegoric coherence, and perhaps such a romantic reading would seem too artfully self-circling for more practically minded students. Yet such a reading might account for the deadly earnestness of the game Dickinson plays with language. It would account for the peculiarly disembodied voice of the poem, and for the owner's transience, and for the owner's own need for power in the world (which comes from claiming the gun and allowing it to speak for him or her, a need we seem to enact in our search for meaning). Those of us in the business of teaching poetry do it because we believe that people "die miserably every day / for lack / of what is found there" (Williams). If Dickinson's poems radically and consistently challenge us to undo the versions of truth by which we try to bring coherence to the poems, they also desperately ask us to keep trying, for our own sakes as well as for the sake of the poetry. The final gesture of "My life had stood" reminds us, remarkably modestly for Dickinson yet characteristically on a slant, that it is through our search for understanding that the poem comes to have a place in the world; and in the attempt to "identify" it, we also identify ourselves and claim what power we can.

DICKINSON'S POEMS IN THEIR OWN CONTEXTS

Voice, Tone, and Persona in Dickinson's Love Poetry

Nancy Walker

Students are apt to find the poetry of Emily Dickinson initially perplexing for several reasons—particularly her elliptical style, eccentric punctuation, and unusual diction and syntax. In addition, they frequently bring to the poetry stereotypical notions of nineteenth-century women in general and Dickinson in particular that preclude an understanding of Dickinson as a complex, courageous woman with a variety of attitudes, moods, and, consequently, poetic voices. Close attention to the multiplicity of her approaches to a single major theme allows students to understand the concepts of voice, tone, and persona in poetry generally, as well as helping them to respect the essential humanity of Emily Dickinson. Her poetry that deals with love is especially appropriate for a study of her many voices because of her deep ambivalence about the role of love in her life. Although she acknowledged its preeminence among human emotions, as in "Love—is anterior to Life" (917), she had difficulty coming to terms with love as it entered into her relationships with both men and women. In speaking of love and sexuality in her poetry, Dickinson is sometimes reverential, sometimes despairing, sometimes cynical, and sometimes playful; discussion of these differences in tone and attitude as well as of the poetic devices used to convey them allows the student access to both the artistry of her poetry and the complexity of her thought.

Although students at a women's college, such as the one at which I taught for a number of years, tend to have a well-developed sense of personal ambition and independence regarding their careers, they are nonetheless socialized to be passive and dependent in love relationships. Because of this socialization, they initially identify most closely with Dickinson's yearning "Daisy" voice rather than with the strongly independent voice that also appears in her love poetry. This response is heightened by the students' assumption that women of earlier periods were incapable of making choices about their own lives. When asked to examine, read aloud, and listen to those poems in which Dickinson is playful or renunciatory about love, they quickly begin to comprehend the range of her—and potentially their—responses to relationships as mature individuals. This approach also helps to dispel the notion that the "I" in the poem is always the poet herself. Students have a tendency to read literature in general as though it were simply the record of the individual writer's life and emotions; when they perceive that Dickinson contradicts herself, approaching the same subject from a variety of stances and emotional states, they begin to understand that the speaker is a created persona who may or may not reflect the attitudes of the writer.

Dickinson's poems about love, like those about her other major themes, tend to reveal the feelings of a person immediately engaged in one of its manifestations rather than reflecting upon it afterward. The poems deal with three principal circumstances: absence or rejection of a loved one, flirtation and sexuality, and marriage. Those having to do with absence or rejection are primarily, though not uniformly, serious in tone and sometimes despairing; the flirtatious poems are typically playful and imaginative; and the poems about marriage reveal the greatest range of attitudes, from reverence to deep skepticism. The persona or voice in these poems varies from the self-assured woman who refuses to justify her love in " 'Why do I love' You, Sir?" (480) to the submissive bride in "Forever at His side to walk" (246) to the playful child-woman of "Did the Harebell loose her girdle" (213).

To achieve these different voices, Dickinson uses variations in metrical pattern, diction, and sound, but most distinctive is the variation in imagery. In poems about sexuality, for example, the imagery comes commonly from the natural world, from the playful harebell and bee to the more ominous worm/snake of poem 1670, "In Winter in my Room." In poems about marriage, the imagery is more apt to be religious, as in "The World—stands—solemner—to me" (493), and in those that deal with distance from a loved one, she employs the aprons, dresser drawers, and other household images that reinforce the sense of Dickinson squarely "at home" throughout her poetry. Thus the joys of flirtation and sexuality require the voice of the innocent child in nature, whereas marriage is associated with the solemnity of religious commitment, and missing a loved one is for her so ordinary a circumstance that it takes place amid the familiar items of the household.

Despite much theorizing about Dickinson's relationships with various men and women, it is almost impossible for the contemporary reader to know by whom an individual poem was inspired or to whom—if anyone—it is addressed. In addition, because of the nineteenth-century conventions of language and the strong influence of the Bible on Dickinson's poetic language and imagery, it is frequently difficult to know whether she is addressing a mortal or a deity, as in poem 473, "I am ashamed—I hide," in which she could either be speaking of becoming the bride of Christ or imagining an earthly wedding. In *Women Writers and Poetic Identity*, Margaret Homans speaks of Dickinson's intuition that all discourse is an invention, an arbitrary expression of assumptions rather than the revelation of truth: "if she can speak in one invented style, all forms of address may be fictive" (168). Nonetheless, love in its various manifestations is a common theme in her poetry, and the variety of her poetic personae reveals the complexity of her response to this basic human emotion. Students comprehend this complexity most readily when they are presented with poems that are thematically similar but quite different in tone and approach. Pairs of poems that deal with sensuality, marriage, and lost or renounced love introduce a variety of personae representing a rich array of emotional states.

Poems with a flirtatious or sensual emphasis occur throughout Dickinson's canon, and the relative accessibility of some of these poems makes them a good point at which to begin a study of the poet's method and range. Perhaps the clearest example of Dickinson's flirtatious voice and method is poem 213, "Did the Harebell loose her girdle," which combines coquettishness and sensual imagery. She transfers the age-old question *Will you respect me in the morning?* to the world of bees and flowers that is frequently a child's introduction to reproductive processes, and in this innocent guise she addresses the sexual double standard. The speaker in the poem is thus both child and adult; the simple imagery of the poem and the lilting rhythm of the short lines, coupled with the repeated "e" sounds, mask the seriousness of the adult query.

When students read this poem aloud, they not only discover the playful rhythms but also become aware of the ambiguity of the syntactical relation between "Bee" and "Harebell" in the third line. "Would the Bee the Harebell *hallow*" can be read either as "would the bee respect the harebell" or, if Dickinson is using inverted syntax, as she so frequently does, "would the harebell respect the bee." The former reading seems to be supported by the third line of the second stanza, if Eden refers to the purity of the Garden of Eden; that is, if the bee loses respect for the flower, it is because she has allowed her purity to be soiled. Dickinson, however, commonly uses "Eden" to mean joy or ecstasy, as in 211, "Come slowly—Eden!" which also deals with the union of a bee and a flower. This fact and the question about the status of the "Earl" in the last line of the poem support the second reading of the "hallow" line, which in turn places the female element in the poem—the harebell—in the position of judgment, the dominant position, able to withhold nobility from the male. A discussion of these two possible readings is a good introduction to the ambiguity that is so common in Dickinson's poetry. Furthermore, that Dickinson may here be placing the female in the dominant position—especially in a mock-sexual encounter—suggests that she did not view women as necessarily submissive. The poet reveals herself as capable of imagining an alternative reality in which women are not only entitled to sensual pleasure but also free from being disgraced by it. The flirtatious harebell is in any case far removed from the abject, submissive "Daisy" with which Dickinson identifies herself in the "Master" letters.

In a much later poem, "In Winter in my Room" (1670), Dickinson adopts a completely different tone and persona to explore again the sensual relation between male and female. Students need only a slight acquaintance with Freudian psychology to comprehend the phallic imagery of the poem, but they may not as readily understand the complexity of the speaker's stance—a stance established by sound, diction, and the creation of an atmosphere of mystery. This poem, like "Did the Harebell loose her girdle," uses elements of nonhuman nature to objectify human sensuality, but the speaker here is a first-person narrator recounting a dreamlike experience, which gives the poem a sense of personal immediacy that contrasts with the playful fantasy of the harebell poem. The dreamlike quality is enhanced by the repeated sounds of *m* and *n*, which have a droning, almost mesmerizing effect, and by the nearly uniform metrical pattern of the lines in each stanza.

Dickinson uses diction and meter, in particular, to convey the ambivalence of her persona. In the first stanza of the poem, the tone is solemn, yet calm; the worm is not threatening but merely presumptuous ("And worms presume"), and the speaker ties him to something "neighboring" and goes along without further thought. The tone of unconcern continues into the second stanza with the word "Trifle," but as the speaker sees the worm become a snake, she speaks with "creeping blood" in describing him as "ringed with power." Even in the presence of the snake, however, the speaker does not panic but attempts to flatter him—"How fair you are"—and when he asks whether she is afraid, she simply replies that she offers him "no cordiality." It is only when the snake begins to move—when the sexual identity of the image becomes clear in "He fathomed me," suggesting both understanding and sexual penetration—that the speaker flees, and the shorter lines of the third stanza reinforce her breathless flight to "Towns on from mine."

By ending "In Winter in my Room" with the flat statement "This was a dream," Dickinson stresses that the poem is an invention and therefore her persona is an invention. It is easy to interpret the poem as expressing a fear of sexuality, but if the "I" in the poem is assumed to be someone other than—someone created by—Dickinson, then it is clear only that she can imagine the fear, not that it is hers. To make this point more forcefully, one can turn to Dickinson's "Wild Nights—Wild Nights!" (249), which also features the first-person speaker but which celebrates an imagined sensual union through the regenerative imagery of the sea and leaves the speaker "moored" in her lover in an Eden of bliss.

Dickinson's poetry about marriage offers even more striking evidence of her ability to speak in a variety of voices. Like most of her poetry, the marriage poems are imaginative re-creations of emotional states, and Dickinson's speakers experience marriage sometimes as a rite of passage from childhood to adulthood ("I'm ceded—I've stopped being Theirs" [508]), sometimes as a frightened bride ("I am ashamed—I hide" [473]), and sometimes in terms of religious conversion ("Title divine—is mine!" [1072]). Two facts about Dickinson's life help establish these poems as inventions rather than autobiographical descriptions: one is her status as a single woman and the other is her lifelong resistance to full religious conversion. With this information, students can more readily appreciate the power of Dickinson's imagination as she addresses the idea of marriage.

One of the most illuminating contrasts within the group of marriage poems is that between 461, "A Wife—at Daybreak I shall be," and 732, "She rose to His Requirement." From a cultural standpoint, these poems reveal Dickinson's understanding of the myth and the reality of marriage for women in the nineteenth century: on the one hand, marriage conferred adulthood on women; on the other, it merely reduced women to a different childlike state because it subsumed a woman's identity under that of her husband. When Dickinson uses a first-person speaker, as she does in most of the marriage poems, including "A Wife—at Daybreak," she assumes the anticipatory, even ecstatic attitude of the young woman who is finally about to be confirmed as an adult; but when she adopts the external stance of the third-person narrative, her tone is detached, cool, even critical.

The speaker in "A Wife—at Daybreak" is exultant about the transition she is about to make from "Maid" to "Bride"; it represents "Victory." She marvels at "How short [a time] it takes to make a Bride," and her passage is attended by angels—a presence that testifies to the holiness of marriage and the speaker's delight in its approach. In fact, the poem moves from the imagery of victorious battle in the first stanza—"Sunrise—Hast thou a Flag for me?"—to the solemnity of religious conversion in the second. On the threshold of adulthood, the speaker "fumbles" at "Childhood's prayer" as she approaches "Eternity"; and her future husband is a "Savior." The fusion of marriage and religious conversion is on one level simple enough: in Christianity, marriage is a sacrament, and traditionally the union was assumed to endure beyond earthly life. Seen in another light, however, the religious imagery reinforces the subordination of female to male in the conventional view of marriage—a subordination implied by the speaker's use of the word "Sir" in the penultimate line.

The suggestion in this poem that marriage is a time of loss for women is amplified in "She rose to His Requirement." Here Dickinson speaks as an observer, watching rather than participating in the ritual passage of a woman from child to wife. When teaching this poem, I have found it useful to refer students to some of Dickinson's letters to Susan Gilbert before Susan married Dickinson's brother, Austin. The two young women exchanged ideas about marriage, among other topics, and in one letter Dickinson expresses serious doubts about the happiness of married women:

> . . . but to the *wife*, Susie, sometimes the *wife forgotten*, our lives seem dearer than all others in the world . . . Oh, Susie, it is dangerous, and it is all too dear, these simple trusting spirits, and the spirits mightier, when we cannot resist! . . . I tremble lest at sometime I, too, am yielded up.   (*L* 1: 210)

Dickinson's resistance to marriage, at least as indicated in this letter, reflects her view that it is not a union of two equals but a yielding of "simple trusting spirits" to "spirits mightier"—the assuming, by women, of a position of socially sanctioned inferiority.

It is the "*wife forgotten*" that Dickinson describes in "She rose to His Requirement." The "she" is unidentified; the woman that the poet's voice describes could be generic, like the wife Dickinson mentions in her letter to Susan, or she could be an individual whom Dickinson had observed. Like the bride in "A Wife—at Daybreak," this woman is transformed from child to adult by marriage: she drops the "Playthings of Her life" to assume "the honorable Work / of Woman and of Wife." Yet the emphasis of the poem is on what she has lost, not on what she has gained, which lends irony to the phrase "honorable Work": the honor of being a wife is an external reward in exchange for which the woman loses what Dickinson terms "Amplitude" and "Awe." Or, rather, she seems to lose them, for the speaker continues in an oblique, ironic fashion. The second and third stanzas hinge on the word "If," and the wife's true feelings "lay unmentioned" as though at the bottom of the sea.

The metaphoric submerging of the wife's dreams and aspirations echoes Dickinson's phrase "yielded up" in her letter to Susan about ten years earlier, and the similarity suggests that this poem more nearly expresses her attitudes toward marriage than do most others. If this is so, it makes the personae of her other marriage poems all the more fictive, all the more illustrative of her ability to enter imaginatively into multiple experiences and states of mind.

By far the most common, and certainly the most poignant, theme in Emily Dickinson's love poetry is loss or renunciation. Although such poems have often been used to perpetuate the image of Dickinson as lonely and love-starved, they can be more productively viewed as evidence of her ability to feel deeply and to express that emotion in poetic language that conveys the complexity of human relationships. Further, these poems are seldom sentimental or maudlin; Dickinson's quick intelligence and skepticism frequently counteract the emotionalism of the subject matter. The variety of personae in these poems further demonstrates Dickinson's skill in bending language to her purposes; the mood of the speakers ranges from docility to anguish, from submissiveness to renunciation.

Most students have had some experience with the ending of a close relationship and identify easily with the sentiments expressed by the speaker in "I got so I could take his name" (293). The violence of the imagery in the first three stanzas underscores the speaker's great emotion; the thunder, torn sinews, and "staples" represent the tumult and pain of loss. Yet when, in the last three stanzas, the speaker seeks the consolation of prayer, the skepticism about religion that also appears elsewhere in Dickinson's poetry saves the poem from sentimentality. God is viewed as more remedy than deity—"Renowned to ease Extremity" might come from the label on a jar of liniment—and her interaction with the object of her prayers is crisp rather than abject: "My business, with the Cloud." The very existence of God is in fact in doubt, for the last six lines of the poem depend on the word "if": "If any Power behind it [the cloud], be," then she will appeal it to ease her "Misery." Not only does this sense of religious skepticism save the poem from sentimentality; it also makes the persona a complex individual who feels loss keenly, yet has the ability to analyze her own attempts to find solace.

In later poems Dickinson's speaker attempts to turn loss into deliberate renunciation and to find consolation in stoicism rather than in a questionable deity. In poem 640, for example, the speaker begins bravely by stating, "I cannot live with you," but it soon becomes apparent that in renouncing a person she is renouncing life itself, which has been placed "over there— / Behind the shelf." This life is described in domestic terms, as cracked china "Discarded of the Housewife"; the speaker seems closely related to this homely image, suggesting that it is she who has been put on the shelf in favor of something new. This sense of unworthiness persists as the speaker asserts that just as she cannot live with her loved one, neither can she die or "rise" with him because of his greater worthiness. The last stanza suggests that the relationship continues as a distant one—"You there—I—here," with the speaker taking a perverse comfort in the "White sustenance—Despair."

Yet despite the quiet anguish of the speaker, the poem is organized as though it were an argumentative essay, which serves to intellectualize and objectify the emotional burden. The speaker explains rationally why she cannot live, die, and "rise" into immortality with her loved one. Further, she explains that if her lover were condemned to hell and she to heaven, she would be in hell because of the anguish of separation. The concluding stanza functions as does the concluding paragraph of an essay, drawing on the evidence offered to propose that the two must remain apart "With just the Door ajar." Despite the differences between this poem and "I got so I could take his name," both present a persona whose ability to think, to intellectualize, saves her from being overcome by an intense sense of loss.

Because Emily Dickinson's poems about love deal with a range of emotions familiar to most people, they constitute an effective starting point for a discussion of the variations in tone, voice, and persona in her poetry. Once students understand the multiplicity of her approaches to this theme, they are prepared to investigate how differences in mood and attitude necessitate different choices of image, meter, and syntax, and thus to comprehend the artistry of her poetry. Such an approach both assumes and reinforces the complexity of Dickinson's vision and helps to dispel the sentimentalized mythology surrounding her life and her work.

A Posthumanist Approach to Teaching Dickinson

William Galperin

My approach to teaching Dickinson developed from two distinct causes: my training in British Romanticism and my attempt as a fledgling instructor to make Dickinson—one of two obligatory women in an obligatory introduction-to-poetry course—part of the so-called visionary company. Convinced of the autonomy and sanctity of the individual perceiving subject, I endeavored initially to show how poems such as "I heard a Fly buzz" (465) and "Because I could not stop for Death" (712) were essentially about imagination or the ability of Dickinson's speaker to annex the world imaginatively rather than be annexed by it. The lines "Because I could not stop for Death— / He kindly stopped for me" shrewdly announced, I discovered in one class, that the poem was not about "Death" (as customarily interpreted) but about Death stopping, or the "Immortality" that the speaker gained ("Since then—'tis Centuries") by refusing to succumb to the impositions placed on her by the material world. Similarly, the emphasis in 465 on the fly perceived, "with Blue—uncertain stumbling Buzz," registered, as I first taught it, the subject's refusal to imitate her various "witnesses" in allowing death precedence over an inner, imagined world, which persists and predominates as long as the speaker can "see to see."

Still, no sooner did I make Dickinson an autonomous seer in the tradition of Blake and Shelley (Bloom 1–131, 282–362) than it became clear that the authority of her speaker was inseparable from the subject's authority as a woman, so that humanism—the promotion of the individual imagination—remained, in a peculiar sense, both the cause and the effect of the subject's refusal to live in the world. Accordingly, the "Immortality" that the speaker achieves for refusal to "stop for Death" is preceded in the poem's narrative by a recognition, a "surmise" as Dickinson describes it, that the subject's suitor was Death: that in marrying him, as she presumably intended, the house or domestic sphere to which she would have been consigned was equivalent to a grave, "A Swelling of the Ground." In this way, the immortality to which the speaker is subsequently privy was no longer immortality per se any more than death so-called signified the end of life. Rather, by redefining death so that it meant a woman's co-optation by culture, the poem similarly redefined immortality as a woman's self-possession, or the result, in turn, of a refusal to allow "society" the prerogative of selecting her.

It is on this nexus, then, of humanism and feminism that my approach to teaching Dickinson—which I call "posthumanist" to distinguish it from other kinds of feminism—has continually turned. For if Dickinson is sufficiently a "Romantic" to oppose society in the way she does, she is sufficiently circumspect not only to yearn for the world she has renounced but also to recognize—and this has particular relevance to the current critical scene—that the act of appropriating the authority formerly consigned to society makes her as much an authority in her own right as an opponent of the dominant order. The key text documenting these stations of awareness is, for my purposes again, "Because I could not stop for Death," which moves from a celebration of the speaker's autonomy, to a nostalgia for what she has renounced, to a recognition finally that the immortality gained for refusal to stop for Death implicates the subject in the very system, indeed the very narrative or "intentional structure" (de Man 65–77), headed "toward Eternity" (Galperin 68–72). As a result, I begin my Dickinson component not with this poem but with poems leading to the conflation of feminism and humanism before the posthumanism (or the deconstruction of humanism) in which the poetry ultimately issues. Further, I always preface my discussion with a brief lecture on women in the nineteenth century, describing the kind of life that awaited Dickinson in a high-bourgeois marriage, whose foremost purpose remained the insurance of heirs, not infrequently at the woman's peril. Marriage, in other words, which was clearly an option for Dickinson (no "Belle of Amherst" she!), would remain, as she rightly envisioned, inimical to her "labor" and "leisure" both. (The boldly "naturalistic" photograph of a woman who might or might not be Emily Dickinson [Sewall, *Life* 752] is particularly helpful in disabusing students of the myth that Dickinson was a woman scarcely human.)

The poems I begin with include "To hang our head—ostensibly" (105), "I'm 'wife'—I've finished that" (199), "For each ecstatic instant" (125), "How many times these low feet staggered" (187), and "Just lost, when I was saved" (160). One virtue of these poems is their relative brevity. Moreover, these works variously anticipate "Because I could not stop for Death" in their protest against marriage and the domestic sphere ("I'm 'wife' " and "How many times") as well as in their treatment of the immortality myth. The forced contrition in "To hang our head," a posture apparently dictated by culture, is perceived as such only after the recognition that this is not the posture "of our immortal mind." Here, then, the question of gender, of the immortality or grace arguably denied women ("*our* . . . mind"), is seemingly key, though not always to the exclusion of men. If anything, Dickinson, as students often realize, is determined to extend the paradigm, turning in the second part to another reader ("You—too"), who, regardless of gender, may resemble the speaker either by sharing her understanding or, even worse, by concealing it.

Similarly, in "Just lost, when I was saved," a state of immortality from which the speaker has been rescued is enlisted in the service of a still incipient feminism. The eternity, in effect, from which the speaker has returned or, as she implies, has just escaped is not always the terrible state that the narrative of her salvation would indicate. Indeed, it is a place the speaker might wish to inhabit a little longer, not only for its exotic offerings, but, more important, for its privacy, for the fact that she can function there "by Ear unheard / Unscrutinized by Eye." Again, it must be emphasized that without the more overtly feminist poems, the allegories of the other texts are latent at best. Yet I find that once encouraged by the feminist poems, students are less daunted by the more cryptic ones, which demand in any case that they venture an interpretation.

The second sequence of poems that I assign—"There's a certain Slant of light (258), "I felt a Funeral, in my Brain" (280), "A Clock stopped" (287), "The Soul selects her own Society" (303), " 'Hope' is the thing with feathers" (254)—represents a reality unsupported by mythology or the difficulty, quite simply, of being in eternity without always knowing that it is immortality. The central text here is "The Soul selects her own Society," which oscillates between a desire for what has been forsaken and a recognition that what has been renounced remains, regardless of its immediate consequences, eminently forsakeable. These poems are not, in the main, cheerful documents, yet their strength—and their appeal for students—is in the candor with which Dickinson describes both the assets and the liabilities of her life alone, which is increasingly a life of the mind. ("When she wins, she loses," I recall one student observing.) Thus, the celebration of imagination in "There's a certain Slant of light," the ability of the perceiving subject to reconstitute the winter *seen*, is freighted simultaneously with despair, which is created rather than overcome. So, too, the more extreme appropriations of "I felt a Funeral" and "A Clock stopped," where whole worlds are reinvented in the speaker's mind, testify all the same to the prisonhouse of subjectivism.

Having urged, then, both the power of Dickinson's imagination and the circumspection of her vision, I am able with the next group of poems to return to the feminist theme, which owes increasingly to a conviction that the self, for better or worse, is all the speaker has or needs. The subject's refusal, for example, to be an object of male delectation in "I cannot dance upon my Toes" (326) stems less from the recognition that such behavior is untoward than from a conviction in the adequacy of her own "Art"—"full as Opera." This confidence is reflected equally in " 'Tis not that Dying hurts us so" (335), which depicts life—that is, life in marriage ("behind the Door")—as infinitely less supportable than the relative freedom by which the barnyard birds of marriage are transformed, in Dickinson's allegory, into migratory ones that fly. Correspondingly, the despair that was so immediate in the previous sequence is more belated here, having evolved into a state to which the speaker is becoming reconciled. A way to illustrate this difference would be to compare "I felt a Funeral" with "After great pain, a formal feeling comes" (341), in which a similar experience is contextualized and, as the latter poem attests, "outlived." Nor must Dickinson always deal explicitly with the question of autonomy versus marriage or the growing need to be a bird of flight rather than a barnyard animal. In "God is a distant—stately Lover" (357), the rather confident detachment through which the poet increasingly approaches her own life is brought to a more generalized subject: the double bind to which religion (and culture) continually subjects one. If Dickinson, then, is becoming more confident in her vocation, her confidence is everywhere apparent, making the world, by turns, a variation on the marriage theme.

At this juncture I move to a series of poems whose celebration of the poetic imagination marks them as Dickinson's most confident and humanistic. Out of context, "The Brain—is wider than the Sky" (632), "Out of sight? What of that?" (703), and "I dwell in Possibility" (657) can seem outrageous or vainglorious to students. But in the trajectory of Dickinson's autonomy as we have followed it, they come off as genuinely celebratory and of a piece with Dickinson's most ferocious renunciations of conjugal life: "Because I could not stop for Death" and "I heard a Fly buzz—when I died." That the latter poem, like the former, is about marriage (that is to say, marriage as death) is almost always the great revelation of this sequence and one that students gravitate toward. They are particularly impressed by the way an ostensible deathbed scene can just as easily be a marital scene, in which the bride, like the dying invalid, will have signed away "what portion of [her] be / Assignable."

I therefore usually reserve "I heard a Fly buzz" for discussion after a more directed treatment of "Because I could not stop for Death." And yet, it is on the latter poem, as I have indicated, that my approach to teaching Dickinson depends. For if it has been the purpose of the Dickinson component to enable students to see that this poem is about immortality, about the prelapsarian grace where "labor" is tantamount to "leisure," it is my purpose now to have Dickinson teach them—as the speaker would herself learn when she "first surmised the Horses' Heads / Were toward Eternity"—that the eternal death that awaited her had she followed a suitor is no less a defeat than the immortality she gained for failure to "stop for Death" in the first place: that the "eternities" belong, no matter their dialectic, to one system of hierarchies and correspondences (Galperin 71–72).

Thus, the poems I conclude with—"Of Consciousness, her awful Mate" (894), "My Life had stood—a Loaded Gun" (754), "What mystery pervades a well!" (1400), and " 'Nature' is what we see" (668)—clearly differ from the previous poems in their reluctance to participate in the appropriate or authoritative system (Homans, *Women* 162–214). This participation is, of course, brilliantly allegorized in "My Life had stood—a Loaded Gun," in which the speaker imagines herself an instrument of destruction in the sway of masculine control. The other poems proceed from this awareness by systematically resigning the authority previously exerted. The well that encloses a mystery is effectively demystified by Dickinson, as is a male orientation, which, seeking to appropriate nature (and woman), is inevitably confounded by, and consequently compelled to mystify, the aspects of "her" beyond control. Likewise, in " 'Nature' is what we see" Dickinson privileges contingent observation, or what Julia Kristeva has called the "semiotic," over the more masculinized orientation or the "symbolic," where the effort to give meaning, to exert control, is rendered "impotent" by nature's "simplicity." Thus, the feminist trajectory in Dickinson, which begins in the attempt to gain authority and to be a woman writer (Gilbert and Gubar, *Madwoman* 581–650), leads in the end to the renunciation of authority and the liberation of poetry from the constraints of humanism.

One very important implication of the "narrative" I have just constructed is its simultaneous resistance to narrative, to a totalizing structure on which interpretations of Dickinson's poetry—my own included—are invariably grounded. Although Dickinson's most radically feminist poems were probably written after her more humanistic ones, it is more important that her poems are sufficiently close in their dates of origin to militate against any notion of an interpretable or otherwise definable oeuvre. Like "Because I could not stop for Death," which is really a series of revisions or transformations, Dickinson's works are continually subject to other works of hers, giving corrigibility, as it were, precedence over interpretability. While Dickinson continues to lend herself to critical reconstructions of one kind or another, any a priori reading is ultimately little more than grist for her mill. And this work against an oeuvre is finally the most radical resistance to authority, the poet's own included, that Dickinson's poetry wages.

Dickinson as Comic Poet

Dorothy Huff Oberhaus

Because many of Emily Dickinson's greatest poems concern mutability and death, poems on these subjects are frequently those chosen for classroom discussion. As a result, students are often given the false notion that Dickinson is an unremittingly morbid poet, a kind of belles lettres version of Mark Twain's Emmeline Grangerford. To counter this misconception and to convey some sense of the scope and complexity of her canon, we as teachers need to pay more attention to her comic poems and to her considerable wit—which her best friend and literary confidante, Susan Gilbert Dickinson, described as "a Damascus blade gleaming and glancing in the sun" (Leyda 473; Oberhaus). Within the time limits of introductory, American literature, and poetics courses, reading such comic poems as "I'm Nobody! Who are you?" (288) and "I taste a liquor never brewed" (214) along with such somber ones as "Because I could not stop for Death" (712) and "Pain—has an Element of Blank" (650) gives a more complete view of Dickinson's art, a perspective that can be explored more fully in Dickinson seminars by devoting several weeks to a whole cluster of her comic poems. To the initial surprise of many students, I also include a selection of Dickinson's comic poems in my courses Comedy, Wit, and Humor and American Humor, both interdisciplinary humanities courses designed for all undergraduates.

The Comedy course considers the comic mode as expressed by such diverse writers as Aristophanes, Shakespeare, Austen, Twain, Dickinson, Thurber, Flannery O'Connor, and Beckett. These writers are viewed in the light of comic theorists like Aristotle, Bergson, Freud, Koestler, Wylie Sypher, and Harvey Cox. I introduce Dickinson about two-thirds of the way into the course, after students have read the theoretical works and the playwrights and novelists through Twain. Reading Dickinson in this context both illuminates her comic spirit and illustrates significant aspects of the comic, thereby increasing students' understanding of the complexity of the comic as mode and as worldview.

By the time we reach Dickinson, students have been introduced to the classic comic heroes, including the *eiron*, the ostensibly self-deprecating little figure who stands outside society but remains undefeated and often asks impious questions. Socrates is often cited as the epitome of the *eiron*, and students have little difficulty identifying this stock comic type in its more recent manifestations, Huck Finn, Walter Mitty, and Charlie Chaplin. Because Dickinson's tone is elusive, however, and because students, like many of her other readers, want to read her poems as confessional rather than as poetic texts, more professorial guidance is required to help them discover that the speaker of "I'm Nobody! Who are you?" is also a kind of *eiron*.

As in many other Dickinson poems, this "Nobody" speaker addresses the reader immediately and intimately and therefore comically, for, as Bergson notes, the comic is by its very nature social and implies an understanding and complicity between speaker and hearer (64–65). With unconcealed delight in the private life that students find it difficult not to pity, Dickinson's speaker conspiratorially invites the reader to share in deflating authority figures, a recurring comic inversion from *Lysistrata* to the Keystone Cops. Her chief means of deflation is animalism, a comic trope from *The Parlement of Foules* to Mickey Mouse (Veron 323): to the nobody speaker, and by implication the nobody reader, the somebodies of this world are no more impressive than frogs who tell their names—and the frog's croak does sound like its name—to the general public, here similarly deflated as a "Bog." This poem's comic tone, as in many of her other witty poems, is reinforced by its uneven metrics, its frequent pyrrhics, and Dickinson's typical condensation and brevity.

"I taste a liquor never brewed" similarly demonstrates Dickinson's comic spirit while illustrating comic themes, strategies, and figures. Its ecstatic speaker, though drunk on life rather than on liquor, is still a drunk, another stock comic type from Falstaff to W. C. Fields. That the entire poem is an extended play on words, with no fewer than fifteen words having to do with drinking and drunkenness ("liquor," "brewed," "Tankards," "Frankfort Berries," "Alcohol," "Inebriate," "Debauchee," "Reeling," "inns," "Landlords," "drams," "drink," "Tippler," and "Manzanilla"), furnishes concrete evidence that the comic is often found in words themselves in the form of pun, a favorite of Dickinson, and other verbal plays (Bergson 127–29). The poem's fantastic element, particularly its "Tankards scooped in Pearl" and its alternate final line, in which the persona is "Leaning against the—Sun" as other drunks lean against lampposts, illustrates the importance of fantasy to the comic (Cox 59–68). The witty impertinence with which she treats heavenly residents—"Seraphs" swinging their halos, here "snowy Hats," and "Saints" running to the windows of heaven—reflects similarly comic treatment of sacred subjects in medieval mystery and morality plays, Georges Rouault's portrait of Christ as clown, and more recently the play *Godspell* (Cox 139). Moreover, as Constance Rourke points out in her discussion of Dickinson as "a comic poet . . . in a profound sense," the ascending movement of this and other Dickinson poems is that of all comedy (209–10).

An important goal of Comedy, Wit, and Humor is to allow students to discover that, as most comic theorists argue, the comic is no less serious than the tragic and other solemn forms. Dickinson's famous train poem (585) nicely illustrates this, as well as Bergson's observation that comedy is a return to childhood, a temporary vacation from adult life (104–05). The poem playfully poses a riddle and challenges the reader to guess what "it" is that "laps the Miles," "peer[s] in Shanties," "neigh[s] like Boanerges," then "Stop[s]—docile and omnipotent / At its own stable door." Students like accepting this challenge and quickly recognize that the poem, a single long, extravagantly compounded sentence, conveys movement. After some wild, off-target guesses, they usually come to the conclusion that "it" is a horse, which is, of course, close to the poem's controlling metaphor, the iron horse. Finding that the poem depicts a train provokes laughter—or at least a smile—demonstrating the close relation between laughter and discovery (Koestler 87–96). We then carefully reread the poem together line by line and in doing so discover that the poem is not simply one of "silly playfulness" as Yvor Winters posits (29) but a serious commentary on the possible negative impact of the industrial society the train represents. "Prodigious," "supercilious," "Shanties," "Complaining," "horrid," and "hooting" are negative words foreshadowing the last stanza's conclusion: after the spondee whose first syllable is "Stop," the train at rest is "docile," but ominously "omnipotent," a word Dickinson usually uses in relation to Deity (e.g., in 420) and one that means, according to her beloved lexicon, "possessing unlimited power" (Webster, 1848 ed.). The poem, then, is both a cartoon of the train and social criticism.

The seriousness of the comic is more easily seen in its forms of irony and satire, and Dickinson is frequently an ironic observer of the passing scene. Her satiric portrait of her contemporary "Gentlewomen" (401) is profitably read in the light of Jane Austen's caustic portraits of Mrs. Bennet and Lady DeBourgh in *Pride and Prejudice*, an earlier course reading. But Dickinson's speaker not only rejects haughty gentlewomen in the here and now; she also concludes, alluding to Scriptures, that because of their arrogant self-righteousness they will be rejected in the hereafter, thereby anticipating a recurring theme of Flannery O'Connor, who is represented later in the course.

Dickinson's poem includes many comic strategies, beginning with its first two lines, which provide an excellent instance of verbal irony. For while "Soft," "Cherubic," and "Gentlewomen" might at first seem complimentary, the following lines show they are used pejoratively. These initial lines also introduce a central paradox of the poem: though the ladies regard human nature with contempt, they themselves are but "Creatures," that is, human beings, and, as the penultimate line puns, "Brittle," not only abrasive, but also easily broken or perishable, that is, mortal. The poem finally addresses a single lady who is representative of the entire group—not a unique individual, as in tragedy, but a type, as in comedy (Bergson 166). Its early lines introduce the binary opposition between non-human images for the lady, which expose her artificiality, and the human nature she abhors. First she is "a Plush," the fabric of an overstuffed Victorian sofa, then "a Star," beautiful to look at but coldly distant from the human perspective, both images contrasted sharply with the verbs "assault" and "violate," with their overtones of sexuality. Stanza 2 similarly contrasts her "Convictions," which are "Dimity"—a flimsy white fabric—with "Human Nature," which is "freckled"—imperfect, but solidly real.

The lady has "Such Dimity Convictions" and "A Horror so refined / Of freckled Human Nature" that she is ashamed of Deity, who both created human nature—including her "Brittle" self—and assumed it himself in the person of the human-divine Jesus. The first sentence of the final stanza mimics the way the lady might express her disdain for Christianity: "It's such a common—Glory— / A Fisherman's Degree." "Common" means both ordinary and belonging to many, and "Fisherman" alludes both to Peter, a fisherman, and to Christ, who told the apostles, "I will make you fishers of men"—of all human beings, not a privileged few as the lady would prefer (Matt. 4.19). The speaker concludes, paraphrasing Scriptures, that on judgment day "Redemption," a metonym for Christ, will be ashamed of the lady as she in this life was ashamed of "me and of my words," his commandment to love one another in Christian humility (Luke 9.26, 48).

A nineteenth-century preacher, a personification of the church of Dickinson's day, is similarly cut down to size in "He preached upon 'Breadth' till it argued him narrow" (1207). In comic anapests and long lines wittily expressing his long-windedness, the speaker scathingly satirizes the preacher, contrasting his narrowness, lies, and "counterfeit presence" with the "Breadth," "Truth," and "Simplicity" of the church's original tenets. This incongruity, "the essence of comedy" (see, e.g., Rubin in Veron 256–57), culminates in the paradox of the final two lines: if the "innocent Jesus" were to meet this preacher, representative of the nineteenth-century American church, he, the church's eponymous founder, would be covered with "confusion" and, by implication, totally out of place.

As social commentaries on nineteenth-century America, this poem and the train riddle are particularly well suited to the American Humor course. But since as Dickinson herself says, she sees "New Englandly" (285), any of her comic poems is a valuable addition to the course, a study of humor in the United States as expressed by such nineteenth-century humorists as Petroleum V. Nasby and Artemus Ward; by Twain in *Huckleberry Finn*, James in *Daisy Miller*, and Melville in "The Operation"; by Thurber, O'Connor, and Salinger in the twentieth century; and as commented on by such theorists as Constance Rourke and Louis Rubin. American humor in many ways resembles other comic traditions, but, having originated in the frontier of the Southwest, it is a more broadly humorous form. Some Dickinson poems reflect this American tradition; several even echo the American tall tale with its shrewd deadpan speaker who is seemingly unaware of the outrageous elements of the story and therefore is the object of the joke as well as its teller (Bergson 71). He or she often irreverently challenges authority, even that of Scriptures, by putting revered subjects to the test of Yankee common sense. Thus the colloquial, reflective speaker of poem 597 concludes that by not allowing Moses to enter the land of Canaan, God behaved as a bully. In a further comic inversion of authority, she suggests her own solution, which she offers as superior to God's: she would have "banned the Tribes," who were "doubtless" at fault, and ceremoniously "ushered Grand Old Moses," decked out in "Pentateuchal Robes," into the promised land.

In another distinctly American poem, 357, Dickinson finds in Longfellow's *Courtship of Miles Standish* an outrageously humorous but apt analogy for the Christian mystery of the Trinity. Here God the Father, like Miles Standish, is "distant" and "stately," though still a "Lover" and "[bride]Groom." As Standish sent John Alden to court Priscilla, so God "Vicarious[ly]" "Woos" the "Soul" by "His Son," the "Envoy." The sly suggestion in the second stanza is, of course, that the soul, like Priscilla, might well choose the attractive and appealing emissary rather than the distant and stately suitor. To avert this possibility, Dickinson's God "Vouches with hyperbolic archness" that God-Standish and Son-Alden are "Synonyme." Students are delighted with the unconventionality of this poem, but because it *is* so unconventional they assume at first that it is blasphemous. Comparing it with 817, a more solemn poem, corrects this assumption and illustrates that the comic can be a pose assumed to express a serious idea. The speaker of 817 declares herself "Bride" of the Trinity, "Father," "Son," and "Holy Ghost"; she thus, like the speaker of 357, uses the language of sacred parody, marital or sexual love as metaphor for divine love, a recurring trope in biblical and Christian poetry (e.g., the Song of Solomon and John Donne's tenth "Divine Meditation"). Moreover, while humorous, the portrait of the Trinity in 357 is far more conventional than it seems initially. As the Christian Bible tells us, God sent his Son because of his love for his creatures; the Son is the mediator, Logos, or, as Dickinson wittily expresses it, "Envoy" (John 4.9). According to Christian doctrine, the persons of the Trinity are separate and distinct, yet one or "Synonym." The poem, then, is still another illustration of one of the most important theses of both comedy courses: the comic is not a frivolous form but as serious in its own way as more solemn literary modes.

Reading this poem with the humorously irreverent criticism of God's treatment of Moses, the conspiratorial "I'm Nobody," the ecstatic "I taste a liquor," the playful train riddle, the satirical "Gentlewomen" and preacher poems demonstrates Dickinson's wit and humor as well as her astonishing

variety. Conveying a sense of this variety to students is a difficult task even
in a semester-long Dickinson seminar; as Richard B. Sewall observed at a
recent conference commemorating the centennial of her death, she is "in-
exhaustible" (Folger Library, 2–3 May 1986). Still, students should know
that Dickinson is far more than simply a poetically gifted prefiguration of
Emmeline Grangerford, whose sole interest and poetic subject was death
and who, as Huck comments, is therefore probably happier being dead
and in the graveyard. By contrast, the poet who wrote "I taste a liquor
never brewed" and who said to T. W. Higginson, "Living for me is ecstasy—the mere sense of living is joy enough" (*L* 2: 474), transcends the
notion that she wrote only of pain and death. When students find Emily
Dickinson on the syllabus of either the Comedy or American Humor
course, they are taken aback, even incredulous. But by the end of the
term, they perceive her in a new way as a poet who is playful as well as
meditative, witty as well as serious, and comic as well as tragic. Students
respond enthusiastically to Dickinson's comic poems and should be introduced to her comic spirit.

Certain Slants of Light:
Exploring the Art of Dickinson's Fascicle 13

Douglas Novich Leonard

The capstone experience for students in my upper-level undergraduate course on Walt Whitman and Emily Dickinson at Gustavus Adolphus College is a grapple with one of Dickinson's fascicles. Students who study Whitman intensively first, as mine do, find that by the time they are confronted with Dickinson's fascicles, they have already acquired many of the skills they need to analyze those bundles of poems as poetic sequences. As in a first reading of Whitman's "Song of Myself," initially the whole mass of a fascicle swims together in the mind without apparent structure. In time, with teaching and with reading of critical works on the structure of "Song of Myself," students realize how parts interact and how meaning develops in a shifting and incremental fashion. Images, themes, tones, and even metrical and syntactical patterns echo and resonate across the entire lyrical sequence.

As we turn to Dickinson in the second half of the course, I describe the manner in which she tied approximately one-third of her poems into packets of around twenty each. Then I bring students up-to-date on the critical debate about the purpose and nature of the fascicles. Are the groupings motivated primarily by practical considerations, a roughly chronological filing system for finished poems? Or do the arrangements of poems have larger aesthetic purposes? My answers to these questions are far less important to my teaching than what I hope to help students learn about reading poetry. The beauty of teaching Dickinson's fascicles is that no orthodox view can be discovered in the library and then parroted in a paper. Students find themselves high and dry, forced to rely on their own observations and intuitions.

Before I ask them to look at the fascicles, however, I find two preliminary activities of great benefit. First, because they need a general sense of Dickinson's themes and techniques, I take two or three weeks to explore, in Johnson's *Complete Poems*, several of Dickinson's "flood subjects," including nature, art, love, self, death, and immortality. Then I try to lead my students further in their thinking about the principles involved in the formation of a lyrical sequence. Besides "Song of Myself," most students have read Blake's *Songs of Innocence* and *Experience*, Wordsworth's Lucy poems, Tennyson's *In Memoriam* or *Maud*, Eliot's *Waste Land* or *Four Quartets*, Pound's *Cantos*, or Berryman's *Dream Songs*. And of course we have looked not only at "Song of Myself" but at the whole of *Leaves of Grass* as a lyrical sequence. I ask students to outline what it is that makes these works sequences. We compare lists and come up with a number of agreed-upon principles, technical and thematic. I do not impose any of my own ideas at this point.

Then I give students a fascicle of Dickinson's—one I consider interesting but not excessively difficult—as reconstructed by R. W. Franklin. Last year I used fascicle 13. I ask them to read and consider the poems, paying particular attention to the ways, if any, in which the fascicle seems to be a sequence. Following are the principles of lyrical sequence my students of last semester extracted after thinking about the sequences of other poets (especially Whitman) and looking at fascicle 13. (By this time they had read a number of critical views, as well. Two were music students and one was an art student; their valuable contributions were also informed by analogies in their own disciplines.)

1. Introductions and conclusions. Poets, like musicians, frequently use beginnings and ends in significant ways. Often a beginning poem of a sequence introduces or suggests a range of themes or techniques, as in an overture. Whitman's "Inscriptions" to *Leaves of Grass* serves this purpose. A final poem might work as conclusion, postscript, or coda. It rarely opens new areas of tension or conflict.
2. Transitions between adjacent poems. Sometimes adjacent poems share a subject or a voice that connects them in an obvious way. Sometimes the connection is made through a juxtaposition of opposites.
3. Tonal dynamics. Tones change from poem to poem in a sequence, sometimes in harmony, sometimes in contrast.
4. Clusters, repetitions of thematic or technical features, words, images, tone, ideas. While a single thread of theme or image occasionally links every poem in a sequence, poets more often employ clusters, smaller groupings of poems related by theme or technique. The clusters, in turn, interact with other clusters.
5. Patterns of literary, classical, or biblical allusion.
6. Movements from the general to the particular and vice versa.
7. Climactic positioning of what are clearly major poems.
8. Repeated metrical patterns.

Working intensely together for a little more than two weeks, my class developed a shared interpretation of fascicle 13 as a lyrical sequence and found that all the principles of sequence previously arrived at were used by the fascicle. Let me recount our (I played a role too) final interpretation of fascicle 13 to exemplify the value of this approach in teaching Dickinson. Although we arrived at a particular view of fascicle 13, what is more important is the validity of seeing the poems of a fascicle working together in numerous artful ways. First I list the nineteen poems in their fascicle order, with the Johnson numbers following the first lines:

1. I know some lonely Houses off the Road   (289)
2. I can wade Grief   (252)
3. You see I cannot see—your lifetime   (253)
4. "Hope" is the thing with feathers   (254)
5. To die—takes just a little while   (255)
6. If I'm lost—now   (256)
7. Delight is as the flight   (257)
8. She sweeps with many-colored Brooms   (219)
9. Of Bronze—and Blaze   (290)
10. There's a certain Slant of light   (258)
11. Blazing in Gold—and   (228)
12. Good Night! Which put the Candle out?   (259)
13. Read—Sweet—how others—strove   (260)
14. Put up my lute!   (261)
15. There came a Day—at Summer's full   (322)
16. The lonesome for they know not What   (262)
17. How the old Mountains drip with Sunset   (291)
18. Of Tribulation, these are They   (325)
19. If your Nerve, deny you   (292)

On encountering this group of nineteen poems initially, one is struck by the presence of five poems wholly dominated by sunset imagery: 8 (219), 11 (228), 12 (259), 16 (262), and 17 (291). Since sunset is Dickinson's most common symbol of dying and since death is the first phase of her flood subject, immortality, there are a great many sunsets in Dickinson's poetry. Yet no other fascicle contains so many. Hence we immediately suspect a special concern with death and dying in fascicle 13. Barton Levi St. Armand calls Dickinson's sunset "the ultimate dress rehearsal for death" (295). The eighth poem of the fascicle is its first sunset poem:

> She sweeps with many-colored Brooms—
> And leaves the Shreds behind—
> Oh Housewife in the Evening West—
> Come back, and dust the Pond!
>
> You dropped a Purple Ravelling in—
> You dropped an Amber thread—
> And now you've littered all the East
> With Duds of Emerald!

> And still, she plies her spotted Brooms,
> And still the Aprons fly,
> Till Brooms fade softly into stars—
> And then I come away—

Although this poem makes no obvious allusion to death as the other sunset poems do, it provides an initial view of the sunset. The speaker's amused pretense of chastising the clumsy "Housewife in the Evening West" turns, in the last stanza, gently melancholy without explanation or resolution. While it is possible to dismiss the poem as a clever lyric whose tone inexplicably varies at the end, one is rewarded by giving the poet the benefit of the doubt and considering the poem within its fascicle setting.

Without knowledge of "She sweeps with many-colored Brooms" and the larger context of fascicle 13, one might, like Brita Lindberg-Seyersted, assume that in the sixteenth poem, "The lonesome for they know not What," the "Amber line" is "sunrise," in contrast with the "purple Moat" of "sunset." One might thus read the poem as saying that the dead long to come back to their lives and loved ones (82–83). Read in the context of the fascicle's other sunset poems, though, the poem's meaning seems quite different:

> The lonesome for they know not What—
> The Eastern Exiles—be—
> Who strayed beyond the Amber line
> Some madder Holiday—
>
> And ever since—the purple Moat
> They strive to climb—in vain—
> As Birds—that tumble from the clouds
> Do fumble at the strain—
>
> The Blessed Ether—taught them—
> Some Transatlantic Morn—
> When Heaven—was too common—to miss—
> Too sure—to dote upon!

Here is not postmortem longing for a return to mortal existence; rather, the poem is about the living who yearn for the fulfillment of immortality. It refers to people as "Eastern Exiles," living their mortal lives on this side of the "amber line" and "purple moat" of the sunset (death). We have already seen both purple and amber associated with the sunset in "She sweeps with many-colored Brooms." In "The lonesome for they know not What," Dickinson explores the familiar Romantic notion that the living half-remember a blissful state of being before mortal existence. The sub-merged allusion to Adam and Eve suggested in "Eastern Exiles" connects the idea of a lost paradise in the usual Christian sense with the idea of lost love in the speaker's life, so the past paradise in the poem can refer at the same time to God's paradise and the paradise of human love. In the con-text of the fascicle, the allusion to romantic love in "The lonesome for they know not What" is unmistakable; the poem immediately following is the love poem, "There came a Day—at summer's full."

My students quickly noticed these five sunset poems, a good beginning to a full interpretation of the fascicle. In deciding what to make of these poems, they followed several leads beginning with the poems' positions and imagery.

The five sunset poems seem clustered from the middle to the end of the fascicle. The first occurs just before the middle, and the fifth is the second-to-last. If the fascicle were a musical composition, one might say that the theme of the sunset occurs fairly late in the piece but then rises to a climactic dominance of the whole work.

At least two of the poems deal directly with domestic images—the sun-set is a "housewife." A student following up domestic imagery in fascicle 13 will find it in six poems: 1 (289), 5 (255), 8 (219), 11 (228), 12 (259), and 17 (291). At least two of the sunset poems use painting imagery, especially the last one, "How the old Mountains drip with Sunset." The painting or art motif recurs in several other poems in the fascicle: 9 (290), 14 (261), 17 (291), and 18 (325). Of the other patterns of imagery, the most significant is the sunset itself, which led students to consider the imagery of light. At the very center of the fascicle is the famous poem beginning "There's a certain Slant of light," which is tuned exclusively to the light motif. Its position and its power emphasize its importance in the fascicle.

From this point, even before closely interpreting the individual poems, my students could begin to count the poems that include light imagery. Surprisingly, sixteen of the nineteen poems draw distinct images involving light or its perception—various kinds of light at various times of day and at various seasons, producing a range of emotional and aesthetic effects. Clearly, the fascicle is working with slants of light both as image and as metaphor. The poems are slants of light on death and grief. In elegiac fash-ion, the fascicle presents different perspectives on the loss of a loved per-son. Although the focus may be outward toward the dead one, this outward looking is just another way of looking inward. Of course, the En-glish elegy is traditionally concerned with the emotional adjustment of the grieving speaker, but for Dickinson it is especially true that objective events, whether a death or a sunset, mirror and then find expression in the subjective consciousness.

After some analysis, a careful student will discover that the light motif of fascicle 13 can be grouped into five periods, each suggestive of a spiritual or psychological state. First, there is midnight, when the light is either absent or dim, generally signifying despair or spiritual blindness, represented by three poems (289, 253, 290). Second, there is sunrise, symbolic of spiritual illumination and resurrection (289, 261). Third, there is noon, a metaphor of love and spiritual transcendence in this life, represented by the famous love poem "There came a Day at Summer's full." Fourth, there is the afternoon, a winter afternoon, symbolic of a long period of mourning, rendered memorably in "There's a certain Slant of light." And fifth, there is the sunset, which, as it figures in the imagery of five poems, dominates the fascicle as a whole, suggesting that the poet's chief concern here is the transition from life to death.

The tenth poem in fascicle 13 is a powerful meditation on grief, which relies on its unusual imagery for its haunting effects:

> There's a certain Slant of light,
> Winter Afternoons—
> That oppresses, like the Heft
> Of Cathedral Tunes—
>
> Heavenly Hurt, it gives us—
> We can find no scar,
> But internal difference,
> Where the Meanings are—
>
> None may teach it—Any—
> 'This the Seal Despair—
> An imperial affliction
> Sent us of the Air—
>
> When it comes, the Landscape listens—
> Shadows—hold their breath—
> When it goes, 'tis like the Distance
> On the look of Death—

"There's a certain Slant of light" is the lowest point in the elegiac movement of fascicle 13. At least four of the poems that precede it speak directly of grief or loneliness (252, 253, 255, 256), while another implies a present state of grief by looking backward to a lost happiness of love (257). Four subsequent poems in the fascicle refer specifically to either the death of or the separation from the loved one (259, 260, 261, 322). Of all the grief poems in the fascicle, however, none is more profound than the pivotal "There's a certain Slant of light." In this poem (even just in the last stanza) Dickinson's surreal personification, juxtapositions of the concrete and abstract, "pictureless" imagery, and bold and multiple metaphorical suggestion prove her a literary pioneer no less original than Whitman or Hopkins. Yet, for all its innovation, there is something about the final stanza that seems entirely accessible and familiar.

Throughout the poem, the speaker expresses her estrangement from the natural world, a world that, however acutely she observes it, has been drained of meaning. Still, in their very opacity, the images are especially appropriate to her mental state. The seemingly interminable cold light of a winter afternoon is an objective correlative of her grief, as is the oppressive music of the funeral church organ. In the tradition of the elegy, the last two stanzas contemplate the inscrutable providence of the situation, with the poem ending on the significant word "Death." In the course of the fascicle, the speaker will eventually climb out of these depths of pain. Although at first she moves counter to the cycles of nature, gradually she will find herself in increasing harmony with them. This harmony achieved will not cancel the anguish of grief, yet somehow even the grief will be affirmed. Through her meditation and her art, the speaker will come to terms, at least for the time being, with the fact that life goes on and the seasons advance in beauty, even lovelier after the blasting winter. There will be reassurance, too, that immortality holds a farther summer to compensate the long winter life.

Following the tradition of the elegy, the speaker of fascicle 13 comes into harmony with nature primarily by accepting the fact that people die. If nature were consistently ugly and villainous, things would be easier: one could maintain a proud defiance. But nature is also very lovely, the model and source of all art and beauty. Even in grief, perhaps especially in grief, the speaker notices again and again the gaiety of a sunset.

"Of Bronze—and Blaze," the poem that follows "She sweeps with many-colored Brooms," expands more profoundly on the ambiguity of nature by describing the speaker's response to the northern lights. Nature itself interrupts the midnight darkness to create the sublime beauty of the aurora borealis, apparently for no audience but itself. The poet, though she finds herself moved and inspired by the show of light, realizes finally that her art cannot compete with nature.

> Of Bronze—and Blaze—
> The North—Tonight—
> So adequate—it forms—
> So preconcerted with itself—
> So distant—to alarms—

An Unconcern so sovereign
To Universe, or me—
Infects my simple spirit
With Taints of Majesty—
Till I take vaster attitudes—
And strut upon my stem—
Disdaining Men, and Oxygen,
For Arrogance of them—

My Splendors, are Menagerie—
But their Competeless Show
Will entertain the Centuries
When I, am long ago,
An Island in dishonored Grass—
Whom none but Beetles—know.

The speaker recognizes that nature is simply the better poem, God, the superior artist. "The noise in the pool, at Noon," Dickinson wrote to her sometime mentor Thomas Higginson, "excels my Piano" (*L* 2: 404). "Of Bronze—and Blaze—" moves from a high Romantic, Promethean aesthetic almost to a chastened repudiation of art in the face of the cold memento mori of the aurora borealis. For human art, steeped in pride, imperfectly mimics nature's easy sublimity and soon passes away.

In the seventeenth poem, fascicle 13 culminates its running meditation on the relation between nature and the artist. Here nature's two great talents—art and murder—are fused; in the end the human artist is slain by beauty. The speaker finally comes to terms with nature, then, not so much because she derives a sustaining insight through her struggles as because nature itself constitutes its own excuse for being. The Lord responded to Job's arguments out of a whirlwind; nature speaks to the artist of fascicle 13 in a sunset. The quality of the imagery in this poem might be termed painterly in its appropriate culmination of the frequent references to art throughout the fascicle:

How the old Mountains drip with Sunset
How the Hemlocks burn—
How the Dun Brake is draped in Cinder
By the Wizard Sun—

How the old Steeples hand the Scarlet
Till the Ball is full—
Have I the lip of the Flamingo
That I dare to tell?

Then, how the Fire ebbs like Billows—
Touching all the Grass
With a departing—Sapphire—feature—
As a Duchess passed—

How a small Dusk crawls on the Village
Till the Houses blot
And the odd Flambeau, no men carry
Glimmer on the Street—

How it is Night—in Nest and Kennel—
And where was the Wood—
Just a Dome of Abyss is Bowing
Into Solitude—

There are the Visions flitted Guido—
Titian—never told—
Domenichino dropped his pencil—
Paralyzed, with Gold—

"How the old Mountains drip with Sunset" resolves the anxiety of "Of Bronze—and Blaze." Yielding to nature, the speaker finds a higher tranquillity. Nature proves itself superior to her in every way, but in the end the speaker meets a glorious defeat at its hands.

The sunset, here, is orchestrated by the supreme Artist. The speaker, an artist of the language, is again relegated to humble admiration of design above her powers to reproduce or even conceive. The poem's connection to the larger plan of fascicle 13 is that the experience of the artistic speaker is precisely analogous to the experience of the grieving speaker elsewhere in the fascicle. As the artist is humbled and stilled by a new awareness of God's design, so the griever is silenced by an awareness that providence maintains its benign supremacy, in spite of apparent neglect. The griever may find the will of God unfathomable, but she may find as well certain moments of transcendence that justify God's ways and reveal the intricacies of divine love and beauty. Traditionally, the English elegy works toward saying that, despite this particular death, "God's in his heaven; all's right with the world." Dickinson's approach, though oblique, is emphatic in "How the old Mountains drip with Sunset." God's peerless artistry in the sunset proclaims his glorious providence in all areas of life. The ineffable beauty of the sunset stops both the hand of the imitating artist and the mouth of the doubting griever.

By the end of the fascicle, again in a way qualitatively different from her elegizing contemporaries Tennyson and Whitman, the speaker remains in mourning even though she expresses a firm hope of being reunited with her loved one in heaven. The fascicle's penultimate poem, which is placed immediately after "How the old Mountains drip with Sunset," contemplates the final victory of those who have suffered in this life. In the meantime, the speaker will endure the purifying tribulation of her loneliness and her art. In the fascicle's last poem, "If your Nerve, deny you," the speaker adopts the comic mode to exhort herself to live fearlessly, wittily suggesting that nothing is more of a spur to life than the fact of death. The flexibility of her form enables Dickinson to let the opposing states of grief and triumph, tragedy and comedy, coexist. Her lyrical sequence, though coherent and artfully orchestrated, sustains a separation among the poems and the force of autonomy for each poem. Tennyson's *In Memoriam*, much more than Milton's "Lycidas," for example, shares with Dickinson's fascicles a modern tendency toward the coexistence of contradictory emotional states in spite of a larger spiritual resolution.

What I have just described is the experience of one year's class with fascicle 13. Perhaps another class will come to quite different conclusions—though I believe the essentials of this interpretation will hold. After the class as a whole worked through fascicle 13, I asked each student to select a fascicle of his or her choice for analysis as a final project for the course. A few of these analyses were very good, some of them creatively incorporating analogues from music or the visual arts. For the most part, though, I found two weeks insufficient for even good students to do justice to a fascicle. To give my students the fullest possible experience with poetry on their own, I am reluctant to provide more structure or guidance in the future as a way of shortcutting their analyses of the fascicles. Instead, I will probably give students a little more time and allow them to work in pairs.

LITERARY, CULTURAL, AND BIOGRAPHICAL CONTEXTS

The Role of Dickinson's Biography in the Classroom

Frank D. Rashid

Whenever I teach Emily Dickinson's poetry, I find it helpful—although somewhat daunting—to recall my own undergraduate response to it. I was put off by Dickinson's preoccupation with death, her apparent refusal to become involved in the world, her concentration on the childlike, her absorption in "little things." I liked my literature alive, political, important, grand. My classmates and I had grown up in the sixties, and when one student walked out of an American literature survey in protest against Dickinson's "irrelevant" poems (such theatrical displays were not uncommon in those years), I confess that I shared his sentiments, although I also confess that I lacked his courage.

Later my interest in Dickinson increased, but I was more attracted to her life than to her work. The biographical "myths" fascinated me. I wanted to know whether or not she had a lover and who that lover might have been, why she didn't try to publish more, why she wore white, why she refused to leave her house. Only when I was forced—by a latent New Critic—to concentrate on the texts themselves did I finally feel the power of Dickinson's poetry. I suspect, however, that my knowledge of her life— not only the myths but also the facts of her daily existence—added to the intensity of the experience.

Even though my undergraduate students seem far removed from the influence of the sixties, their first responses to Dickinson do not differ much from mine and those of my classmates. Some students consider the poems anachronistic or strange; others become so interested in Dickinson's life that they treat the poems only as her autobiographical minichapters, each one disclosing some new secret. I suggest that some in-class attention to Dickinson's biography can help teachers capture the interest of the first group of students, while redirecting that of the second. Dickinson's life, properly emphasized, can be an entry to her poems.

Most poetry teachers would rather spend class time on poetry than on a dull recitation of the facts of the writer's life. Many teachers have philosophical problems with mixing biography and literary criticism. It *is* possible to teach the work of some poets with little or no reference to their biographies. But Dickinson's life will not go away. No matter how much a teacher might prefer to concentrate on the poems, two of Dickinson's distinctive features inevitably lead students to questions about her life.

The first has to do with Dickinson's characteristic way of using biographical details in her poems. Much is known about her life, but she cleverly disguises its most provocative elements: the "Terror since September," the identity of "Master," the particular sources of her delight and despair. Nevertheless, she wrote constantly about the effects of these elements. Her poems persistently invite the reader inside, and then close the door to the inner rooms. Because she concentrated on effects rather than causes, the curious can only speculate about the sources of the "funeral in the brain," the "cleaving in the mind," the "great pain" that precedes "a formal feeling"; similar perplexity attends references to "moments of escape" and "rapture." Dickinson's letters are not very helpful. They are full of choice bits of news, entertaining details, and witty, epigrammatic remarks, but once they hint at the sources of her thrill and trauma, they can be as cryptic and elliptical as the poems. Enough clues remain to suggest that something remarkable happened to this woman. Many of her readers—students, teachers, and critics—feel that whatever it was lies at the center of her creative impulse. Curiosity about her life therefore rivals interest in her poems and complicates the task of the teacher who wishes to concentrate on them.

The second distinctive feature arises from the first. Several oversimplifications and distortions about Dickinson's life have emerged from attempts to explain the biographical "gaps." For understandable reasons, the unusual in Dickinson's life is exaggerated; the usual, ignored. The "mythic" Dickinson—Amherst's reclusive "white moth"—emerges from its cocoon. Because of such popular caricatures, many students—even those unfamiliar with Dickinson's work—enter the classroom with some preconceptions about her. Besides causing other problems, these notions can give to her biography an emphasis missing from the study of other poets.

Teachers of Dickinson's poetry should take advantage of this emphasis rather than allow themselves to feel obstructed or offended by it. Biographical elements—with cultural, religious, social, and psychological background—can add depth to students' understanding and appreciation of the poems. Teachers can use students' interest in Dickinson's life to help build an interest in the poetry and can show uninterested students that Dickinson was aware of much of what troubles them, that she made conscious use of it in her work.

The popular myths can provide a useful context for this endeavor. The "real" Emily Dickinson may have been less weird than the mythic one, but she was just as interesting. Part of the job of the undergraduate instructor in Dickinson should be to qualify many of the popular preconceptions about the poet and to present something of what we know of the actual experiences that may underlie her poems. Much of the scholarship since Richard B. Sewall published his *Life of Emily Dickinson* in 1974 has continued the important task of making Dickinson, the person, more real and less fabulous. Researchers have shown that she was more involved in the world, more gregarious and magnetic, even in her seclusion, than the myths portray her. Feminist critics have argued persuasively that Dickinson was less the victim of a repressive society than a woman who consciously chose a way of life that allowed her ultimately to triumph over that society. New theories about Dickinson's possible love relationships and her states of mind reveal something of the intensity of her feelings and the courage of her behavior. A discussion about Dickinson, the person, can thus introduce students to a poet whose choices they can understand, whose character they can respect rather than pity, and for whom they can feel a "transport of cordiality," not distance. Knowledge of her life should liberate, not obstruct, her work.

Nothing in my experience of teaching Dickinson illustrates the usefulness of biography better than my repeated attempts to explain her preoccupation with death. Students meeting Dickinson for the first time in introductory literature and poetry classes usually are greeted by two or three of her most popular poems: "I heard a Fly buzz" (465), "Because I could not stop for Death" (712), "I felt a Funeral, in my Brain" (280). Although we may privately wish for more variety from anthologists, these poems are worthy of inclusion in any book of poetry. But the teacher may notice that all this death imagery puts off many students. I have sometimes responded to this tendency by becoming defensive about Dickinson (which only convinces the students that I am just as morbid as she is) or by trying to place her within the poetic tradition of concern with death (which only convinces them that all poets are morbid).

Some understanding of Dickinson's life, however, can make her concern with death much more understandable. Cynthia Griffin Wolff's *Emily Dickinson* provides the most recent reminder of the pervasiveness of death in nineteenth-century New England. The threat of consumption (tuberculosis) was constant; the Norcrosses (Dickinson's mother's family) were particularly vulnerable to the disease, as were many of young Emily's schoolmates. Pregnancy and childbirth were hazardous; common illnesses often turned into killers. Ever watchful for signs of consumption, Emily's parents, as Wolff says, fretted over illnesses like the flu that often beset their daughter (68). Moreover, the role of women—and even of girls—as watchers of the dying made them particularly conscious of death. Emily's memorable visit, at age thirteen, to the deathbed of her friend Sophia Holland was not unusual, and the poet's presence at other death vigils clarifies a cluster of powerful poems of which "I heard a Fly buzz" is the best known. As Wolff observes, "Few in Emily Dickinson's world could put death out of mind . . . " (69). Students, seeing death as Dickinson must have seen it, are far more tolerant of her concern with it, and they can approach "Because I could not stop for Death" with heightened sensitivity to death's intimacy with her.

Biography is well employed, too, to explain other choices of subject matter or ways of handling them. Students find her frequent treatment of nature's "little things" less bothersome when it is tied, not only to the poetic fashions of her day, but also to the relatively strong background in the natural sciences given to the future poet at Amherst Academy. Students are also more sympathetic to her concern with transience and loss when it is traced to her lifelong residence in one locale. In this context, they understand her intense feelings for her childhood friends who moved away from Amherst and even her association of their absence with death. They see that this feeling of acute loss may have bearing on her later concentration on the passing of things, her hunger for something "steadfast," her sensitivity to late summer and autumn, her preoccupation with loneliness. It adds resonance to the experience of many of her poems, revealing both a dimension she has in common with other people and a profundity of feeling that is uniquely hers. It does not, however, *explain* "These are the days when Birds come back" (130), "I shall keep singing" (250), "Further in Summer than the Birds" (1068), or "The last of Summer is Delight" (1353), and it should only create a context for careful analysis of these poems in class, not replace it. Nor should biographical facts be presented in such a way as to inhibit students' freedom of interpretation.

Biography, then, may be used to help explain those general dimensions of her poetry, like her concern with death, that most bewilder students. Biographical details may, of course, also aid in the interpretation of specific poems and lines, although perhaps less than they would with other poets. It may be helpful, when discussing "I started Early—Took my Dog" (520), for the teacher to mention Dickinson's close relationship with her dog, Carlo, but this knowledge is less essential than, say, the fact that Sylvia Plath had a horse named Ariel.

In discussing Dickinson's life, the teacher need not feel obligated to advocate a single explanation for her absorption in her art or her choice of a way of life. The many theories about Dickinson's motivations cannot be ignored; taken together they provide fascinating testimony to her complexity. But presenting a single view as definitive can oversimplify her life and limit unnecessarily students' experience of her poems. Few individuals could explain a choice of life-style or vocation by the single fact of gender role, parental rejection, or love affair. Each theory about Dickinson's life contradicts, qualifies, or supplements other theories. John Cody's persuasive application of psychoanalytic principles to Dickinson's home life and familial relations in *After Great Pain: The Inner Life of Emily Dickinson* is persuasively questioned by feminist critics who dispute the fundamental assumptions of psychoanalytic criticism. William H. Shurr's fascinating attempt to find in the structure of Dickinson's fascicles the clues to the romantic mystery in her life, while often praised, is not universally accepted by other Dickinson scholars.

My intention is not to question the validity of biographical or psychological scholarship but merely to point out the potential hazards of oversimplifying Dickinson for our students. Some years ago, I taught a student whose only knowledge of Dickinson came from hearing of Rebecca Patterson's hypothesis about the poet's possible lesbian love affair (*Riddle*). This explained "everything," the student felt. Even if the potential validity of this theory is granted (and later critics have argued convincingly about a "homoerotic strain" in Dickinson's work), such an introduction, presented without any qualification, unnecessarily channels reading and interpretation in a single direction. Suzanne Juhasz, while strongly advocating a feminist view of Dickinson, comments on the limitations of any single approach to the poet who "is, after all, so large" (*Feminist Critics* 20). Other scholars like Cody and Shurr who advance single-explanation hypotheses carefully note their limitations and the possible validity of alternative approaches.

Students often ask me questions about Dickinson's life that I can best answer by briefly presenting one of the theories about her familial relationships or her possible love affairs. I am careful to explain the evidence and reasoning behind the theory but also careful to qualify it by mentioning any contrasting views. I use the same procedure when I am submitting my own ideas. Moreover, I try to distinguish between the established facts of Dickinson's life and the theories about it. Even if one theory seems particularly persuasive, presenting it as gospel can erect an unnecessary barrier between the students and the poems. I aim not to be noncommittal but to provide students with the most accurate biographical information I have. Far from being confused by the proliferation of biographical theories, most students seem to enjoy them. Introduced properly, the different theories can involve the students in the mysteries surrounding the poet and can encourage them to form and test their own ideas about her.

I think—and this, of course, is a theory—that Dickinson understood the need to touch the reader's life, that she disguised the details of her existence, not to provoke questions about it, but to draw attention to the subject matter of her work. Few poets who turn inward are as successful in hiding the crucial events of their lives. The exact identity of a poet's lover, for example, may remain a mystery, but we can at least be fairly certain of the existence, and usually the gender, of such a person. Dickinson leaves all in doubt, both because of deliberate concealment and because of her tendency to leap immediately from fact to metaphor and from cause to effect. Unlike modern "confessional" poets, Dickinson does not tell all; she eliminates all but "essential oils." Specific causes are masked; effects dominate. She reveals much more of what she thinks and feels than she does of the circumstance to which she is reacting. Through metaphor she extracts the universal out of the particular, isolating it and defining it. Where contemporary poets often emphasize the significance of the literal experience itself, Dickinson hides the literal beneath layers of metaphor.

Omission of the literal and causal can have a liberating effect. Dickinson's universality, her ability to write on several levels at once and to appeal to different readers as she does so, results from this capacity to project literal experience into figurative terms that can be applied to many different situations:

> The nearest Dream recedes—unrealized—
> The Heaven we chase,
> Like the June Bee—before the School Boy,
> Invites the Race—
> Stoops—to an easy Clover—
> Dips—evades—teases—deploys—
> Then—to the Royal Clouds
> Lifts his light Pinnace—

Heedless of the Boy—
Staring—bewildered—at the mocking sky—

Homesick for steadfast Honey—
Ah, the Bee flies not
That brews that rare variety! (319)

Her use of the boy and the bee seems almost a conscious attempt to direct attention to the subject and away from the poet. However, in-class speculation about Dickinson's own possible "nearest dreams" can enhance understanding of the poem and provide a basis from which to approach poems that are less accessible or more obscure. Such an exercise can also involve students who are initially deterred by Dickinson's apparently childlike or archaic subject matter. Perhaps her "heaven" was a visit from a lover or friend, or publication of her work and recognition as a poet. It may have had something to do with mystical union with nature or even God, as suggested by the poem's imagery. Perhaps her heaven was the object of all these dreams or of none of them. The search for the fact behind the metaphor can make students work more intensely on poems like this one. Such an inquiry should encourage them to apply the poem to their own "nearest dreams." Eliciting such a response seems to be at least one motive behind Dickinson's leap from literal experience to its rendering into metaphor. Her combination of abstract and concrete images invites personal involvement in the poem at several levels. If, as recent scholars have suggested, there is a central, personal myth that helps explain Dickinson—as there is with Plath, for example—this myth is not restrictive or self-centered. Her metaphors allow her to translate and extend her experience to others and to do so in ways particularly close to the concerns of many students.

Dickinson can be seen as a spokesperson for such concerns. In many poems like "The nearest Dream," she ponders the same questions that perplex young adults: questions about the effects of experience, the pursuit of pleasure, the desire for something absolute, the relation of the individual to society. Persistently skeptical of the status quo, Dickinson refuses to accept the easy answer, to conform readily to established patterns. Certainly this outlook is true in her life as well as her work. It is one thing to express such skepticism on paper, but quite another to make it a code of behavior in life. Perhaps my classmates and I would have been more open to Dickinson's poems had we recognized in them not only the letter to the world but the protest against it. The student who walked out of our session on Dickinson might have found the poems more "relevant" had he known of the writer's refusal to conform to the mid-nineteenth-century religious enthusiasms that eventually swept up everyone else in her school and family.

Dickinson's biography is a useful tool. It does not replace close reading of the poems or attention to the elements that make them pertinent to students' lives today. The poetry, finally, is what makes Dickinson's life noteworthy. The poems may or may not provide the clues to the mystery that surrounds her life, but they definitely reveal the "marrows" of her mind and the depth of the ideas that absorbed it. Much of the reward in studying Dickinson comes from recognizing how much of life she actually experienced, despite the limitations of her situation. Her mind traveled, even as she stayed at home. She still refuses to be trapped. We may think that the secrets of her life will allow us to grasp her at last. But these are only easy clovers. The mind of Dickinson "dips—evades—teases—deploys—" and makes bewildered "schoolboys" of us all.

A Feminist Critic Responds to Recurring Student Questions about Dickinson

Cheryl Walker

The questions that concern students when they encounter Dickinson's work are not so different from the critics' questions. In fact, many of our best critics acknowledge that teaching has refined their sense of priorities. In the remarks that follow, however, I want to suggest not how teaching has improved my criticism but how feminist criticism has affected my teaching. Like most other feminist critics, I read a great deal that is not feminist, and in the classroom I often employ analytical techniques that made their appearance long before the revolution in women's studies. But my assignment here is to clarify how a specifically feminist critic might answer frequently asked student questions by drawing on recent feminist research. I confine myself to three questions about the poet's life and three about the poetry.

"Why did Emily Dickinson become a recluse?"

Students want to know the answer to this question because they find the life of a recluse unfathomable. As a feminist critic, I use history to resurrect the experience of gender. In an article in 1895, Rebecca Harding Davis wrote that in the "Gray Cabins of New England" were many such women. Davis's exemplar had not let a human being cross the threshold for five years, yet "nobody thought her conduct odd or remarkable" (621). We know that Lavinia, her sister, did not find Emily's seclusion startling. She said that it occurred gradually, became habitual, and was not the result of any one experience.

Instead of concentrating on the losses Dickinson sustained in her retreat, recent feminist criticism endeavors to make the poet's withdrawal seem like a positive choice. Works like Mary Kelley's *Private Woman, Public Stage* and my *Nightingale's Burden* provide a context for the drive toward seclusion by exploring nineteenth-century society's insistence that women remain within the private sphere. Suzanne Juhasz celebrates Dickinson's choice to "live in the mind" in *The Undiscovered Continent*, and Wendy Martin makes an extensive response to the question of withdrawal in *An American Triptych*:

> Paradoxically, by simplifying her world—by remaining single, by excluding random social encounters, by always wearing white—she remained receptive to the intricate patterns and complicated textures of her experience. In order to protect herself from social obligations, Dickinson turned the code that confined nineteenth-century women

to the private sphere into a privilege that permitted her time and space to write.   (127)

"*Why did she wear a white dress?*"

Students will enjoy looking at the picture of Emily's white dress in Jean McClure Mudge's *Emily Dickinson and the Image of Home*. The dress is not at all nunlike; to our eyes it looks bright and even stylish. Working out from the visual signifier helps counteract an impression often left with us by traditional male critics who speak of the poet's "protestant self-excruciation in life's name" (Sewall, *Critical Essays* 85). Unlike an R. P. Blackmur, feminist critics emphasize the ambiguity in the poet's conception of "a woman white." In *The Madwoman in the Attic*, Sandra Gilbert and Susan Gubar provide a whole series of interpretations of her, such as maid, virgin, nun, bird, madwoman, corpse, and ghost.

This ambiguity may at first seem intimidating to students, many of whom would prefer a simple answer they could apply to their reading of the poems. But the poems themselves insist on no less than a circle of significations. It should be possible to explore such a circle by considering the poet's use of metonymy. The "polar privacy" of 1695 ("There is a solitude of space") exists in tension with the queenly white of such "ermine poems" as 117 ("In rags mysterious as these") and 704 ("No matter—now—Sweet") where the color has social and political significance. We should not forget that Elizabeth Barrett Browning's Aurora Leigh, one of Dickinson's favorite heroines, wore white when she chose poetry over love. Other nineteenth-century women poets like Maria Brooks and Christina Rossetti dressed in white. What is the "White Election" Dickinson speaks of in 528? Perhaps it is literary ascendancy. Seen from this vantage point, the white dress comes to represent almost the opposite of what many thought it before: not the nun's renunciatory impulse, but the politician's hunger for inclusion and the earl's arrogance of claim. "I think that what we *know*—we can endure that others doubt, until their faith be riper" (*L* 2: 419), Dickinson once wrote. The white dress can evoke the confident poet as well as the nunlike mask.

"*What was the nature of Emily Dickinson's sexuality?*"

An heir to romantic notions about sexuality herself, Emily Dickinson uses highly charged rhetoric when addressing both males and females, raising questions in students' minds about the nature and range of her sexual interests. Since undergraduates are likely to be concerned about their own sexuality, these questions are often loaded. It is hard for many students to accept homoeroticism in a writer they wish to admire. It is equally hard for lesbian students not to dismiss Dickinson's heterosexual passion as a mask.

Helpful perspectives on nineteenth-century female friendships can be found in Carroll Smith-Rosenberg's classic article "The Female World of Love and Ritual" and Lillian Faderman's *Surpassing the Love of Men*. Vivian Pollak faces squarely the possibility that the poet had the homoerotic feelings she expresses in some poems and letters but says that carnality "was not the major focus of her relationship with Sue" (79) and that Susan Gilbert Dickinson was Emily's most intense female love object.

Since critics continue to imagine a heterosexual love plot for Dickinson's life, feminists provide useful ballast in their insistence on the importance of women to Emily's intellectual and moral growth. Adalaide Morris discovers that same-sex relations in Dickinson's poems point toward an ethic of mutual empowerment whereas male-female relations take form within a patriarchal hierarchy where the woman may achieve at best a subversive role reversal.

Dickinson expresses a good deal of curiosity about sexual matters in both poems and letters. As a feminist, I find her range and flexibility (taking us from the horror of "In Winter in my Room" [1670] to the exultation of "Wild Nights—Wild Nights" [249]) more intriguing than the identity of the beloved whom she addresses in the "Master" letters. Students often share this protean territory of desire and prefer its exploration to the biographical guessing game.

"Why does the poet write so many poems about death, about God?"

Growing up in a secularized and sanitized environment where both God and death are carefully segregated from daily life, few students have suffered over religious doubts or watched with fascination to see the "glee glaze." After reminding a class about the intensity of religious concern during the Second Great Awakening, after discussing death rates, deathbed watches, and the poet's own experiences with loss, I try to make students focus on the politics of death and belief in Dickinson's poems. What kinds of human interactions does she use to model her imagined encounters with the absolute?

Long ago Albert Gelpi suggested that Dickinson's relation to the "papa above" might be derived from the poet's interactions with her father (*Mind of the Poet*). Barbara Clarke Mossberg followed up this lead with her formulation of the "daughter construct" in *When a Writer Is a Daughter*. Psycholinguistic feminists like Mossberg focus on the development of Dickinson's psyche, seeing in the various coy, submissive, and resentful postures she assumes with the deity a variety of psychological survival strategies.

Theorists like Margaret Homans and Joanne Feit Diehl interpret the poetry as a feminine response to a masculine tradition. Homans believes that the discovery of the fictiveness of language freed Dickinson from the burdens of the past and resulted in a liberated theology. In *Women Writers and Poetic Identity* Homans writes, "She uses that linguistic power first to reverse the ordinary direction of power between a feminine self and a masculine other, and then, as in the poems where she undoes antithetical language, uses it to discard the idea of dominance altogether" (201). Discussing the poet's relations to muse, God, and death, Diehl demonstrates how Dickinson appropriates the terms of authority for her own use and refuses to be overwhelmed.

The tactic I'm most familiar with, however, is that of placing Dickinson in a female poetic tradition. After exposing a class to selected passages from *The Nightingale's Burden*, I might ask them to compare a poem about death by Lydia Sigourney with a poem about death by Dickinson. It is useful if they can discover on their own the way Sigourney aims to confirm her reader's expectations, Dickinson to surprise and confound them.

"Why does she use so many odd images, like those from commerce, law, medicine, military science, and politics?"

Like Dickinson's geography of Tunis, Himmaleh, and Timbuctoo, her vocabulary can seem exotic to some students. They need encouragement, however, to use a dictionary and to risk their own interpretations in discussion. Once hooked, they may become demon devotees of *Webster's*.

But vocabulary—like other aspects of Dickinson's style—can be a different stumbling block for the feminist teacher. The ease with which Dickinson enters verbal territories historically off-limits for women may seem to undermine an argument urging gender divergence. Critics have used recent French theory to make a number of arguments about Dickinson's linguistic behavior, but a feminist critic like Cristanne Miller uses it to locate Dickinson's language within a gendered linguistic system. Applying a set of theories about *l'écriture féminine* to the American poet's work and drawing on the writings of Julia Kristeva, Hélène Cixous, and Luce Irigaray, Miller identifies Dickinson's style as explosive, protean, hard to categorize, and always changing. *L'écriture féminine* makes comprehensible Dickinson's sudden shifts from domestic imagery, nature metaphors, and metaphysical conceits to worldly talk of guns, microscopes, and legal documents. Yet Miller also insists on Dickinson's particular female historical existence. That existence created the alembic in which the poet distilled "essence expressive of her life."

Another question to consider is how Dickinson imagined her audience. Karl Keller answers with the masculine pronoun: "Imagining her audience to be male gave Emily Dickinson opportunity to play the deviant. Perhaps she could have played that among women, too, but she would not have had to be as brisk, as nasty, as coy, as teasing, as sure. These postures were created by the men in her mind" ("Notes" 69–70).

Students have fun examining a poem like 1466 ("One of the ones that Midas touched") from the point of view of how it would strike them if written by the "rural man" the poet claims to be. Knowing what we do about Dickinson, we might ask, how does the poem affect us differently? How does persona determine audience and how does an educated audience determine persona?

"Why does the poet speak of herself as male?"

Even the common and uncontroversial "A narrow Fellow in the Grass" (986) brings the students face-to-face with Dickinson's use of the male pronoun. Refusing to be silenced by the oft-repeated comment that all voice in the lyric belongs to a persona, the feminist critic is likely to agree with Susan Gubar that literary cross-dressing is never completely innocent. Even Dickinson's insistence to Higginson that her poems were not personal should be assessed in terms of its strategic potential.

The feminist teacher might ask students what specific activities seem to Dickinson to require a male pronoun: the "plashing in the pools" of 652 or the barefoot roaming of 986? These activities surely have their counterparts in the free play of the imagination Dickinson valued so highly. Wendy Martin explains the poet's habit of personifying herself as male in terms of "an acute conflict between her active and passive and creative and conventional selves" (103). Adrienne Rich, in "Vesuvius at Home," also interprets the poet's choice of the male pronoun in these terms: "Since the most powerful figures in patriarchal culture have been men, it seems natural that Dickinson would assign a masculine gender to that in herself which did not fit in with the conventional ideology of womanliness" (Gilbert and Gubar, Shakespeare's Sisters 105). One poem that might stimulate a very interesting discussion along these lines is 196, "We don't cry— Tim and I," long ago analyzed by Rebecca Patterson in "Emily Dickinson's 'Double' Tim."

Piqued by the stimulating analyses I have mentioned and by books like Alicia Ostriker's Writing Like a Woman and Stealing the Language, students in the contemporary classroom should have the opportunity to consider connections between gender and genre. Emily Dickinson is a fascinating example of a poet who both affirms and denies those connections. Her own words are the best incentive for continuing discussion:

> The Poets light but Lamps—
> Themselves—go out—
> The Wicks they stimulate—
> If vital Light
>
> Inhere as do the Suns—
> Each Age a Lens
> Disseminating their
> Circumference—   (883)

"By Birth a Bachelor": Dickinson and the Idea of Womanhood in the American Nineteenth Century

Charlotte Nekola

In the past ten years, historians have offered us new insights on what it meant to be raised according to concepts of middle-class womanhood in the American nineteenth century. Their writings, paired with Emily Dickinson's correspondence and poetry, can broaden the context of her life and work by enabling students to investigate her relation to the ideology of gender. Her letters clearly both echo and reject its edicts, and her poetry carries on a dialogue, both directly and indirectly, with its ideas. Feminist critics such as Nina Baym, Joanne Feit Diehl, Terrence Diggory, Joanne Dobson, Albert Gelpi, Sandra Gilbert and Susan Gubar, Margaret Homans, Suzanne Juhasz, Wendy Martin, Helen McNeil, Cristanne Miller, Vivian R. Pollak, and Adrienne Rich have given us important discussions on Dickinson and questions of gender; Cynthia Griffin Wolff and Barbara Antonina Mossberg have taken a biographical route to these issues. My approach to teaching Dickinson combines literary, biographical, and historical perspectives in order to place Dickinson within the contradictions of a culture that posed an important dilemma for women writers: how to claim self within an ideology of self-denial. This debate was in particularly high relief in Dickinson's time—literary culture embraced the individual, the self, as index, while womanhood was defined as absence of self.

Students who use a historical, biographical, and literary approach to issues of gender gain another perspective on Dickinson's place in the nineteenth century, one which suggests that her task as a poet necessarily differed from that of such contemporaries as Emerson, Whitman, or Wordsworth. The historians Nancy F. Cott, Carl N. Degler, Ann Douglas, Barbara Leslie Epstein, Mary P. Ryan, Kathryn Kish Sklar, Carroll Smith-Rosenberg, and Barbara Welter, among others, investigate nineteenth-century ideas and institutions important to any female writer of the period: the cult of true womanhood, the depiction of fame as devastation for women, equations of the female imagination with selfishness, the goals of education, and movements toward religious conversion, for example. Dickinson's letters comment on all these phenomena.

The starting point for most undergraduates is neither a blank slate nor a solid familiarity with a representative sampling of Dickinson's poetry. Rather, what comes to mind is the unavoidable cultural mythology surrounding Dickinson: the mad recluse, the spinster-versifier, cloistered in her room writing strange poems. One strong reason for teaching background on the ideology of womanhood in the American nineteenth century is to evaluate these myths in the context of Dickinson's culture. We can see that Dickinson and other women writers of her class, race, and time worked not only under their own private dilemmas of identity but also under the influence of pervasive ideas of gender that hindered rather than fostered the development of ego, voice, and imagination. To preserve herself as a writer, Dickinson was forced to reject much of her culture: the ideal of "true" womanhood, conventional marriage, evangelistic conversion, schooling in submission and piety. Aspects of that culture may have made reclusion attractive: the idea of separate spheres for men and women cast the world as dangerous for women; fame in that world was portrayed as emotional devastation. Once we view the popular mythologies that surrounded her in the context of such contemporary gender ideology, a different Dickinson may emerge for us—not the fey woman-in-white, the doomed "poetess," but a stubborn writer who worked out a private solution, however idiosyncratic, for writing brilliant verse in a particularly unpromising era for women poets. Examining gender issues in a cultural context thus leads us away from the notion of her personal "madness," a notion that has allowed readers to dismiss poems that seem unreadable, or simply difficult, as the products of the mad myth.

Ideas about writers "transcending" their social milieus may lead readers to think that Dickinson could "rise above" contemporary beliefs that conflicted with her development as a poet. Her letters, however, clearly show that although she may have circumnavigated her culture, she certainly did not escape it. Echoes from the contemporary ideology of womanhood surface again and again in her letters and often become the overt content of her poetry. Consequently, pairing Dickinson's letters with primary and secondary source materials that relate to issues of gender provides a compelling experience for students. They will be able to find those echoes themselves. One method of arranging these materials would be topical: you could organize classes around an aspect of the ideology of womanhood in the nineteenth century, such as the cult of true womanhood or the idea of fame. The following suggestions include materials for historical background, primary sources, and Dickinson's letters and poems that speak to these issues.

Some general background on the cult of true womanhood and the concept of separate spheres for women and men would ground students in the basic ideas of gender that applied to women of Dickinson's class and race. Cott's *Bonds of Womanhood*, Welter's *Dimity Convictions*, and Ryan's essay "Femininity and Capitalism in Antebellum America" all discuss the history and implications of the idea that woman's supreme virtues are piety, submissiveness, propriety, and domesticity. Degler's introductory remarks in *At Odds* (28) might stimulate discussion of how ideology applied to the way men and women lived out their everyday lives. Contemporary primary sources on the idea and status of womanhood can be found in Margaret Fuller's essay "Woman in the Nineteenth Century" (Myerson 82–239). Fuller presents an interesting contrast to Dickinson since she did break most of the conventions of her time and became an essayist, journalist, public speaker, and international political activist. Yet, as her essays show, she was keenly aware of the position of women raised more traditionally than herself. Thomas Wentworth Higginson, the *Atlantic Monthly* editor who corresponded with Dickinson but did not publish her, provides another invaluable source, since he also wrote essays on the status of women in that era. His commentary in the collected *Atlantic Essays* is incisive and often surprisingly radical; he says that in his society "all men are born patrician, all women are legally plebeian" (120).

Dickinson's earlier letters show us that she had been taught the ideology of true womanhood and separate spheres. In letters that mention her place at home, at school, and in her community, she bristles against the ideas of propriety, submission, domesticity, and piety for young women (letters 7, 20, 36, 43, 157, 204).[1] Her tone is often humorous or mocking, suggesting real complaint mixed with a certain amount of distance from convention. At one point, she describes herself as "a Bachelor" (*L* 2: 350). The necessity of defining oneself as of the opposite gender provides interesting fuel for classroom discussion; viewing this need in the light of historical materials encourages a cultural, rather than a personal, interpretation of its implications.

Students might then want to consider what alternative visions of womanhood contemporary education may or may not have offered. According to Cott's *Bonds of Womanhood* and Barbara Leslie Epstein's *Politics of Domesticity*, education for women, based on the idea of separate spheres, chiefly trained them to return home to their "true" vocation rather than to take up other vocations in the world outside. As Higginson said, a woman like Margaret Fuller escaped because she had been educated as a boy (*Essays* 110). Both Higginson's essays and Fuller's "Woman in the Nineteenth Century" provide commentary on women's education. Other useful primary sources are letters and records collected in Jay Leyda's *Years and Hours of Emily Dickinson* that relate to Dickinson's school years at Mount Holyoke, including the journal of the Mount Holyoke school recorder. These documents give us glimpses of Dickinson's days at college. With regard to the Mexican-American war, for example, the Mount Holyoke recorder of 3 March 1848 says that "we know little of the political world . . . I sometimes think too little," suggesting a certain amount of insularity and lack of emphasis on "the world" at this academy (Leyda 1: 139). Over and over, the Mount Holyoke recorder recounts the daily investment in religious conversion—who was saved, who was not, what happened at school-wide assemblies aimed at conversion. Dickinson's early and later letters show that her experience at school was strongly colored by training in conventional womanhood and by pressure to convert. In short, in her letters, teachers and study appear to be exhilarating (letters 6, 8, 9, 13, 14, 15, 19). But while pressures to convert (letters 33, 39, 35, 30) and messages to conform to appropriate female roles (letters 6, 22) alternately amused, annoyed, and distressed her, she clearly felt that women should be educated (letters 87, 225), though perhaps in some other way.

When Dickinson discusses religious conversion in her letters and when she discusses marriage in both her letters and poetry, a common concern emerges: the subordination of self to another. When the issue is conversion, she resists, as she says, the moment when she would "give up" (L 1: 67). Similarly, she balks at the idea of a married life "henceforth to him" (L 1: 210). Yet her position is not easy. Dickinson was neither "true" woman nor true "bachelor." Her difficulty at definition is understandable when we look at the goals of both contemporary evangelistic movements and of contemporary marriage. According to Cott and Epstein, women outnumbered men in the rush to religious conversion. It involved a giving up of self to a Higher Authority and was commonly expressed in daily life as selfless good works in the community. Dickinson scorned both the cult of conversion and the cult of good works, but her scorn is occasionally undercut with doubts and self-recriminations (letters 23, 39, 35, 30).

According to Cott, marriage in Dickinson's time also presented a troubling paradox: a "voluntary choice" amounting to "self-abnegation" (78). In the letters and poems Dickinson ponders this dilemma. Her ambivalence over marriage and over the giving up of self in marriage can best be evaluated in her famous "man of noon" letter (L 1: 210) and in a group of poems that consider the status of "wife" (16, 271, 732, 1072). The letter, as many commentators note, and the wife poems voice a common concern: the obscurity, silence, and even burial of conventional wives as they subordinate their lives and desires to those of their mates, rising, as Dickinson says, "to His Requirement" (poem 732). These may be Dickinson's most overtly sociological poems, as it is clearly the social role of wife that she probes.

The cult of female selflessness obviously conflicted with the contemporary literary cult of self-reliance. Male authors such as Emerson and Whitman made the self an index to the world and encouraged "the poet" to evaluate that world with an individual, self-reliant sensibility. How likely it would be for a woman to become "the poet" in response to these recommendations is debatable: she was taught to deny herself and to believe that the "world" was not her "sphere." Perhaps because of ideology's negative portrayal of the outside world, women viewed that world far more as a threat to their well-being than as a challenge to their poetic powers. Cott's, Ryan's, Welter's, and Epstein's historical works all offer background on the cult of domesticity that fostered ideas of home as haven and world as wasteland.

Dickinson's is certainly one of America's most famous retreats from the world. Her personal hermitage, however, can be viewed in the context of her time and its ideas. Dickinson's response to her culture's messages is far more ambivalent than popular mythology would have it: she both rejects and longs for the world outside, hardly the stance of one simply born to reclusion. Sometimes her letters echo contemporary sentiment about the sanctity of home (letters 59, 123, 145); she seems deeply upset by the idea of leaving her home or by the prospect of homelessness (letters 86, 182). There are, however, unmistakable notes of yearning for what she misses when she considers her brother's life in Boston (letters 91, 116), thinks about a friend who has become a schoolteacher (letter 73), or even looks out her window (letter 318). Dickinson's idea of home was probably mixed with issues of gender and identity; to leave it could be both alluring and dangerous. For another example of this conflict, we may look to the diary of Margaret Fuller. We find that despite her success in leaving home for the world outside, she was plagued with doubts about her womanhood (Chevigny 59–60). Certainly Emerson and Whitman did not experience this dilemma over the incompatibility of their gender with writing about and living in the world.

Fame and publication, ways of setting oneself forth in the world, would naturally have been problematic for those raised on the virtues of self-denial and domesticity. Dickinson's famous dismissal of publication as an "Auction" (poem 709) has often been viewed as an example of her reclusive disposition. But this poem also voices the sentiment of contemporary ideology, which presented fame as a false prize for women, one that would take them away from their true throne in the home and leave them wandering, homeless. Other women poets in Dickinson's era, whom she may have read, such as Helen Hunt Jackson, Felicia Hemans, Adelaide Proctor, Mary E. Hewitt, and Lydia Sigourney, warned against the dangers of women's trying to crown themselves with laurels. Bringing their voices into a public arena violated true womanhood; anonymity was the better virtue. Though Dickinson often echoes contemporary female sentiment on the issue, she wrote at least one poem, "Fame is a bee" (1763), that is much less dismissive of fame than the "Auction" poem is, and some letters express her early desire for recognition (letters 238, 265, 199, 58). She also wrote both poems (593, 148, 312) and letters (234, 389, 940, 742) praising famous women writers. Students can consider the relations between the current ideology and Dickinson's shifting positions by looking at the work of female contemporaries side by side with Dickinson's letters and poems on fame or on the fame of other women writers. Was anonymity truly her choice or simply one that she felt she must adopt, as a woman writer?

Looking at Dickinson's relation to nineteenth-century ideas of womanhood gives us one way of locating her, of bridging the gap between myth and poet. Students will find a writer confronting contradictions between her work and her gender that male poets most likely did not have to consider—contradictions that may have made the writing of lyric poetry an ambivalent enterprise at best. Dickinson would have learned that fame and publication were inappropriate, even devastating, for the woman writer; that the American continent, its marketplaces, ports, rivers, and plains were not the "true" text of womanhood or her poetry; that writing about the self, for a woman, was an indication not of integrity but of "self-ishness" or even madness; that writing poetry, with the writerly ego and authority traditionally required, conflicted with definitions of her gender.

This approach also offers a context for those Dickinson poems concerned with issues of gender. Classroom discussion might begin with poems that most overtly protest the conventions of gender: those in which Dickinson examines the social role of "wife" and its consequences in the silencing of female voice (16, 271, 732, 1072). From there, students can consider poems that involve negotiations between female and male speakers (506, 508, 616, 754). Once seen as a rhetorical strategy instead of a personal aberration, Dickinson's use of male masks takes different forms: the speaker of the poem may wrestle with male authority, borrow the language of a male speaker, or seize her own voice. The attractions and perils for a female speaker's adopting a male "other" have been discussed recently by Diehl, Diggory, Dobson, Gelpi, Gilbert and Gubar, Nekola, and Rich, among others.

Students might then begin to examine the substance and style of Dickinson's poetry in the light of gender. As Cristanne Miller suggests, the problem of gender does offer one explanation of Dickinson's veiled, perplexing "slant" style; the result may be poetry that resists interpretation (1). Having looked at some of her knottier poems, students may consider why a poet, ostensibly intent on communicating with language, would write poems of such difficulty and subterfuge. As Nekola and McNeil discuss, another debate on language emerges in poems that value silence over speaking or telling. These poems (13, 544, 167, 543, 1750) and, conversely, those that portray silence as a horror (250, 486, 613, 1123, 1251) may be explored as reflecting the ambivalent position of the woman poet: writing while constantly involved with the dilemma of silence and speaking. Instructors and students can discuss the uneasy position of female speakers who assume bardic authority in the light of Dickinson's poems that claim authority at the outset and undo that same authority by the end of the poem (384, 1189, 283, 1005, 1247). Or instructors may want to start with the poems and work back to historical and biographical materials.

For further research, students interested in gender issues within a historical frame could pursue other primary source materials, if available. They might look at local newspapers or local correspondence from Dickinson's era to see how prescriptive ideas of womanhood were integrated into daily life. Or they might read some of the sentimental literature, either poetry or fiction, that espoused the ideology of womanhood (see Kelley for fiction, E. S. Watts for poetry). A project that requires less archival work, since the texts are now reprinted, would be to examine the letters and diaries of Margaret Fuller for conflicts between the idea of womanhood and the writer's ambition. Students engaged with the politics of literary criticism might review anthologies to see what kind of Dickinson has been presented over the years: the "tame" Dickinson, for example, with poems on bees and flowers, or the "mad" Dickinson of the consciousness and death poems. Students might also evaluate the critical introductions in anthologies or other works: The central question would be the way criticism has dealt with a cultural myth created in response to the "heresy" of her life and work as a woman writer (solitary, unmarried, therefore mad woman writes mad poetry: solitary, unmarried, therefore sexually crippled woman writes a poetry of repression; and so on). Dickinson was not as "tame" as the ideal of true womanhood, nor was she simply mad if she experienced the inevitable ambivalence her culture offered a woman poet of genius. Advanced students might analyze Dickinson's treatment of more abstract issues, such as time or death, and see if they can be discussed as issues of gender; for example, her concern over the limits of time might be viewed as urgency for an anonymous female voice to be heard. Whatever route students choose, those working with Dickinson and a combination of historical, literary, and biographical materials relating to gender issues can develop new perspectives on the relativity of cultural and literary values.

NOTE

[1]In this essay, letters mentioned or listed, but not quoted, are identified by the numbers assigned them in Johnson and Ward's *Letters of Emily Dickinson.*

"Looking at Death, is Dying": Understanding Dickinson's Morbidity

Barton Levi St. Armand

> Looking at Death, is Dying—
> Just let go the Breath—
> And not the pillow at your Cheek
> So Slumbereth—   (281)

"But she's so *morbid!*" is an often-heard lament from fresh readers of Emily Dickinson's poetry, whether they be sixteen or sixty. Those over sixty, or those who have been exposed to a conservative ethnic background where traditional funeral and mourning customs still prevail and who are familiar with old women dressing completely in black as an outward and visible sign of prolonged inner and immedicable grief, will have less of a problem with Dickinson's stress on the panoply of death and dying. But with modern exequies becoming more and more streamlined, antiseptic, and privatized, as the twentieth century itself begins to put out its last candles, the skull beneath the skin that grins at us in such poems as "Because I could not stop for Death" (712) or "I heard a Fly buzz—when I died" (465) is beginning to seem as remote and as alien as the enigmatic "sign you must not touch" in John Donne's baroque poetry of melancholy and malaise ("The Funeral").

This situation should not surprise us, since Donne and Dickinson are cousins-german in their attitudes toward death, both preaching, as Donne writes in his "Song" ("Sweetest love, I do not go"), that because all must die and all lovers eventually part, it is best to accustom oneself to such inevitabilities and so "by feigned deaths to die." Dickinson did not go as far as Donne, who had himself painted in his winding sheet, "so tyed with knots at his head and feet, and his hands so placed, as dead bodies are usually fitted to be shrowded and put into the grave" (*Death's Duell* 40). Yet her famous white dress, which Dickinson wore exclusively in one form or another later in her life, was a plain-style New England version of Donne's shroud, both wedding gown and winding-sheet in one, a living icon symbolizing that whatever the wearer's ultimate spiritual destiny— celestial marriage or angelic celibacy—she had forcibly put away the world.

Both Dickinson poems cited above are full-stage dress rehearsals for death; moreover, "Because I could not stop for Death" is tinged by an eroticism that had already erupted more boldly and more blatantly in Donne. The Victorian Dickinson is never as explicit as the lusty poet of "To His Mistress Going to Bed," nor does she ring scatological changes on the seventeenth-century pun that made the verb *to die* a slang term for sexual orgasm (significantly, *to spend* did the same duty for her own capitalistic century). But she did fabricate a private love-religion that beatified herself and the object of her passion in much the same manner as Donne's "Canonization." Dickinson's autobiographical "Novel," which she claims is true but so condensed that it remains unread and disbelieved (669), is therefore like Donne's "legend," which is romance, hagiography, and short caption all in one, an intensely abbreviated form that though "unfit for tombs and hearse" is still suitable for poetic devotionals:

> And if no piece of chronicle we prove,
> We'll build in sonnets pretty rooms;
> As well a well-wrought urn becomes
> The greatest ashes, as half-acre tombs;
> And by these hymns, all shall approve
> Us canonized for love. . . .

Just as the American Puritan poet Edward Taylor chose homely spinning wheels and freshly baked loaves of bread as his vehicles of metaphor rather than the elegant compasses of Donne's "Valediction: Forbidding Mourning," so did the no-nonsense Dickinson prefer Isaac Watts's staunch singsong hymn meters over the mannered intricacies of the Petrarchan or Shakespearean sonnet. Yet to make Dickinson's death poetry and its Donne-like emphasis on spiritual autopsies, shuddering night thoughts, and anticipatory funeral rites ("I felt a Funeral, in my Brain" [280]) as understandable as possible to a sometimes fascinated, sometimes horrified, undergraduate audience, I have found it necessary to become myself the kind of collector of the curious, the quizzical, and the eccentric that Donne was. His age excelled in such antiquarian pursuits—one thinks automatically of figures like Sir Thomas Browne, Robert Burton, and John Aubrey—though in dealing with Dickinson's supposed morbidity, I have found that it is imperative for the teacher to go beyond the virtuosity of a "show and tell" approach. One must also set her private hymns against our own contemporary public chronicles of grief and bereavement if Dickinson's poetry of death, love, and love in death is to come fully alive and not simply be exhibited, like Donne's "bracelet of bright hair about the bone," as a grisly memento wrenched from a broken and violated grave ("The Relic").

Donne and Dickinson can be compared not only because they are part of a long and strong tradition of English metaphysical poetry (a quotation from a poem by George Herbert, copied out in Dickinson's hand, was once published as one of her own productions) but because the intimacy and urgency of their art were the result of a similar displacement of, rather than a mere dissociation of, sensibility. Donne was a Catholic whose family's religious heritage automatically cut him off from office holding and public power; in reaction he turned to a mordant poetry of passion, building a closed world of ritualistic, liturgical, rhetorical excess. This excess was one of mood as well as of language, a love-hate relationship with his place, with his God, and with his own escapist eroticism. The result was manic-depressive swings of emotion, combining ecstatic devotion with nihilistic despair, rough-hewn monosyllabic expletive with Latinate polysyllabic cadence. Donne's premature superannuation is symbolized by the "palsy," "gout," and "five gray hairs" that worry stanza 1 of "The Canonization," but this angry young man was eventually replaced by, or rather evolved into, the sober Anglican apologist preferred to the living of the deanship of Saint Paul's by that most learned of monarchs, James I.

Emily Dickinson was, as befits her American-Puritan heritage, a more independent naysayer, but she was no less an outsider in her culture than was the scorned and scornful Donne. Though never imprisoned in the Tower of London for an unlawful liaison, she was equally "Love's martyr," in effect becoming her own jailor, locking herself away in her father's house in Amherst while also locking out the busy, public Whiggish world of Scottish common-sense-school philosophy and unflagging Christian endeavor that Squire Dickinson symbolized. Raised on the cold milk of provincial Congregationalism, heated periodically to scalding temperatures by repeated revivals of religion both at home and at Mount Holyoke Female Seminary, Dickinson thirsted after the velvety clarets and rich port wines of romantic love. Whether she found that love in person or in persona still remains a question, but the result of her displacement as an unorthodox member of a believing community and as a genteel single woman shut out from the spheres of public, literary, and maternal power led to the same kind of confessional, self-dramatizing, consciously liminal art produced by Donne. As a nineteenth-century New Englander and the daughter of one of the Connecticut Valley's powerful "River Gods," Dickinson could at least live her life and choose her fate with more confidence and comfort than her seventeenth-century predecessor; after visiting her in 1870, the much maligned but extremely well read Thomas Wentworth Higginson wrote to his wife that "if you had read Mrs. Stoddard's novels you could understand a house where each member runs his or her own selves. Yet I only saw her" (*L* 2: 473).

The novels of Elizabeth Barstow Stoddard (1823–1902), like her *Temple House* of 1867, are one of the keys to the composite Holinshed's *Chronicles* that the teacher can use to recontextualize the unique character of Dickinson's strict New England nurture as well as to encourage students to

appreciate the rebellious, all-consuming interiority conditioned by that upbringing. As Stoddard observes, "The events of thought and feeling occupy
little time and space; they may be so invisible in the ordinary drama of the
day that the decree which decides the future is made, and the bystanders
only observe that a man is twisting his mustache, or a woman adjusting her
ribbons" (*Temple House* 186). The Dickinson who ties her hat, creases her
shawl, and puts "new Blossoms in the Glass" while realizing that "Existence—some way back— / Stopped" (443); who learns to hear her lover's
name spoken without experiencing "That Stop-sensation—on my Soul— /
And Thunder—in the Room" (293); and who apprehends that it is under
the sign of such "little" things as the shortness of a sigh that "by Trades—
the size of *these* / We men and women die!" (189) well knew from personal
experience the authenticity of Stoddard's novels, though the aristocratic
and condescending Mary Channing Higginson did not.

It was through just such personal experience that Dickinson encountered the reality of death and dying in Victorian America, as expressed in
lines as uncompromising as "She died—*this* was the way she died" (150).
While this reality had its innerness, it also had its finite emblems, hiero-
glyphs, and tokens, all part of a new, elaborate romantic mourning iconography, what Dickinson herself referred to as "the éclat of Death" in her
archly ironic "That short—potential stir" (1307). The best way that I have
found to establish contact with this iconography and the psychic strategies
of consolation that lay behind it is through direct examination of its material remnants, some of which are still embedded in our late twentieth-
century culture. It has been well over twenty years since Jessica Mitford
derided "the American way of death," but the practices she condemned in
1963 were themselves the last gasp of a romantic revival in a modernist
age. Expensive, padded, earthquakeproof caskets, as heavily carved as one
of the American cabinetmaker John Henry Belter's laminated rosewood
armchairs, no matter how out of place they might seem in a world increasingly dominated by Scandinavian design, constituted a technological folk
survival. What was once a popular and normative cultural mode of burial
had remained virtually unchanged since Victorian times. American funeral
practices continue to be largely a code without a codification, a sign with
signification, since the attitude behind them—sentimentality—has with-
ered away without being replaced by any ritual expressive of the invisibil-
ity and oceanic nothingness of today's "death in a minor key" (Ariès,
Images 112).

Emily Dickinson participated fully in the romanticizing of death, though
her tough neo-Puritan upbringing, which enjoined her to examine the dying self as rigorously as the living Word, also taught her to interrogate
steadily and constantly sentimentality's wishful presuppositions ("I mea-

sure every Grief I meet" [561]). As often as she found in this cultural mode intimations of immortality and what Walt Whitman called "whispers of heavenly death" in a late poem by the same name, Dickinson also discovered small-minded hypocrisy ("Safe in their Alabaster Chambers" [216]), blasphemous philosophical lacunae ("I heard a Fly buzz—when I died"), and cosmic chilliness ("Because I could not stop for Death"). I explore her techniques of domestication, exaggeration, and inversion in my chapter on Dickinson and Victorian death rituals in *The Soul's Society: Emily Dickinson and Her Culture*, but they can only be italicized by concrete object lessons drawn from the paraphernalia of American mourning practices. I can still recall a student telling me of her initial repulsion after I had brought in a part of my own small collection of jewelry made from human hair, photographs of the dead, and silver coffin plates—all mementos of mourning designed to be hung on the self or on the wall—and then how she realized that these were not repugnant relics but rather legitimate tokens of a whole lost consciousness and sensibility. Moreover, this sensibility was in rebellion against a dry, mechanistic theology that did not look toward consolation of the living but that used the fact of death as an excuse for a public dissection of the deceased's immortal soul and eternal destiny. Such was the hair-splitting rigor of the "New England Theology" that conditioned the ups and downs of Dickinson's youthful manic-depressiveness, embedded not only in the seesaw emotionalism of her early poetry ("If I'm lost—now" [256]) but in the polemical New England novels of her close contemporary Harriet Beecher Stowe, like *The Minister's Wooing* of 1859 and *Oldtown Folks* of 1869. The death of an appealing but unconverted loved one is central to the sentimental vision mythologized by Stowe and by a host of mortuary poets, who preached sanctification through suffering and the panacea of a progressive, cottage-style heaven as welcome antidotes to the "slow poison" of Calvinist doctrine (*Minister's Wooing* 339).

The result was both the spread of a popular literature of consolation, epitomized by the elegies of Lydia Sigourney, Alice and Phoebe Cary, and the Davidson sisters, and a remarkable material constellation of symbols and icons into a full-blown mythology of mourning, that "Dark Parade— / Of Tassels—and of Coaches" Dickinson describes in her crystallized local-color masterpiece, "There's been a Death, in the Opposite House" (389), with its offhand, deliberately gossipy tone. I suggest three approaches, then, that the teacher can take in stimulating students to think about Dickinson's fascination with death not simply as a freakish idiosyncrasy but as a cultural revelation that has resonances and relevancies to our contemporary interest in the tabooing of death, the dynamics of grief, and the treatment of the dying. The first approach, on which I have already touched, is an investigation of the material culture of death. Students are encouraged to write personal narratives and reminiscences of family death customs (photographing the dead is still practiced among some ethnic groups in American society, for example). Individual student involvement can be further deepened by research about and exposure to mourning artifacts often housed in local historical societies and museums. These items include needlework mourning pictures and samplers, mourning jewelry, coffin plates, plaques, shadow boxes featuring designs made of woven human hair, black-bordered mourning stationery ("The letter edged in black"), mourning costumes, funeral elegies, poems, cards, and broadsides—even fancy hearses with carved panels and etched-glass windows to emphasize the baronial character of the antique funeral procession itself ("Because I could not stop for Death" [712]).

The teacher who lives in New England, the attic of America, is fortunate in having easy access to such objects and can often use a wealth of museum resources to trace funeral customs back to the actual rings, gloves, and poems that were regularly distributed at funerals in the seventeenth, eighteenth, and early nineteenth centuries. Happily, fine illustrated books and articles about mourning art exist to supplement or even replace a hands-on experience with the material evidences of the growing romantic cult of death (Morley; Pike and Armstrong; Schorsch). But while every place in America might not have preserved the ephemeral keepsakes of this sentimental *danse macabre*, every place in America has its cemeteries, and these places of interment can be readily used to gauge the changes in tomb sculpture (Barker and Gay; Gillon; Kull; Marion). Styles range from the Puritan boneyard with its uniform ranks of slate tablets incised with grinning winged skulls (social control and natural depravity) to the neoclassic marble balance of urn and willow (pious commemoration and sensibility) to the wild and effusive eclecticism of Victorian times (monumentality and sentimentality), end-stopping with the modified art-deco cubism of the early twentieth century ("less is more"). What are we to make of the even more abstract stelae of our own day, where an opulent three-dimensional symbolism has given way to a new plain-style emblematic mode suited to the flat utilitarianism of the easily mowed suburban lawn (Hijiya)?

All these changes in taste record countervalent changes in attitude, culture, and consciousness, most of them secularizing and many of them quite subtle; as Ariès notes, "For unbelievers and believers alike, the cross has become a part of the common language of our communications code, in which it signifies death. A cross displayed after a name states, quite independent from any (at least conscious) idea of salvation, that the subject has recently died" (*Images* 227). The Victorian idea of the cemetery as a dormitory for the dead ("What Inn is this" [115]), as well as a resort for the

living ("After a hundred years" [1147]) and a place for recreation, meditation, and moral, patriotic, and aesthetic uplift, was a romantic innovation
that united the love of nature with the self-indulgent pleasures of melancholy celebrated in Thomas Gray's "Elegy in a Country Churchyard"
(1751). Garden cemeteries in England and America were soon filled with
marbles as polished as Gray's verses, eventually becoming a study in Victorian clutter as their early picturesque ambiance gave way to the coloniz-
ing demands of the imperial self, though the original purposes of the
movement have been curiously resurrected in California's various Forest
Lawn memorial parks (*Pictorial Forest Lawn*). Dickinson's poems set in
country burying grounds—"Safe in their Alabaster Chambers" (216),
"Where bells no more affright the morn" (112), "Who occupies this
House?" (892), "She laid her docile Crescent down" (1396)—can be fruit-
fully transplanted to this context, while her many elegies and tributes (see
1701, 1702, and 1703 for some undated examples) can be compared and
contrasted with the traditions of the epitaph, seen in its folk, popular, and
elite forms (Enright; Meltzer). Although this tradition has shrunk to an
abbreviated minimalism on modern tomb sculpture, contrasting both to
the poignant, wry, comic or orphic tenseness of the *Greek Anthology* and
to the long-winded eulogia to be found on eighteenth- and nineteenth-
century stones, it still survives in the commemorative verse that can be
seen on the obituary page of almost every local newspaper, especially
around holidays like Memorial Day, Christmas, Mother's Day, and Father's
Day. Funeral directors sometimes distribute books and pamphlets contain-
ing consolatory passages from prose and poetry as part of their services,
and these can be used to trace the modern history of bereavement; the
eclecticism of the selections reflects Americans' penchant for a multichan-
nel, melting-pot approach to the vexing problem of death.

For death today is a problem rather than the visitation, act of God, or
sublime mystery that it once was. Like the breakdown of the family car, it
disrupts our lives, overloads our schedules, and embarrasses us into awkward disclosures about complicated affairs and interpersonal relations better left unuttered and unrevealed. This fact leads naturally to a second
sounding of Dickinson's mortuary preoccupations, which involves tracing
the history of dying itself (Ariès, *Western Attitudes*; Farrell; Stannard,
Death in America) and the concern of such contemporary "thanatologists"
as Elisabeth Kübler-Ross and Ernest Becker with the troubling psychological repercussions stemming from the wholesale twentieth-century "denial
of death" (Dumont and Foss). The only difficulty with this methodology,
fascinating and involving as it may be, is that it tends to develop into a
separate sociological study that can reduce Dickinson's poetry into only
another artifact, document, object, or relic of culture. If kept within

bounds, however, it can be a valuable adjunct in opening up discussion about the searching questions posed in her art, questions of accommodation, compassion, and dignity that mirror the recent tendency to counter the technological alienation of death by both highlighting and ameliorating the visibility of the process (Carr; Russell; S. Stoddard). The success of this approach depends largely on the teacher's ability to digest much of the weighty literature on the subject, some of it highly specialized, and to present it with economy, tact, and a keen eye for selections that students themselves can report on and discuss without sinking under the sheer abundance of professional jargon or historical fact. (Ariès's *Hour of Our Death*, the *summa theologica* of the history of death and dying, is 650 pages long!)

A third and final means of setting Dickinson's poetry in the context of her time and our time is a comparative one; Poe immediately comes to mind as an American contemporary whose obsession with death and its Gothic-revival trappings parallels her own Calvinistically grounded interest in the subject, although the funerary preoccupations of Charles Dickens in such works as *Oliver Twist, Martin Chuzzlewit*, and *Dombey and Son* offer an equally nice, transatlantic perspective. In his poetry, Poe dramatizes the public mythology of the beautiful death ("Annabel Lee," "The Sleeper," "To One in Paradise") as well as exploiting in his more famous tales the horrors of corruption, supernatural trauma, and premature burial (cf. Dickinson's "I died for Beauty" [449], "I felt a Funeral, in my Brain," and "I heard a Fly buzz—when I died"). The taste for Gothic romance and for a gothicizing of experience is a remarkable constant in Western culture, and if, as Sandra Gilbert and Susan Gubar claim, the Gothic is primarily a woman's genre (*Madwoman* 594), lines of relation can be drawn from this central web to many other writers and concerns. As I myself have argued, Dickinson often thought of herself as a heroine of Gothic romance, incarcerated in dungeons ("They put Us far apart" [414]), menaced by monsters ("'Twas like a Maelstrom, with a notch," [414]), and pursued through tortuous mental labyrinths ("One need not be a Chamber—to be Haunted" [670]). Her sisters in terror range from the Emily of Ann Radcliffe's *Mysteries of Udolpho* (1794) to the Clara of Charles Brockden Brown's *Wieland* (1798), though the specter in her path remained metaphysical rather than ectoplasmic. Sometimes it was God, sometimes it was death (see "Bereaved of all, I went abroad" [784], for a singularly Poesque obsession with the image of the grave similar to that of Poe's "Oblong Box"), but she managed to stare both down ("'Tis so appalling—it exhilarates" [281]) through the steadiness and steadfastness of her art. I have had gratifying success in making parallels between Dickinson's Gothicism and that of the Brontës, drawing out a generic thread that stretches to the Harlequin romances of today's airports and drugstores. Since there is a growing and probing secondary literature on this phenomenon, much of it stimulated by the rise of feminist and popular culture criticism, I have not felt alone or eccentric in exploring these filiations between the ancients and the moderns. Certainly one of the best sessions in my undergraduate seminar on Dickinson was a report on Sylvia Plath's poetry, with special emphasis on the biographical parallels with and contrasts to Emily Dickinson's life. By coming freshly to Sylvia Plath as a representative of the 1950s and to that period's conformist stereotypes, these students could use Plath's slow suffocation within the bell jar of convention to understand and appreciate Dickinson's more distant but just as intense Victorian struggle for survival and sanity.

Dickinson's Romantic strategies of subversion gain added power if we consider that in regard to death and bereavement, our contemporary funerary practices have returned almost full circle to the toned-down restraint of a determinedly antiliturgical Puritanism. Funeral rites are more and more anonymous, watching by the dead is increasingly omitted (as are flowers), and mourners are advised not to dwell on the past but to "return to normal" as soon as possible. Like the early Puritans, we simply deposit the body in the grave with no attendant service, or we reduce it to sanitary cinders, since unlike them we expect no day of reckoning or resurrection (Stannard, *Puritan Way.*) Harriet Beecher Stowe charged that the Puritans "swept away from the solemn crises of life every symbolic expression" (*Oldtown Folks* 83); her own Romantic generation reversed this trend by replacing a religion of severity with a religion of sentiment.

It appears that we are once again at a crossroads in sensibility, for the enigmatic, almost mute role of mourning and commemoration in our culture perfectly reflects the postmodern emphasis on fissures, gaps, margins, traces, and erasures of all kinds. The Emily Dickinson who boldy used metonymy, ambiguity, fade-outs, and dashes to confront the excesses of her times may remain, for students and teachers alike, the best practical guide to the attenuated brevities of our own.

Dickinson among the Realists

Elissa Greenwald

Dickinson's place in American literature has been influenced by the context in which she is taught. Since she is frequently treated along with writers of the early nineteenth century, the American Romantics, critics often emphasize the role in her poetry of the autonomous Emersonian self that conquers or annihilates the outer world.[1] I have taught Dickinson in both parts of the nineteenth-century survey, American Romanticism and American Realism, but primarily in the latter half, since it covers the years from 1855–1900. Seeing her in the context not only of Emerson but of her successors among prose writers illuminates the interplay of Romanticism and realism in her works. I have found it especially interesting to treat her in the context of realism since this background opens up new ways of seeing her poetry, as well as realism as a whole.

In teaching this course, I begin by emphasizing Dickinson's connections to American Romanticism, since many of the students have taken the first half of the nineteenth-century survey. I mention that Dickinson is often seen as an Emersonian poet of the consciousness that renounces or conquers external reality; I then suggest that we can modify this view by stressing her links to the writers of the era during and after the Civil War. To do so first requires redefining the term *realism*. Many students assume that realism entails accurate copying of things as they are and that works of the period labeled American Realism will present documentary pictures of the time. Throughout the course, I emphasize that realism needs to be more broadly defined, or even abandoned as a term for describing this era.

Shira Wolosky has demonstrated the links between Dickinson's poetry and her historical context by reminding us that Dickinson is a poet of the Civil War. I emphasize the indirectness of Dickinson's representation of reality as well as her connections to historical events. I focus on the interaction between consciousness and the external world in her poems, especially in poems about or including landscapes. By making clear how physical details are transformed into figurative entities in her poetry, I show how Dickinson begins the transformation of reality from received object to personal impression, a principal characteristic of American fiction after the Civil War. Thus Dickinson becomes a "representative woman" for the era, and the students tend to draw analogies between her works and those of the other writers we study throughout the term.

I spend two and a half weeks on Dickinson. Since the class usually has about forty students, I divide the time equally between lecture and discussion. I begin with poems that celebrate sensual experience, especially the pleasures of poetry, such as "I taste a liquor never brewed" (214) and "I dwell in Possibility" (657). I then alternate poems that treat religious and metaphysical issues, such as "I know that He exists" (338), with apparently simple poems of nature, such as "A narrow Fellow in the Grass" (986), to show how the poems of nature are complicated by metaphysical doubt. I proceed to poems in which Dickinson fuses the physical and the metaphysical, consciousness and the world, especially those concerned with death and immortality: "There came a Day at Summer's full" (322), "I heard a Fly buzz—when I died" (465), and "Because I could not stop for Death" (712). I conclude with poems in which abstractions become concrete, focusing on poems about poetry: "This Consciousness that is aware" (822) and "A Word made Flesh" (1651).

Throughout our weeks of study, I draw students' attention to strategies of mimesis and indirection in Dickinson's verse, particularly in the use of landscape. This subject enables students to grasp Dickinson's use of figuration and the nature of progression in her poetry. After I outline an interpretive model for a few poems, I open the class to discussion on others. By that point students feel capable of interpreting Dickinson on their own. They soon draw analogies between various poems and notice structural aspects such as the transition to a new level of inquiry often introduced in the final stanza. Students begin to point out reversals of subject and object in her use of landscape, which makes them attentive to similar issues of point of view in the novels we read later in the course.

The clearest examples of poems that illustrate the relation of consciousness to the physical world are those about landscapes, especially those in which religious and natural images interact. A crucial work in this respect is "There's a certain Slant of light" (258), which I teach midway through the study of Dickinson. While some of the poems about nature, such as "A Visitor in Marl" (391), emphasize the role of an external force, a power in nature, others emphasize the interaction between a perceiving self and the external world. In "There's a certain Slant of light," the physical attributes of the external world are translated into modes of human perception. In teaching the poem, I begin by asking why "Slant" is capitalized. Students note immediately the possible allusion to religious concerns (reinforced by more explicit religious language later in the poem, such as "Heavenly Hurt") and the way in which capitalization turns the elements mentioned into allegories. The "Slant" that begins as physical fact becomes the source of an inner feeling—the state of mind that feels "oppress[ed]" by "Winter Afternoons." The interchange of outer phenomenon and inward sensation is reflected by the description of the "Heft / Of Cathedral Tunes," a form of synesthesia in which sound is translated into weight and almost made visible.

The slant of light becomes a symbol, not so much of some wound within the self (an "internal difference") as of the gap between the self and the outer world, the gap perhaps constituted by death, of which the light then becomes an objective correlative. The "imperial affliction," the knowledge of death, which comes to us seemingly from nowhere ("Sent us of the Air"), is then projected onto the landscape, which takes on the capacities of human perception toward the end of the poem: "When it comes, the Landscape listens— / Shadows—hold their breath. . . . " Finally, as the image of the sunset implies, human perception and landscape are inter-fused, transformed by the fact of death—the horizon that is both their meeting place and dividing line: "When it goes, 'tis like the Distance / On the look of Death." Death itself becomes ambiguously the subject or ob-ject of the "look" in the last line, as if death could be either a fact in the physical world or an entity within human consciousness.[2]

This work illuminates not only the way consciousness and the physical world interact in Dickinson's poems but the way the status of the physical world changes from stanza to stanza, often through the use of metaphor and personification. Her translation of scenes into figures, and the result-ant meanings for the relation of consciousness to reality (and for the reli-gious question of the possibility of a life beyond the physical one), can then be seen in many of her poems. In poems that explicitly treat landscape in relation to the fact of death, the interpenetration of subject and object suggests the immortality of consciousness as it is reflected in the physical world. The transformation of the details of a scene, such as the setting sun in "Because I could not stop for Death" (712), into a metaphor for the progression of human life reinterprets the physical sunset as a representa-tion of the border between life and death that is transgressed in the very passage of the day. In "Just lost, when I was saved!" (160), the metaphor of the tide as symbol for the border of death gives way to a vision of death as what transcends both borders and metaphors.

Landscape in relation to consciousness is given a different configuration in "Good Night! Which put the Candle out?" (259), in which the candle as a symbol of the soul is translated into physical features such as a light-house. In this poem, the physical world of nature and humanity is trans-lated into symbolic form, reflecting the capacity of the soul to transcend the physical realm. Yet, unlike Emerson, Dickinson does not see nature principally as a symbol of facts of the human soul. Rather, she describes an interchange between human beings and nature, consciousness and the physical world. The emphasis on the shifting status of landscapes and of other physical details in her poems makes students aware that Dickinson uses figurative language to explore metaphysical issues. In other ways as well, Dickinson transforms the elements of poetry to make the mode of representation reflect her themes. For example, one can see her consider-ation of the possibility that consciousness may outlast the physical world in her frequent use of a speaker who speaks from beyond death. Here, too,

Dickinson does not use the power of consciousness to destroy an external reality whose presence she sees, for better or worse, as ineradicable. In "I heard a Fly buzz—when I died," the fly seems to represent the "last infirmity of noble mind," the physical world that cannot be eliminated, that may be what prevents transcendence (or perhaps what enables it). I conclude the study of Dickinson by considering, in "A Word made Flesh" (1651), how the relations of consciousness to reality, of mind to embodiment, are analyzed in reference to language and poetry.

The focus on the "realism" of Dickinson's treatment of landscapes and other physical details enables me to link her to the writers of the rest of the term (notably Whitman, James, Crane, and Jewett). Her consideration of consciousness, as represented in particular by the role of the lyric speaker, gives students added awareness of the use of point of view in narrative. Reading Dickinson introduces the idea of a "slant" vision of the world in which reality is not seen directly, a perspective that can be traced in many of the other "realist" writers. I usually open discussion of these writers by asking students to discuss point of view, the use of the "I" or other narrating voice. Their increasing awareness of this fictive and constructed voice leads them to associate the narrative voice in prose fiction with the speaker in Dickinson's poems.

Attention to aspects of realism in Dickinson also links her more clearly to her contemporary Walt Whitman. Whitman's famous catalogs in "Song of Myself" are often taken as documentary descriptions. Reading Whitman after Dickinson, however, tends to make students more aware of how the voice of the "I" in Whitman transforms the subjects described. Reading Whitman in the light of Dickinson's work also illuminates ironies in the placement, juxtaposition, and sequence of details in his catalogs (as in Dickinson the placement of elements in the sequence of stanzas often defines the metaphysical status of the objects). The famous section 11 of "Song of Myself," in which a "twenty-ninth bather" joins the twenty-eight men, can be seen as a representation of the poet's relation to the physical world, of his poetry as an attempt of the desiring self to unite with the physical world (as the "twenty-ninth bather" may be either the poet or the woman he describes, whose desire the poet helps to fulfill).

In the prose writers, the example of Dickinson helps complicate our notions of the relation of fiction to reality. Reading the first paragraph of Henry James's *Portrait of a Lady* in the context of Dickinson's "There's a certain Slant of light" (a comparison suggested by a student) calls attention to the role of the narrator and the shifting status of the landscape of Gardencourt, which seems alternately an external scene and an impression in the mind of the reader or narrator. The "borderline" sensibility in the Dickinson poem becomes the space in which James writes. Dickinson's dramatizations of speakers can help us understand James's use of third-person narration. Through his frequent intrusions, the narrator makes his presence felt and directs our interpretation of the story. James seems to stand both within and outside his story, turning reality into an impression conveyed by the author to the reader. Whereas Dickinson tends to show the penetration of the physical world into the consciousness that is "where the Meanings, are," James views reality as constituted principally by one's impressions.

James's emphasis on the impression is extended in the works of Stephen Crane. In *The Red Badge of Courage*, the depiction of the battles mainly in retrospect (in Henry Fleming's reflections on events during the war) is reminiscent of Dickinson's focus on the experience of aftermath, how experience strikes the mind after it is concluded, in such poems as "After great pain" (341). Dickinson notes the peculiar effect of retrospection on perception in "My Triumph lasted till the Drums" (1227), in a way that anticipates Crane's view of the ironies of "Glory." Crane's exaggerated depiction of the field of battle that turns its elements into symbols parallels Dickinson's transformation of physical details through the use of figurative language, which is characteristic of her battle imagery. Indeed, in "Inconceivably solemn" (582), she uses various battlefield sights to exemplify "the very Press / Of Imagery" that can make the physical world seem overwhelming, as it often becomes for Henry Fleming. One student recalled the hazy vision of "I heard a Fly buzz" as a corollary to the clouded physical and moral vision of Crane's central character throughout *The Red Badge of Courage*.

A sense of literary depiction as out of joint with reality and an emphasis on impressions are even more central in Sarah Orne Jewett's "Country of the Pointed Firs." Students are quick to realize how the story of the narrator, who remains slightly distanced from her subject—the events and the people of Dunnet Landing—represents the conventions of narrative itself: the distance of the narrator from the story told and the problem of sequential plot (since the story tends to proceed by looping back on events rather than following strict linear sequence). As Dickinson uses the conventions of poetry (speaker, meter, orthography) to question not only poetry but issues such as the relation of the self to the physical world and the soul to the body, Jewett uses fiction to raise similar questions: whether there can be an adequate response of one individual to another or whether we are all isolated; whether the images perpetuated by memory have any permanence. By the end of Jewett's work, the physical world, seen in retrospect, seems to fade away entirely, as the houses and town of Dunnet Landing disappear from the view of the narrator and necessarily of the reader as well: " . . . when I looked back again, the islands and the headland had run together and Dunnet Landing and all its coasts were lost to sight" (160).

Treating Dickinson in terms of realism helps students understand representation in literary creations as an attempt of the creative self to forge a relation with the physical world. Dickinson's poems force us to question any simple acceptance of reality as something that can be described apart from the self. For if the actual seems to stand as a barrier between consciousness and complete knowledge or transcendence ("I heard a Fly buzz"), the self always intervenes in any encounter with the world, making perfect transparence in literary or other representations impossible. Reading Dickinson helps us perceive the "slant" relation to reality in the works of the late-nineteenth-century "realists," especially in their use of impressionism. After analyzing Dickinson's complex use of speakers, we become more keenly aware of how the narrator's stance transforms meaning in prose fiction. Finally, by considering the role of realism and the use of sequence in Dickinson's poems (aspects usually associated with narrative), we can see how Dickinson's transformation of lyric conventions provides a new perspective from which to view the use of voice and the illusion of the representation of reality in prose fiction. Knowledge of how Dickinson transforms the conventions of lyric poetry empowers students in the reading of poetry generally and enables them to understand how lyric is aligned to other forms of representation.

NOTES

[1]On the Emersonian context, see Anderson and especially Porter (*Modern Idiom*). For discussions of Dickinson's transformations of Emersonianism in the name of another kind of power, see Diehl; Homans, *Women Writers*; and Cameron. For a revival of the idea that the poetry reflects a view of the self as antagonistic to the world, see Benfey and Greg Johnson.

[2]On this poem, see Cameron (101–03), who also emphasizes the use of figures, though her perspective differs from mine. See also Weisbuch, especially 11–39, on Dickinson's "analogical habit."

Dickinson Identified:
Newer Criticism and Feminist Classrooms

Mary Loeffelholz

The critical strategies recently grouped under the umbrella term *posthumanism* offer a variety of challenges to other, more traditional approaches to the teaching of Emily Dickinson's poetry. I have taught Dickinson's poems to undergraduate and graduate students at a large midwestern state university, in courses ranging from an introduction to women's studies in the humanities to a survey course in American literature to an almost entirely graduate course in feminist literary criticism and theory. What it means to teach Dickinson's poetry posthumanistically changes to some extent from course to course. In an introductory women's studies course, readings of Dickinson's poems may attend to the poems' appropriation and critical representation of authoritative metaphors of female and male identity in nineteenth-century American culture. In the survey course in American literature, I combine those general concerns with a specific emphasis on Dickinson's critical transformations of Emerson's tropes of the poet as seer and idealist. What these approaches to teaching Dickinson hold in common is the posthumanist critique of identity, the identity both of persons and of poems. To the extent that we can draw these issues into the classroom, the cultural construction of gender (as the women's studies course might put it) and the powerful and contradictory prior texts of literary tradition and the politics of canon formation (as the American literature survey course might see them) discredit the notion that Dickinson's poems immediately express the essence of a unified and transcendent authorial selfhood.

Posthumanist approaches do not forestall discussions of selfhood or subjectivity; they only make such discussions interesting, and interested, ideologically speaking. "Interested," because it is an axiom of many posthumanist schools that ideas of selfhood reflect social power and define the "human" so as to exclude disempowered groups. "Interesting," because once we suggest that subjectivity is a contradictory and socially contingent artifact, it can be analyzed rather than tacitly assumed in the classroom. Posthumanist and particularly feminist approaches welcome "the chance of challenging the ideology of the subject (as male, white, and middle-class) by developing alternative and different notions of subjectivity" (Huyssen 213). I cite two Dickinson poems to explore possible posthumanist readings in both women's studies and English undergraduate classrooms: "Dare you see a Soul *at the White Heat*?" (365) and "The Spirit is the Conscious Ear" (733). Both are, in different ways, poems of self-fashioning. They inherit religious and secular metaphors of power and transcendence. Yet close classroom readings can argue that a transcendental subject (traditionally, of course, a masculine subject) is postulated in, and at the same time undercut by, the actual language of the poems—an insight that will have a different meaning for students in different classes.

A women's studies classroom is in certain ways a posthumanist teaching situation by definition: by creating such a classroom, we undertake a responsibility for querying universal man, the subject of humanism, in all his guises. At the same time, however, feminist scholarship across the disciplines has had a profoundly uneasy relation with posthumanist theory, a relation that might take as its motto Nancy Miller's observation that "only those who have [a signature] can play with not having it" (53). For women historically denied full access to subjectivity, authorial identity, and the signature, the posthumanist critique of identity and the subject may seem at best premature and at worst grotesquely misplaced. (See Homans, "Feminist Criticism"; Moi; Kamuf; and N. Miller for extended discussions of this issue.)

Feminist uneasiness with posthumanist theory is at its most acute, I should imagine, when women's literature enters the women's studies classroom. For readers in such a classroom (and here I include myself with my students), women's writing holds out certain promises of identification, transference, and transcendence—identification with another woman's speaking voice across gulfs of time and space, transference onto the text's superior power to give voice to women's experience, and transcendence of immediate, concrete historical limitations on women's autonomy. If posthumanist approaches to teaching Dickinson's poetry in certain respects put these responses under suspicion, it's fair to ask what they can offer students in return.

I teach a small sampling of Dickinson's poetry, together with a few poems by Charlotte and Emily Brontë, in the University of Illinois course Introduction to Women's Studies in the Humanities. The course is divided into a theoretical introduction to general issues in women's studies, followed by a historical section that surveys the rise of modern feminist movements and thought, with an emphasis on United States history and culture. I decided at the outset to experiment with integrating discussions of women's art and women's literature into their historical contexts, or at least to juxtapose historical and literary reading assignments. I hoped that our reading assignments and classroom discussions could avoid the twin temptations of seeing literature either as sheer passive historical documentation of life in a comfortably distanced elsewhere or as expressions of uniformly timeless essences of women's experience, whether of rebellion or victimization, with which students might immediately and ahistorically identify. (And very often, of course, students jump alternately from one to the other of these temptations, without being conscious of doing so; cross-questioning in class can sometimes bring out the contradictory assumptions entailed in both temptations.) I wanted to make a feminist and posthumanist case that women writers of poems are subjects of history (as are we, students and readers of poems), constructed in their historically specific languages—engaged in struggle, rather than constituted as passive atoms of social totalities or transcendental spirits.

Dickinson's poems, perhaps better than any other literary readings in the course, lend themselves to this approach. The students tend to condescend to Anne Bradstreet, whose poems we read earlier in the semester, by relegating her to the distanced and unregenerated (because Puritan and unfeminist) "elsewhen." My pedagogical challenges to this condescension erode its edges but, I am sorry to say, seldom dislodge its center. When we read contemporary women's poetry, not surprisingly students respond quite differently, celebrating the unqualified immediacy of their identifications with the poetry I assign and the poems they themselves choose and bring into class. Fiction, whether Charlotte Perkins Gilman's or Alice Walker's, seems to allow the class both to identify with the protagonists and to distance the situations of characters as possibly reflecting a specified historical "elsewhen"—the contexts of nineteenth-century medical practices or the civil rights movement. Dickinson's poetry, however, lands in a generic and historical zone where the students themselves become profoundly unsure of their strategies of identification or condescension. From a posthumanist standpoint, as I have suggested, this uncertainty is very much to be valued.

At the outset of our discussion students spontaneously remark their lack of contexts for reading Dickinson's poetry. Confessing, as they think, to their interpretive failure, they actually put into their own words the important critical insight Robert Weisbuch propounded: Dickinson's "sceneless-ness," her "analogical" and "anti-allegorical" poetics. My first task is to enlarge on and validate this response, to take it as a starting point rather than the terminus of interpretation. Reading poems like "Dare you see a Soul *at the White Heat?*" (365) and "My Life had stood—a Loaded Gun" (754) for (usually) the first time, students have every reason to feel that Dickinson aggressively wards off readerly identifications and aggressively cuts herself off from social determinations. I then try to show students that this very feeling—once put into words, generalized, and justified with reference to the texts—can in its turn become the grounds for interpreting Dickinson historically as a woman writer. Dickinson's often aggressive attempts to define herself, for instance, were ventured in a culture that exalted self-sufficient individualism yet that remained thoroughly ambivalent about extending the ideology of human subjectivity to women. The intellectual difficulty of the poems defies the nineteenth-century's uneasiness over women's intellectual powers and its relegation of women to realms of largely unreflective feeling. I mention these historical contexts (which have already been covered) and connect Dickinson's struggles with her culture to students' struggles with her language.

After soliciting initial reactions to the poems, I ask students what they know about Dickinson's biography and work. By this point in the women's studies course, students are self-consciously skeptical about the presentation of women in their prior education experience. They volunteer the well-known facts, which they take with a grain of salt, and ask for more information, often on the writing, publication history, and reception of the poems—information that curiously seems to have been neglected in high school representations of the Dickinson biography. What I can add to their knowledge inevitably foregrounds posthumanist issues of how an author is "constructed" as such and how, specifically, a woman writer comes into being out of the texts Dickinson so equivocally left behind. (For instance, who took over and edited texts not intended for publication? How were the texts initially altered for publication? What biographical stories did people seem to want to hear about a woman poet? How did they feel it necessary to explain her? When and how did Dickinson become a canonical writer?) Not that we, in class, can be innocent of such constructions: we read only a small selection from the poems, and we too try to envision—albeit with the help of the new feminist history—a woman writer as the producer of these poems.

I ask the class to begin with "Dare you see a Soul *at the White Heat*" as a poem that makes problematic both readerly identification and ideas of "experience," two mainstays of humanist (and much feminist) literary criticism:

> Dare you see a Soul *at the White Heat*?
> Then crouch within the door—
> Red—is the Fire's common tint—
> But when the vivid Ore
> Has vanquished Flame's conditions,
> It quivers from the Forge
> Without a color, but the light
> Of unanointed Blaze.
> Least Village has its Blacksmith
> Whose Anvil's even ring
> Stands symbol for the finer Forge

> That soundless tugs—within—
> Refining these impatient Ores
> With Hammer, and with Blaze
> Until the Designated Light
> Repudiate the Forge—

Simply asking students how they feel about the poem's address to its reader in the first two lines underscores the point about identification: the poem challenges its reader instead of courting an immediate merging. The initial challenge draws a line between reader and speaker, engaging them both to some degree in self-definition. The speaker asks something unusual of her audience and so motivates the class's analysis of the poem's succeeding metaphors of self-fashioning.

We discuss the conventional associations of white and red with innocence, experience, and female sexuality; I ask what happens to those associations and their causal order in this poem. I provide them with a text from a familiar author, Anne Bradstreet, as a gloss on the poem's allusively religious vocabulary:

> Iron, till it be thoroughly heat, is uncapable to be wrought; so God see good to cast some men into the furnace of affliction and then beats them on His anvil into what frame he pleases.   ("Mediations Divine and Moral" 31)

Recalling their historical readings, students can by now voice the contradictions in the sexual and religious ideologies that the poem allusively draws on: Puritanism on the one hand maintaining the innate depravity of all people, including women, and nineteenth-century sexual ideology on the other hand maintaining the essential purity of women, in the context of the "feminization of theology" (Douglas). Exploiting this historical contradiction, Dickinson forges a rhetoric of aggressive self-fashioning, making a case for transcendent identity that depends on historical "Ores."

With a glance back at how this poem's rhetoric of self-fashioning revises the students' sense of Dickinson's biography (her decision to wear white, for instance), the class moves on to the much more notorious "My Life had stood—a Loaded Gun," where we face more division and contradiction within the speaker herself, as well as in the languages she exploits and inhabits. By this time students are better able to talk about the complexities of being "identified," the event with which poem 754 begins, and to acknowledge the poem's connections between power, aggression, and identity. These are issues that stay alive throughout the semester's readings. If posthumanist reading strategies tend to deny my women's studies class the vicarious powers of immediate identification, they allow the students instead to think reflectively about identity in language. This accomplishment seems to me wholly consonant with the feminist aims of the class, since women's studies as a discipline works to make the foundations of our everyday identities available for conscious reflection and thus for change.

In the survey course in American literature, students lack the fuller historical context available to the women's studies class but have (by term's end, when Dickinson is taught) a richer literary background to draw on. Many of the same opening moves work for this class, and I similarly use students' prior information about Dickinson and their initial reactions to the poems. These students, too, have read Bradstreet; to a poem like "Dare you see a Soul *at the White Heat*," they can bring not only Bradstreet's "Meditation" but also *The Scarlet Letter*'s symbolic representation of female "experience" and its consequences. To some degree, literary history in this class stands in for more direct political and economic history, and Dickinson's work gets separated from the condition and struggles of most other women of her time. If in the women's studies course I can make a case for Dickinson's broad quarrel with her culture on the basis of historical evidence, in the American literature survey I must accomplish some of the same goals with reference to our literary readings. And this endeavor brings Dickinson's poems, first and foremost, up against Emerson's writings.

Where the New Criticism often (and illuminatingly) saw Dickinson's poems as repeating Emerson, feminist and posthumanist readers and teachers are more likely to see Dickinson as a critic of the Emersonian heritage, someone who repeats with a difference. Sometimes the posthumanist angle on this issue involves nominating a different canon of Dickinson poems; at other times, it involves looking differently at the "Emersonian" poems described by the New Criticism. As an instance of the latter approach, I look, in my American literature survey classroom, at poem 733:

> The Spirit is the Conscious Ear.
> We actually Hear
> When We inspect—that's audible—
> That is admitted—Here—
>
> For other Services—as Sound—
> There hangs a smaller Ear
> Outside the Castle—that Contain
> The other—only—Hear—

Albert Gelpi's exemplary reading (in the light of its focus on intellectual history, a reading scarcely reducible to New Criticism narrowly conceived) saw in this poem a Dickinson "heartily" in agreement with Emerson's idealism of consciousness, his enthroning of the soul as "master" of its body and senses (*Mind of the Poet* 98–99).

My posthumanist classroom strategy allows me to suggest otherwise, maintaining that here Dickinson indeed repeats Emerson, but with a deconstructive difference. Simply reading the poem aloud—hoariest and greatest of all classroom tactics—suffices to set the difference vibrating. Students look up, look down to the text, look up, and try to assess aurally as well as visually the difference between "here" and "hear." The two great nineteenth-century idealist metaphors for the poet's authority—the mastering, creative eye and the certainty of bardic voice—come quietly to loggerheads in this small poem. "Here" and "hear" are both alike and different; alike in voice, different to the eye. A trivially punning deconstructive icon of difference? Surely not, if Emerson's punning "eye/I" icon of sameness is a cultural fiction of hoary authority.

This icon of difference opens the poem's critique of self-presence for classroom discussion. If students are allowed to regard the poem's voice as that of a doubting speaker, rather than a serenely authoritative central consciousness, the speaker's characteristics can be evolved in discussion. This alienated soul virtually treats its senses as servants who do the soul's living for it. It reduces its body to a mere doorknob—the hanging ear—for consciousness. The encastled consciousness needs constant and slightly anxious in(tro)spection in order to know it's alive. The subject of the verb "Contain" is not so clear as it might be; is the soul unambiguously the "container" of presence, when it stoops to language? when, after all, it takes its metaphorical form, the "Conscious Ear," from the despised body? The poem takes the powerful Romantic ideology of solipsistic consciousness (which the students of course know Dickinson acted out to some degree in her life) and linguistically undercuts it. The poem's language, over and against its manifest content, subverts the hierarchies that rank consciousness over the sense, soul over body, mind over matter. This posthumanist reading starts simply from allowing the poem its space in the classroom, as the language-entity it is. Once started, this critique of the transcendental subject in language can be extended into other and better-known poems and related to the historical contexts in which Dickinson found and remade herself as a gendered subject.

In conclusion, having tried to open a difference, I must admit to the similarities between New Critical pedagogy and the pedagogies of posthumanism, particularly deconstruction, which is often charged (in the United States) with warming over New Critical assumptions and practices. The classroom strategies I practice do rely, as does or did the New Criticism, on close textual readings. A strong and growing strand of posthumanist argument contends that it is high time that we held suspect the fetishism of the "reading" and the institutional production of infinitely more readings (Merod). Such fetishism, it is argued, can but reiterate assumptions about the ahistorical, transcendental unity of the poetic object, a unity and transcendence not in practice challenged by deconstruction's purported "dissemination" of language's meaning—a unity and transcendence effectively, if perversely, reconstituted by the continual production of deconstructive, and even newly historical, readings. It seems unlikely that any particular critical strategy can currently inoculate itself from within against such institutional pressures toward readings.

While I take this disturbing criticism seriously, I can see no alternatives to teaching readings that would do otherwise than leave students gaping before literary monuments (and before other cultural artifacts of arguably more importance to them). As a feminist teacher, I particularly do not want to leave my students disempowered and gaping before their culture(s). The feminist and posthumanist participatory readings I can conceive of practicing in the classroom do severely qualify the conditions of reading's promised intelligibility and deny—along with the unity of text and the unity of the subject—any transcendental link between (absolute) power and (absolute) intelligibility. But that still leaves the links between power and intelligibility or knowledge to be read in all their contingent historical specificity; it leaves us readings, history, authors, and readers as conflicted subjects. The subject, as Dickinson puts it, is nevertheless—in its posthumanist contexts—"We." Posthumanist approaches can't close the gaps between Dickinson and her student readers or restore Dickinson to them as a (fictional) full human presence. What they can teach are active interpretations that, if successful, may lead Dickinson's students to ask interpretive questions about their own subjectivity, the conditions of their self-presence and their presence to one another. Posthumanist approaches honor the sheer difficulty of Dickinson's poems, which seems to me important in itself. Beyond that, posthumanist approaches to Dickinson recognize the difficulty of being in and of a culture, using its language, and being its critic at the same time; I can think of nothing I would rather teach (or explore with) my students.

APPENDIX:
SAMPLE ASSIGNMENTS

Assignment for an Introductory Class, *Lynne P. Shackelford*

Pick one stanza from any poem by Emily Dickinson in our text (the *Norton Anthology of American Literature*) and explicate it, commenting on both style and content. The structure of your paper should be as follows:

1. An introductory paragraph that identifies the poem, its general message, and how the stanza you selected fits into the poem as a whole.
2. Several paragraphs commenting on the stanza's meaning and relevant stylistic features. Among the points you might consider are diction (connotation, allusion, repetition, ambiguity, punning, paradox, irony), imagery, metaphor and simile, symbol or allegory, the speaker and tone, the setting and situation, meter and rhyme scheme, sounds (alliteration, assonance, and consonance), theme(s), and the form.
3. A concluding paragraph evaluating the stanza.

Assignment for an Introductory Literary Studies Class, *William Galperin*

Dickinson's poem "A Clock stopped" (287) would appear to develop, and to depend for its effect on, an extended analogy between an external object and an internal condition, between a specific and concrete thing—the clock—and some state of mind or feeling or being. How does the poem establish this connection? What aspects of its language suggest that the clock is something other than—or more than—a physical object? What is the effect of Dickinson's strategy of externalization, and how would you characterize the condition that the clock represents? Is something actually happening to the speaker or is the speaker simply an observer of something happening? How does the language of the poem convey such a condition?

In your reading of "A Clock stopped" pay particular attention to diction, punctuation, and the structure of individual lines. Consider, for example, words such as "Puppet," the conjunction of "Trinket" with "awe," as well as phrases such as "Pendulum of snow" and "Decades of Arrogance." Consider, too, the possible identities of "Him" in the poem's final line. Don't hesitate to consult the dictionary for words that you already know but that may possibly have other meanings in conjunction with the poem. You might begin your essay by stating what you think the purpose of the poem is so that your interpretation will be a way of proving your thesis rather than a way of finding it. The paper should be three to five pages long.

Assignment in a Dickinson Seminar, *Barbara L. Packer*

As you have noticed by now, Dickinson's syntax is as idiosyncratic as everything else about her poetry. English is an analytic rather than a synthetic language; it is quite poor in syntactical markers to indicate case or tense or part of speech and hence is unusually dependent on word order to make syntactic relations clear. Poets have always taken liberties with word order, of course, but the more liberties they take, the more difficult the poems become to understand.

Dickinson helps herself liberally to the poet's freedom to invert or otherwise scramble normal word order—and makes the task of understanding even harder because she removes most ordinary punctuation and substitutes dashes. She then goes on to remove even those remaining markers in English (e.g., writing "he omit" instead of "he omits") or else to substitute one part of speech for another (e.g., using the infinitive of the verb when we would expect a declarative or imperative mood). Her poems thus become elaborate exercises in grammatical decoding.

For next week, select a poem to "unscramble" and parse. The ones listed below are nice, thorny ones, but you may select any you like. Write the sentences out in normal English prose, and identify the parts of speech, the mood and tense of the verbs, and so on. Be sure to indicate any violation of normal usage—such as when a normally intransitive verb is made transitive or when what is normally a preposition is treated as a noun. If two wholly different readings of a line are possible, give both.

448, 455, 464, 471, 499 (last 3 stanzas), 515, 544, 552, 628, 630, 645, 667, 721, 740, 741, 745, 774.

Two Creative Assignments for Undergraduates, *Paula Uruburu*

One out-of-class assignment I have found productive and enlightening for students is to ask them to write a poem in Dickinson's style (or in what they perceive as her style). This allows students to express themselves more creatively than they might in an essay or research paper and helps them appreciate the effort involved in literary creation. Even the least enthusiastic students will usually pick up on Dickinson's random use of capitalization, dashes, uncommon vocabulary, and themes like death or immortality. Some students may throw in abstractions to make their poems seem more like Dickinson's. Others will analyze those themes and add their own points of view. In comparing their poems with Dickinson's in class, students discover that truly great poetry, like all successful writing, requires careful attention to diction, syntax, and the overall structure and logic involved in developing an idea. They realize, too, the added dimensions that biblical, historical, and literary allusions give to a work. They see how essential it is to revise and rework ideas.

Another successful assignment, better suited to students who have discussed Dickinson extensively in class, is to have them create their own fascicle. I bring in a copy of an original fascicle from Franklin's *Manuscript Books*, and we examine its structure: arrangement, progression of ideas, movement toward a conclusion. We discuss why Dickinson might have chosen to collect certain poems, often arranged around a theme, into those small books, why she might have included a particular poem, and what underlying method there could have been in its organization. I might ask students, for example, whether the individual poems are arranged like steps in a process of meditation.

I then ask students to choose five poems and organize them with an eye to some sort of progression or resolution to a question. Depending on the situation, I will either give them a list of poems dealing with general subjects like love, death, immortality, or nature or ask them to come up with five poems they believe are thematically related. Johnson's edition of the

Complete Poems contains a helpful subject index to which students can refer. We then analyze each poem and explain the similarities, differences, and connections among them, noting changes in word choice, usage, images, and tone. I ask students to explain their choices and to compare them to the choices Dickinson made in the fascicle we examined earlier.

Questions for an Oral Exam on Criticism in a Dickinson Seminar, *Cheryl Walker*

In this seminar, what kinds of critical positions have been represented? What questions does each critic find most compelling in dealing with Dickinson's work? Describe the critical conversation among these critics concerning the issues of nature, God, and style.

> What place does Dickinson occupy in American traditions of literature, for example, vis-à-vis Hawthorne, Emerson, Thoreau?
>
> In what sense is Dickinson a Puritan, and in what sense does she defy Puritanism?
>
> Using the criticism we have read, describe Dickinson's peculiar kind of language and be ready to discuss at least two different responses to her success with it.
>
> Discuss the chronological changes in attitudes toward Dickinson among the critics we have read.
>
> What is the value of reading criticism like this for the study of Emily Dickinson? (Be specific. Refer to critics by name and by point of view.)

In studying for this oral examination, you should review the criticism we have read and your notes from class discussion. Be ready to specify which approaches belong to which critics, dates of critical articles, relations among authors—especially where critics refer to one another or disagree with one another. This exam will be open book. You should refer to specific passages. Prepare for all the above questions. You may, and in fact should, discuss them among yourselves; one person's success will not jeopardize another's; "the consummation devoutly to be wished," as Hamlet says, is that all should do well.

SURVEY PARTICIPANTS

This volume would not have been possible without the generous responses of the survey participants. Their observations, suggestions, and shared experience have taught us much about Dickinson and about teaching. We thank them all for their contributions.

Robert Bain, University of North Carolina, Chapel Hill; Wendy Barker, University of Texas, San Antonio; Richard Benvenuto, Michigan State University, East Lansing; Martin Bickman, University of Colorado, Boulder; E. Miller Budick, Hebrew University of Jerusalem; Jack L. Capps, US Military Academy, West Point; Jean Ferguson Carr, University of Pittsburgh; J. Donald Crowley, University of Missouri, Columbia; Carlos Daghlian, Universidade Estadual Paulista, Brazil; Joanne Feit Diehl, University of California, Davis; Margaret Freeman, State University of New York College, Old Westbury; August J. Fry, Free University, Amsterdam; William Galperin, Rutgers University, New Brunswick; Maryanne Garbowsky, County College of Morris; Elissa Greenwald, Rutgers University, New Brunswick; Jonnie G. Guerra, Mount Vernon College; James Guthrie, North Central College; Judy S. Hager, University of Maine, Fort Kent; Darryl Hattenhauer, Bemidji State University; Margaret Homans, Yale University; Rowena Revis Jones, Northern Michigan University; Suzanne Juhasz, University of Colorado, Boulder; Amy Kaplan, Mt. Holyoke College; Lynn Keller, University of Wisconsin, Madison; M. Jimmie Killingsworth, Memphis State University; Helene Knox, Muhlenberg College; Douglas Novich Leonard, Gustavus Adolphus College; Ann Lilliedahl, Texas Southern University; Diane Lichtenstein, College of St. Thomas; Mary Loeffelholz, Northeastern University; John Mann, Western Illinois University; Wendy Martin, Queens College, City University of New York; Toni A. H. McNaron, University of Minnesota, Twin Cities; Cristanne Miller, Pomona College; Jonathan Morse, University of Hawaii, Honolulu; Mary L. Morton, Nichols State University; Charlotte Nekola, William Paterson College; Dorothy Huff Oberhaus, Mercy College; Larry Olpin, Central Missouri State University; Barbara L. Packer, University of California, Los Angeles; Robert W. Peckham, Sacred Heart Seminary; Alice Hall Petry, Rhode Island School of Design; David Porter, University of Massachusetts, Amherst; Frank D. Rashid, Marygrove College; John Reiss, St. Michael's College; Lee J. Richmond, St. John's University; David Robinson, Oregon State University; Katharine M. Rogers, Brooklyn College, City University of New York; Nicholas Ruddick, University of Regina; Barton Levi St. Armand, Brown University; Richard B. Sewall, Yale University; Lynne P. Shackelford, Furman University; William Shullenberger, Sarah Lawrence College; William H. Shurr, University of Tennessee, Knoxville; Regina Siegfriend, ASC, Aquinas Institute; Bess Stark Spangler, Peace College; David H. Stewart, Texas A&M University; Paula Uruburu, Hofstra

University; Inez Wager and Willis Wager, King College; Cheryl Walker, Scripps College; Nancy Walker, Vanderbilt University; David Watters, University of New Hampshire, Durham; Shira Wolosky, Hebrew University of Jerusalem

WORKS CITED

Alexander, Bonnie. "Reading Emily Dickinson." *Massachusetts Studies in English* 7.4 and 8.1 (1981): 1–17.

Anderson, Charles. *Emily Dickinson's Poetry: Stairway of Surprise.* Westport: Greenwood, 1982.

Ariès, Philippe. *Images of Man and Death.* Trans. Janet Lloyd. Cambridge: Harvard UP, 1985.

———. *The Hour of Our Death.* Trans. Helen Weaver. New York: Knopf, 1981.

———. *Western Attitudes toward Death.* Trans. Patricia M. Ranum. Baltimore: Johns Hopkins UP, 1974.

Barker, Felix, and John Gay. *Highgate Cemetery: Victorian Valhalla.* Salem: Salem House, 1984.

Baym, Nina. "God, Father, and Lover in Emily Dickinson's Poetry." *Puritan Influences in American Literature.* Ed. Emory Elliott. Urbana: U of Illinois P, 1979. 193–209.

Becker, Ernest. *The Denial of Death.* New York: Free, 1973.

Benfey, Christopher. *Emily Dickinson and the Problem of Others.* Amherst: U of Massachusetts P, 1984.

Bercovitch, Sacvan. *The Puritan Origins of the American Self.* New Haven: Yale UP, 1975.

Bergson, Henri. "Laughter." *Comedy.* Introd. and appreciation Wylie Sypher. Garden City: Doubleday, 1956. 59–190.

Blake, Caesar R., and Carlton F. Wells, eds. *The Recognition of Emily Dickinson.* Ann Arbor: U of Michigan P, 1968.

Bloom, Harold. *The Visionary Company: A Reading of English Romantic Poetry.* Ithaca: Cornell UP, 1971.

Bogan, Louise. "A Mystical Poet." Sewall, *Collection.* 137–43.

Bradstreet, Anne. *The Works of Anne Bradstreet.* Ed. Jeannine Hensley. Cambridge: Harvard UP, 1967.

Brooks, Cleanth, and Robert Penn Warren. *Understanding Poetry.* New York: Holt, 1960.

Buckingham, Willis J. *Emily Dickinson: An Annotated Bibliography.* Bloomington: Indiana UP, 1970.

———. "Emily Dickinson's Dictionary." *Harvard Library Bulletin* 25 (1977): 489–92.

Cameron, Sharon. *Lyric Time: Dickinson and the Limits of Genre.* Baltimore: Johns Hopkins UP, 1979.

Capps, Jack L. *Emily Dickinson's Reading: 1836–1886.* Cambridge: Harvard UP, 1966.

Carr, Arthur C. *Grief: Selected Readings.* New York: Health Sciences, 1975.

Chevigny, Bell Gale. *The Woman and the Myth: Margaret Fuller's Life and Writings.* Old Westbury: Feminist, 1976.

Cody, John. *After Great Pain: The Inner Life of Emily Dickinson.* Cambridge: Belknap-Harvard UP, 1971.

Cott, Nancy F. *The Bonds of Womanhood: "Woman's Sphere" in New England, 1780–1835.* New Haven: Yale UP, 1977.

Cox, Harvey. *Feast of Fools: A Theological Essay on Festivity and Fantasy.* New York: Harper, 1969.

Dandurand, Karen. "New Dickinson Civil War Publication." *American Literature* 56 (1984): 17–27.

———. "Why Dickinson Did Not Publish." *DAI* 45 (1984): 3130A. U of Massachusetts, Amherst.

Davis, Rebecca Harding. "In the Gray Cabins of New England." *Century Magazine* 49.4 (1895): 620–23.

Degler, Carl N. *At Odds: Women and the Family in America from the Revolution to the Present.* New York: Oxford UP, 1980.

de Man, Paul. "Intentional Structure of the Romantic Image." *Romanticism and Consciousness.* Ed. Harold Bloom. New York: Norton, 1970. 65–77.

Dickinson, Emily. *Acts of Light.* Paintings by Nancy Ekholm Burkert. Appreciation by Jane Langton. Boston: New York Graphic Soc., 1980.

———. *The Complete Poems of Emily Dickinson.* Ed. Thomas H. Johnson. Boston: Little, 1960. London: Faber, 1970.

———. *Final Harvest.* Ed. Thomas H. Johnson. Boston: Little, 1961.

———. *The Letters of Emily Dickinson.* 3 vols. Ed. Thomas H. Johnson and Theodora Ward. Cambridge: Belknap-Harvard UP, 1958.

———. *The Manuscript Books of Emily Dickinson.* 2 vols. Ed. R. W. Franklin. Cambridge: Belknap-Harvard UP, 1958.

———. *The Master Letters of Emily Dickinson.* Ed. Ralph W. Franklin. Amherst: Amherst Coll. P, 1986.

———. *The Poems of Emily Dickinson.* 3 vols. Ed. Thomas H. Johnson. Cambridge: Belknap-Harvard UP, 1955.

———. *Selected Letters.* Ed. Thomas H. Johnson. Cambridge: Belknap-Harvard UP, 1971.

———. *Selected Poems and Letters of Emily Dickinson.* Ed. Robert N. Linscott. Garden City: Anchor-Doubleday, 1959.

Diehl, Joanne Feit. *Dickinson and the Romantic Imagination.* Princeton: Princeton UP, 1981.

Diggory, Terrence. "Armored Women, Naked Men." Gilbert and Gubar, *Shakespeare's Sisters* 135–50.

Dobson, Joanne. " 'Oh, Susie, it is dangerous': Emily Dickinson and the Archetype of the Masculine." Juhasz, *Feminist Critics* 80–97.

Donne, John. *Death's Duell*. Ed. Geoffrey Keynes. Boston: Godine, 1973.

————. *The Elegies* and *The Songs and Sonnets*. Ed. Helen Gardner. Oxford: Clarendon Press, 1965.

Donoghue, Denis. *Emily Dickinson*. U of Minnesota Pamphlets of American Writers 81. Minneapolis: U of Minnesota P, 1969.

Douglas, Ann. *The Feminization of American Culture*. New York: Knopf, 1977.

Duchac, Joseph. *The Poems of Emily Dickinson: An Annotated Guide to Commentary Published in English, 1890–1977*. Boston: Hall, 1979.

Dumont, Richard G., and Dennis C. Foss. *The American Way of Death: Acceptance or Denial?* Cambridge: Schenkman, 1972.

Eberwein, Jane Donahue. *Dickinson: Strategies of Limitation*. Amherst: U of Massachusetts P, 1985.

Enright, D. J., ed. *The Oxford Book of Death*. New York: Oxford UP, 1983.

Epstein, Barbara Leslie. *The Politics of Domesticity: Women, Evangelism, and Temperance in Nineteenth-Century America*. Middletown: Wesleyan UP, 1981.

Faderman, Lillian. *Surpassing the Love of Men: Romantic Friendship and Love between Women from the Renaissance to the Present*. New York: Morrow, 1981.

Farrell, James J. *Inventing the American Way of Death, 1830–1920*. Philadelphia: Temple UP, 1980.

Ferlazzo, Paul J., ed. *Critical Essays on Emily Dickinson*. Boston: Hall, 1984.

————. *Emily Dickinson*. Boston: Twayne, 1976.

Franklin, Ralph W. *The Editing of Emily Dickinson: A Reconsideration*. Madison: U of Wisconsin P, 1967.

Galperin, William H. "Emily Dickinson's Marriage Hearse." *Denver Quarterly* 18.4 (1984): 62–73.

Gelpi, Albert. "Emily Dickinson and the Deerslayer: The Dilemma of the Woman Poet in America." *San Jose Studies* 3.3 (1977): 80–95. Rpt. in Gilbert and Gubar, *Shakespeare's Sisters* 122–34.

————. *Emily Dickinson: The Mind of the Poet*. Cambridge: Harvard UP, 1966.

Gilbert, Sandra. "The Wayward Nun beneath the Hill: Emily Dickinson and the Mysteries of Womanhood." Juhasz, *Feminist Critics* 22–44.

Gilbert, Sandra, and Susan Gubar. *The Madwoman in the Attic: The Woman Writer and the Nineteenth-Century Literary Imagination*. New Haven: Yale UP, 1979.

————, eds. *The Norton Anthology of Literature by Women*. New York: Norton, 1985.

————, eds. *Shakespeare's Sisters: Feminist Essays on Women Poets*. Bloomington: Indiana UP, 1979.

Gillon, Edmund V. *Victorian Cemetery Art*. New York: Dover, 1972.

Griffith, Clark. *The Long Shadow: Emily Dickinson's Tragic Poetry.* Princeton: Princeton UP, 1964.

Griswold, Rufus W., ed. *The Female Poets of America.* Philadelphia: Carey, 1849.

Gubar, Susan. "Blessings in Disguise: Cross-Dressing as Re-Dressing for Female Modernists." *Massachusetts Review* 22 (1981): 477–508.

Hagenbüchle, Roland. "Precision and Indeterminacy in the Poetry of Emily Dickinson." *ESQ: A Journal of the American Renaissance* 20 (1974): 33–56.

Hemans, Felicia. *The Poetical Works of Felicia Dorothea Hemans.* London: Oxford UP, 1914.

Higginson, Thomas Wentworth. *Atlantic Essays.* Boston: Osgood, 1871.

———. "Letter to a Young Contributor." *Atlantic Monthly* 9 (1862): 401–11.

Hijiya, James. "American Gravestones and Attitudes toward Death." *Proceedings of the American Philosophical Society* 125 (1983): 339–63.

Homans, Margaret. "Feminist Criticism and Theory: The Ghost of Creusa." *Yale Journal of Criticism* 1.1 (1987): 153–82.

———. *Women Writers and Poetic Identity: Dorothy Wordsworth, Emily Brontë, and Emily Dickinson.* Princeton: Princeton UP, 1980.

Howe, Susan. *My Emily Dickinson.* Berkeley: North Atlantic, 1985.

Huyssen, Andreas. *After the Great Divide: Modernism, Mass Culture, Postmodernism.* Bloomington: Indiana UP, 1986.

Jackson, Helen Hunt. *Poems.* New York: Arno, 1972.

Jewett, Sarah Orne. *The Country of the Pointed Firs and Other Stories.* Garden City: Anchor-Doubleday, 1956.

Johnson, Greg. *Emily Dickinson: Perception and the Poet's Quest.* University: U of Alabama P, 1985.

Johnson, Thomas H. *Emily Dickinson: An Interpretive Biography.* Cambridge: Belknap-Harvard UP, 1955.

Jordan, Mary Augusta. "Emily Dickinson's Letters." Blake and Wells 57–61.

Juhasz, Suzanne, ed. *Feminist Critics Read Emily Dickinson.* Bloomington: Indiana UP, 1983

———. "Reading Emily Dickinson's Letters." *ESQ: A Journal of the American Renaissance* 30 (1984): 170–92.

———. *The Undiscovered Continent: Emily Dickinson and the Space Within.* Bloomington: Indiana UP, 1983.

Kamuf, Peggy. "Replacing Feminist Criticism." *Diacritics* 12.2 (1982): 42–47.

Keller, Karl. "Notes on Sleeping with Emily Dickinson." Juhasz, *Feminist Critics* 67–79.

———. *The Only Kangaroo among the Beauty: Emily Dickinson and America.* Baltimore: Johns Hopkins UP, 1979.

Kelley, Mary. *Private Woman, Public Stage: Literary Domesticity in Nineteenth-Century America.* New York: Oxford UP, 1984.

Kintgen, Eugene. "Nonrecoverable Deletion and Compression in Poetry." *Foundations of Language* 9 (1972): 98–104.

Koestler, Arthur. *Act of Creation: A Study of the Conscious and Unconscious in Science and Art.* New York: Dell, 1964.

Kristeva, Julia. *Revolution in Poetic Language.* Trans. Margaret Waller. New York: Columbia UP, 1984.

Kübler-Ross, Elisabeth. *On Death and Dying.* New York: Macmillan, 1970.

Kull, Andrew. *New England Cemeteries: A Collector's Guide.* Brattleboro: Greene, 1975.

Levin, Samuel R. "The Analysis of Compression in Poetry." *Foundations of Language* 7 (1971): 38–55.

———. "Reply to Kintgen." *Foundations of Language* 9 (1972): 105–12.

Leyda, Jay. *The Years and Hours of Emily Dickinson.* 2 vols. New Haven: Yale UP, 1960.

Lilliedahl, Ann. *Emily Dickinson in Europe: Her Literary Reputation in Selected Countries.* Washington: UP of America, 1981.

Lindberg-Seyersted, Brita. *The Voice of the Poet: Aspects of Style in the Poetry of Emily Dickinson.* Cambridge: Harvard UP, 1968.

Lubbers, Klaus. *Emily Dickinson: The Critical Revolution.* Ann Arbor: U of Michigan, P, 1968.

Lucas, Dolores Dyer. *Emily Dickinson and Riddle.* De Kalb: Northern Illinois UP, 1969.

MacLeish, Archibald. "The Private World: Poems of Emily Dickinson." Sewell, *Collection* 150–61.

Marion, John F. *Famous and Curious Cemeteries.* New York: Crown, 1977.

Martin, Wendy. *An American Triptych: Anne Bradstreet, Emily Dickinson, Adrienne Rich.* Chapel Hill: U of North Carolina P, 1984.

Marx, Leo. *The Machine in the Garden: Technology and the Pastoral Idea in America.* New York: Oxford UP, 1964.

Matthiessen, F. O. *American Renaissance: Art and Expression in the Age of Emerson and Whitman.* New York: Oxford UP, 1941.

———, ed. *Oxford Book of American Verse.* New York: Oxford UP, 1950.

McMichael, George, ed. *Anthology of American Literature.* 2 vols. 3rd edition. New York: Macmillan, 1985.

McNeil, Helen. *Emily Dickinson.* New York: Pantheon-Virago, 1986.

Meltzer, David, ed. *Death: An Anthology of Ancient Texts, Songs, Prayers, and Stories.* San Francisco: North Point, 1984.

Merod, Jim. *The Political Responsibility of the Critic.* Ithaca: Cornell UP, 1987.

Miller, Cristanne. *Emily Dickinson: A Poet's Grammar.* Cambridge: Harvard UP, 1987.

Miller, Nancy. "The Text's Heroine: A Feminist Critic and Her Fictions." *Diacritics* 12.2 (1982): 48–53.

Miller, Perry. *Nature's Nation*. Cambridge: Belknap-Harvard UP, 1967.

————. *The New England Mind: From Colony to Province*. Cambridge: Harvard UP, 1953.

————. *The New England Mind: The Seventeenth Century*. New York: Macmillan, 1939.

Miller, Ruth. *The Poetry of Emily Dickinson*. Middletown: Wesleyan UP, 1968.

Mitford, Jessica. *The American Way of Death*. New York: Simon, 1963.

Moi, Toril. *Sexual/Textual Politics: Feminist Literary Theory*. London: Methuen, 1985.

Monteiro, George, and Barton Levi St. Armand. "The Experienced Emblem: A Study of the Poetry of Emily Dickinson." *Prospects* 6 (1981): 186–280.

Morley, John. *Death, Heaven and the Victorians*. Pittsburgh: U of Pittsburgh P, 1971.

Morris, Adalaide. " 'The Love of Thee—A Prism Be': Men and Women in the Love Poetry of Emily Dickinson." Juhasz, *Feminist Critics* 93–113.

Mossberg, Barbara Antonina Clarke. *Emily Dickinson: When a Writer Is a Daughter*. Bloomington: Indiana UP, 1982.

————. "Emily Dickinson's Nursery Rhymes." Juhasz, *Feminist Critics* 45–66.

Mudge, Jean McClure. *Emily Dickinson and the Image of Home*. Amherst: U of Massachusetts P, 1975.

Murphy, Francis, and Hershel Parker, eds. *The Norton Anthology of American Literature*. Vol. 1. 2nd ed. New York: Norton, 1985.

Myerson, Joel, ed. *Margaret Fuller: Essays on Life and Letters*. New Haven: College and University P, 1978.

Nekola, Charlotte. "Emily Dickinson and the Poetry of Silence." Diss. U of Michigan, 1984.

Oberhaus, Dorothy Huff. "In Defense of Sue." *Dickinson Studies* 48, bonus issue (1983): 1–25.

Ostriker, Alicia. *Stealing the Language: The Emergence of Women's Poetry in America*. Boston: Beacon, 1986.

————. *Writing Like a Woman*. Poets on Poetry. Ann Arbor: U of Michigan P, 1983.

Parker, Richard Green. *Aids to English Composition*. New York: 1845.

Patterson, Rebecca. "Emily Dickinson's 'Double' Tim: Masculine Identification." *American Imago* 28 (1971): 330–62.

————. *Emily Dickinson's Imagery*. Ed. and introd. Margaret H. Freeman. Amherst: U of Massachusetts P, 1979.

————. *The Riddle of Emily Dickinson*. Boston: Houghton, 1951.

Pearce, Roy Harvey. *The Continuity of American Poetry*. Princeton: Princeton UP, 1961.

Petry, Alice Hall. "The Ophidian Image in Holmes and Dickinson." *American Literature* 54 (1982): 598–601.

Pickard, John B. *Emily Dickinson: An Introduction and Interpretation.* New York: Holt, 1967.

Pictorial Forest Lawn. Glendale: Forest Lawn Memorial Park, 1970.

Pike, Martha V., and Janice Gray Armstrong. *A Time to Mourn: Expressions of Grief in Nineteenth Century America.* Stony Brook: Museums at Stony Brook, 1980.

Pollak, Vivian R. *Dickinson: The Anxiety of Gender.* Ithaca: Cornell UP, 1984.

Porter, David. *The Art of Emily Dickinson's Early Poetry.* Chicago: U of Chicago P, 1966.

———. *Dickinson: The Modern Idiom.* Cambridge: Harvard UP, 1981.

Poulet, Georges. *Studies in Human Time.* Trans. Elliott Coleman. Baltimore: Johns Hopkins UP, 1956.

Pound, Ezra. *The Spirit of Romance.* New York: New Directions, 1968.

Proctor, Adelaide. *The Poems of Adelaide Proctor.* Boston: Ticknor, 1866.

Rich, Adrienne. "Vesuvius at Home: The Power of Emily Dickinson." *Parnassus* 5 (1976): 49–74. Rpt. in *On Lies, Secrets, and Silence: Selected Prose 1966–1978.* New York: Norton, 1979. 151–83.

Richards, I. A. *Practical Criticism: A Study of Literary Judgment.* New York: Harcourt, 1929.

Rilke, Rainer Maria. "Fifth Elegy." *Duino Elegies.* Trans. J. B. Leishman and Stephen Spender. New York: Norton, 1963. 46–53.

Rosenbaum, S. P., ed. *A Concordance to the Poems of Emily Dickinson.* Ithaca: Cornell UP, 1964.

Rourke, Constance. *American Human: A Study of the National Character.* Garden City: Doubleday, 1931.

Russell, Ruth O. *Freedom to Die: Moral and Legal Aspects of Euthanasia.* New York: Dell, 1976.

Ryan, Mary P. *Cradle of the Middle Class: The Family in Oneida County, New York, 1790–1865.* Cambridge: Cambridge UP, 1981.

———. "Femininity and Capitalism in Antebellum America." *Capitalist Patriarchy and the Case of Socialist Feminism.* Ed. Zillah R. Eisenstein. New York: Monthly Review, 1979. 151–72.

St. Armand, Barton Levi. *The Soul's Society: Emily Dickinson and Her Culture.* New York: Cambridge UP, 1984.

Schorsch, Anita, "A Key to the Kingdom: The Iconography of a Mourning Picture." *Winterthur Portfolio* 41 (1979): 41–71.

Sewall, Richard B. *The Life of Emily Dickinson.* 2 vols. New York: Farrar, 1974.

———. *The Lyman Letters: New Light on Emily Dickinson and Her Family.* Amherst: U of Massachusetts P, 1965.

———, ed. *Emily Dickinson: A Collection of Critical Essays.* Twentieth Century Views. Englewood Cliffs: Prentice, 1963.

Showalter, Elaine, ed. *The New Feminist Criticism.* New York: Pantheon, 1985.

Shurr, William H. *The Marriage of Emily Dickinson: A Study of the Fascicles.* Lexington: U of Kentucky P, 1983.

Sklar, Kathryn Kish. *Catherine Beecher: A Study in American Domesticity.* New York: Norton, 1973.

Smith-Rosenberg, Carroll. *Disorderly Conduct: Visions of Gender in Victorian America.* New York: Knopf, 1985.

———. "The Female World of Love and Ritual: Relations between Women in Nineteenth-Century America." *Signs: Journal of Women in Culture and Society* 1 (1975): 1–30. Rpt. in Smith-Rosenberg, *Disorderly Conduct* 53–76.

Stannard, David E. *Death in America.* Philadelphia: U of Pennsylvania P, 1975.

———. *The Puritan Way of Death: A Study in Religion, Culture, and Social Change.* New York: Oxford UP, 1977.

Stevens, Wallace. "The American Sublime." *The Collected Poems of Wallace Stevens.* New York: Knopf, 1969. 130–31.

Stoddard, Elizabeth. *Temple House.* New York: Johnson Reprint, 1971.

Stoddard, Sandul. *The Hospice Movement.* New York: Random, 1978.

Stowe, Harriet Beecher. *The Minister's Wooing.* Ed. Sandra R. Buguid. Hartford: Stowe-Day Foundation, 1978.

———. *Oldtown Folks.* Ed. Henry F. May. Cambridge: Harvard UP, 1966.

Tate, Allen. "New England Culture and Emily Dickinson." *Symposium* 3 (Apr. 1932): 206–26. Rpt. as "Emily Dickinson" in Sewall, *Collection* 16–27. Rpt. with original title in Blake and Wells 153–67.

United States Information Agency. *Highlights of American Literature.* Washington: USIA, 1983.

Veron, Enid, Ed. *Humor in America: An Anthology.* New York: Harcourt, 1976.

Waggoner, Hyatt H. *American Poets from the Puritans to the Present.* Boston: Houghton, 1968.

Walker, Cheryl. *The Nightingale's Burden: Women Poets and American Culture before 1900.* Bloomington: Indiana UP, 1983.

Wasserman, Marion. "Inhalation—Exhalation." Class essay. Sarah Lawrence Coll., 1985.

Watts, Emily Stipes. *The Poetry of American Women from 1632 to 1945.* Austin: U of Texas P, 1977.

Watts, Isaac. *The Psalms, Hymns and Spiritual Songs of the Rev. Isaac Watts, D.D.* Boston: Crocker, 1834.

Webster, Noah. *An American Dictionary of the English Language.* 2 vols. New Haven: Webster, 1841.

———. *An American Dictionary of the English Language.* 2 vols. Amherst: Adams, 1844.

———. *An American Dictionary of the English Language.* 2 vols. Springfield: Merriam, 1845.

————— . *An American Dictionary of the English Language.* 1848 ed. Ann Arbor: University Microfilms International, 1979.

Weisbuch, Robert. *Emily Dickinson's Poetry.* Chicago: U of Chicago P, 1975.

Welter, Barbara. *Dimity Convictions: The American Woman in the Nineteenth Century.* Athens: Ohio UP, 1976.

Whicher, George Frisbie, ed. *Poetry of the New England Renaissance, 1790–1890.* New York: Holt, 1967.

————— . *This Was a Poet: A Critical Biography of Emily Dickinson.* New York: Scribner's, 1938.

Wilbur, Richard. "Sumptuous Destitution." Sewall, *Collection* 127–36.

Williams, Oscar, and Edwin Honig, eds. *The Mentor Book of Major American Poets.* New York: NAL, 1962.

Williams, William Carlos. "Asphodel, That Greeny Flower." *Pictures from Brueghel and Other Poems.* New York: New Directions, 1967.

Winters, Yvor. "Emily Dickinson and the Limits of Judgment." Sewall, *Collection* 28–40. Rpt. in Blake and Wells 187–200.

Wolff, Cynthia Griffin. *Emily Dickinson.* New York: Knopf, 1986.

Wolosky, Shira. *Emily Dickinson: A Voice of War.* New Haven: Yale UP, 1984.

Yeats, William Butler. "Byzantium." *The Collected Poems of W. B. Yeats.* New York: Macmillan, 1973.

Recordings

Copland, Aaron. *Twelve Poems of Emily Dickinson.* Adele Addison, soprano; Aaron Copland, piano. New York: Boosey, 1951. Columbia M30375.

Emily Dickinson: A Self-Portrait. Read by Julie Harris. Caedmon, S-2026, 1968.

Poems and Letters of Emily Dickinson. Read by Julie Harris. Dir. Howard Sackler. Caedmon, TC 119, 1960.

Poems of Emily Dickinson. Read by Nancy Wickwire. Original music composed and played by Don Feldman. Spoken Arts, 1959.

Sprenkle, Elam. *Six Songs for Mezzo-Soprano and Brass Quintet.* 1981. On *Synthesis.* Annapolis Brass Quintet, with Elaine Bonazzi. Sedro Wooley, Washington. Crystal, S 219, 1985.

Films and Tapes

The Belle of Amherst. Play. By William Luce. Prod. KCET. LC 83-700199. Dist. IFEX.

Emily Dickinson. New York Center for Visual History.

Emily Dickinson: A Certain Slant of Light. By Jean Mudge and Bayley Silleck. 29 min. Dist. Pyramid Films.

Emily Dickinson. Voices and Visions. Written by Judith Thurman. Dir. Veronica Young. Prod. Jill Janows. 60 min. New York Center for Visual History, 1988. Videotape available from Annenberg Corp. for Public Broadcasting.

Four Generations of Women Poets. Audio Sketches of American Writers. 45 min. National Public Radio Service, ME-80–11–28, 1980.

Terris, Virginia. *Emily Dickinson as a Woman Poet.* Everett Edwards, Inc., Box 1061, DeLand, FL, 32720.

The World of Emily Dickinson. Filmstrip. Guidance Associates, Communications Park, Box 3000, Mount Kisco, NY 10549-3000.

INDEX OF FIRST LINES

Following each first line, in parentheses, is the number assigned to the poem by Thomas H. Johnson.

INDEX OF NAMES